BEFORE
FANFICTION

BEFORE FANFICTION

RECOVERING THE LITERARY HISTORY
OF AMERICAN MEDIA FANDOM

Alexandra Edwards

Louisiana State University Press
Baton Rouge

Published by Louisiana State University Press
lsupress.org

DESIGNER: Barbara Neely Bourgoyne
TYPEFACE: Arno Pro

COVER ILLUSTRATION: *The Book Worm and Her Favorite Book,* by Will Houghton, from *Puck* (May 16, 1914).

Portions of chapter 2 first appeared, in somewhat different form, in "Literature Fandom and Literary Fans," in *A Companion to Media Fandom and Fan Studies,* ed. Paul Booth (John Wiley & Sons, 2018). An excerpt from chapter 3 first appeared, in somewhat different form, as "'Entre Nous': Rawlings's Pre–World War II Fan Mail," *Journal of Florida Literature* 25 (2017): 51–61.

LIBRARY OF CONGRESS CATALOGING-IN-PUBLICATION DATA
Names: Edwards, Alexandra, author.
Title: Before fanfiction : recovering the literary history of American media fandom / Alexandra Edwards.
Description: Baton Rouge : Louisiana State University Press, [2023] | Includes bibliographical references and index.
Identifiers: LCCN 2022058694 (print) | LCCN 2022058695 (ebook) | ISBN 978-0-8071-7362-6 (cloth) | ISBN 978-0-8071-8027-3 (paperback) | ISBN 978-0-8071-8032-7 (pdf) | ISBN 978-0-8071-8028-0 (epub)
Subjects: LCSH: American literature—Women authors—Appreciation. | American literature—20th century—Appreciation. | Popular literature—United States—History and criticism. | Fans (Persons)—United States—History—20th century. | Fan fiction—History and criticism. | Literature and society—United States—History—20th century. | LCGFT: Literary criticism.
Classification: LCC PS152 .E39 2023 (print) | LCC PS152 (ebook) | DDC 810.9/92870904—dc23/eng/20230807
LC record available at https://lccn.loc.gov/2022058694
LC ebook record available at https://lccn.loc.gov/2022058695

For the girls who loved so much they rewrote the world

CONTENTS

ILLUSTRATIONS

ACKNOWLEDGMENTS

This book has traveled with me around the United States as I pursued the sometimes exciting and often frustrating life of an early-career scholar. As I have worked on it, I have accrued a long list of people who kindly offered their support and expertise, to whom I am incredibly grateful:

My advisors, Susan Rosenbaum, Roxanne Eberle, and Douglas Anderson, who graciously supported me in writing the work I wanted to write; my Athens crew, including Courtney Hoffman, Henna Messina, Holly Gallagher, Holly Fling, and Tareva Johnson, who read the earliest drafts; the librarians and archivists at the University of Florida, the University of Georgia, and the Renaissance Society at the University of Chicago; the staff and volunteers at the Marjorie Kinnan Rawlings State Historic Site; Corey Goergen, Molly Slavin, Ben Bergholtz, and Kent Linthicum, who read the middle drafts, and all of the Brittain Fellows who were comrades in trying times; my union mates in the United Campus Workers of Georgia Local 3265; the attendees and presenters at the first annual Fan Studies Network North America conference, especially Abigail De Kosnik and Rukmini Pande, for their insightful and generous comments; Paul Booth, who included an early draft of chapter 2 in *The Companion to Media Fandom and Fan Studies;* the staff at LSU Press, especially Jenny Keegan, who championed this little book; my family, especially my partner and our pets; and finally, the fanfic writers, fan artists, and other fan-people who have been my friends for decades, especially Emily, Chelle, Gina, Sara, Kat, Layne, and Esther.

BEFORE FANFICTION

Fanaticism, Yes!

Fanaticism? No. Writing is exciting
and baseball is like writing.
   —MARIANNE MOORE, "Baseball and Writing," 1966

But at the heart of it all I think there's a fundamental ability to see a spectrum of
opportunity in anything (and everything) coupled with the willingness to engage
with those opportunities. Politics, sports, songs, shows, people, situations—we see
not only what exists or is portrayed but the roads not taken or the decisions not
addressed and we play in the space between. Without a culture there can be no
subculture, and *what we are is the subculture of possibility.*
   —ROSSETTI, blog post, circa 2009

Marianne Moore loved baseball, but she didn't want to be called a "fan."
Writing in 1966, the modernist-poet-turned-midcentury-literary-doyenne disavowed any "fanaticism" in her regard for the sport—and in doing so, sought
to distance herself from an American cultural lineage stretching back to the
1880s, when newspaper writers covering baseball first shortened the word
"fanatic" to "fan." The ancestry to which Moore says no continues through
the early-century birth of the film industry, film fans, and fan magazines,
includes the literary periodical press's adoption of the term "fan" to describe
book lovers, and reaches all the way into her present moment, the year CBS
debuted *Star Trek,* a television series whose fans would build an underground
literary movement dedicated to queer romance that is still innovating on the
cultural fringes today.
   Moore's no is, in a way, relatable, especially for fans and scholars who have
spent years arguing against a pathological reading of their interests and practices. In another way, it is disheartening—at least, it is to me, a fan and scholar

who sees the poet's cut-and-paste method as one tool in the kit of fans' trans-formative literary practices. But her "no" is also instructive. It points to a partic-ular anxiety around American popular culture and the enjoyment thereof, an anxiety tied up in the literary and print marketplaces of the twentieth century. Like Moore, many critics and writers have attempted to force a separation be-tween literature and fan cultures or practices: literature was serious (even if, per Moore, it could also be exciting), whereas fans were frivolous. Even the fast-growing field of fan studies, where fanfiction and fan art are worthwhile objects of academic inquiry, has tended to obscure the relationship between fan cultures and literature. No literary history of fandom has yet been written, despite being sorely needed.

I blame this lack on what I call the "fandom creation myth." From the semi-nal works of fan studies in the early 1990s to recent pop scholarship, one creation myth about fandom has been repeated time and again. Western media fandom, this myth tells us, might have gained popularity in the 1960s and 1970s as female audiences mimeographed and mailed each other *Star Trek* fanzines, but it owes its creation to the male-dominated world of the 1930s science fiction pulps.[1] But this version of history ignores the rich fan cultures of the early twentieth century, and it erases the many women writers, readers, and film fans who trans-formed American culture by their participation in early forms of fandom. This book examines the work of popular American women writers working outside of the genre of science fiction, and the fan responses to these women's work, in order to argue for a literary counterhistory of American media fandom—one that returns women to center stage while pointing to historical continuities that better explain how we got from there to here.

It was inspired, as so many fanworks are, by obstinacy.

I found Western media fandom when I was thirteen years old, searching the internet for information about my favorite television show, *Buffy the Vam-pire Slayer* (*BtVS*). It was 1998; the show was in its second season and gaining popularity. I stumbled onto the Bronze, a *BtVS* fan message board hosted by the show's network.[2] Here, I was quickly initiated into a sprawling, exciting, creative community of women who gathered via the internet—at the Bronze but also at their own websites and online archives—to analyze, critique, and imaginatively expand the media we loved. These women wrote fanfiction (fanfic or fic), edited each other's stories (beta reading), drew fan art, created mixtapes (fanmixes), made manipulated images (manips), wrote analytical essays (meta), edited television and film clips into music videos (fanvids), sewed costumes to wear at fan conventions (cosplay), crafted replica props, coded and maintained fanfiction archives, recorded audio versions of fanfiction stories (podfic), campaigned against misogyny and rape culture on television (fan activism), and much else besides. They were passionate and productive, and above all they refused to let any possibility pass them by, relentlessly rewriting every single given fact of the show. Writing *was* exciting, but unlike Marianne Moore, these women proudly owned their "fanaticism."

Fandom became part of my life. It was—and still is—both my community and a collection of practices that taught me how to engage with texts, how to analyze them, and how to marry that analysis with my own emotions in order to creatively expand, alter, or entirely rewrite them. Fandom prepared me for my career as a literature scholar—but when I began my graduate studies, I was surprised and dismayed to learn that fans and literature scholars rarely realized that they spoke the same language. English as a discipline seemed largely unaware of fandom and its creations. Fans, even the "acafans" who studied fandom, stressed the primacy of television as the foundational fannish medium. Media studies scholars maintained fandom's "creation myth," the oversimplified and historically inaccurate idea that fandom was created by a small group of white male science fiction fans who, while reading the pulp magazine *Amazing Stories,* somehow spontaneously invented fan conventions, fan magazines, and fanfiction in the 1930s.[3]

But I saw fan practices everywhere in literature! I saw the ancestors of my *BtVS* posting board friends in Jane Austen, who practiced "face-casting" the characters in her books; in the Brontë sisters, who as children filled small handmade "zines" with elaborate, interconnected stories; in Louisa May Alcott, who refused to unite the couple her fans "shipped" in her work-in-progress ("WIP"); in Anita Loos, whose books and films included intertextual references to her other films and books; in H.D., who transported the poetry of Sappho to Pennsylvania; in Nella Larsen, who rewrote a Sheila Kaye-Smith story to "racebend" the characters; and yes, in Marianne Moore, who cut up newspapers to create her densely allusive, scrapbook-like poems. These women— writing before, during, and after the supposed "invention" of Western media fandom—prefigured both the spirit and the specific textual practices of the fan communities in which I grew up.

In contrast to the male-dominated creation myth, the chapters that follow investigate fan cultures surrounding the shared media of early twentieth-century American literature, with a focus on white and African American women writers and their fan communities. The first half of the twentieth century saw several media revolutions—from large (the creation of the film industry) to small (modernist little magazines)—that fundamentally altered the American literary marketplace and the ways that readers interacted with literature. Though the rich print culture of the nineteenth century had encouraged a certain amount of "interactivity" between authors and their readers, twentieth-century media and consumer culture invited a form of consumer participation that compelled concrete, often textual, responses to cultural products. This shift in the cultural landscape would make it possible for the especially passionate to name and claim an identity that expressed their affective connections to certain texts: the identity of the "fan." It would also formalize a set of fannish reading and writing practices that have shaped popular and literary culture over the last hundred years.

Fans don't just love; they read, reread, master, share, compare, critique, appropriate, extend, transform, and talk back. By closely examining these practices and their textual traces in published works and archives, I aim to revise the ways we think about both fandom and the literature of the twentieth century, beyond hierarchical categories like highbrow, middlebrow, and lowbrow; modernism and mass culture; and avant-garde, realism, and regionalism. Though such categories undoubtedly existed in the field of literary production, scholarship has tended to overdetermine their boundaries and use them to reinforce hierarchies of gender, race, and class. The devalued forms are always linked explicitly to women writers and readers, and even attempts to celebrate these forms reify their position in opposition to the masculine, culturally serious texts of modernism. But fan responses to texts often complicate supposed distinctions and oppositions, more accurately representing the strange networks of the cultural and literary marketplace, as well as their profound effects on women readers and writers.

This is not the stultifying, passive consumption that Theodor Adorno and Max Horkheimer claim the culture industry requires. These products encouraged fan participation. The early twentieth-century press brimmed with "calls to action," specific ways for fans to talk back to the cultural products they consumed. In the process, the culture industry helped to educate and encourage the public to see themselves as savvy participants in a cycle of creation and exchange. Fan cultures broke down barriers between producers and consumers, and their infusion into the literary marketplace helped a diverse range of readers develop a set of reading and writing practices that could, and often did, serve as a form of literary apprenticeship. Fan cultures, I argue, worked to democratize cultural production, and in the process opened a variety of paths to both personal expression and professional distinction—neither of which hold any more or less intrinsic value than the other.

In writing this book, I set out to tell a different origin story for "media fandom," that loose network of communities of interest and practice whose genesis has been so underdocumented. It was not a simple task. There was no Book-of-the-Month Club fanfiction archive to visit, no comprehensive fandom history text to read, no simple search term to plug into library catalogue searches or even to use when scouring for literary antiques on eBay. The prehistory of fanfiction is culturally specific and largely lost, and so I had to search instead for its traces—in archives, published texts, and contemporary literary scholarship. For this reason, I have had to look beyond a literary-critical reading of "fanfiction" (which, in any case, was a word not coined until the 1940s).[4] I speak of "fan cultures" in this book because it is nearly impossible to speak of "fanfiction," or even self-identified literary "fandoms," in the early twentieth century. Though literary fans were developing their own cultural practices and communities, they did not necessarily use those words.

I could have told this story in a number of ways, but I made three choices that fundamentally shape this short book. First, like many fanfiction writers, I let my critique guide me. I chose the three interrelated claims of the "fandom creation myth" that rankled me the most—that white male science fiction fans of the 1930s created fan conventions, fan magazines, and fanfiction—and shaped my chapters around refuting them each in turn. To do so, I have divided each chapter into two major sections: I begin by synthesizing current research on the fan culture or practice being addressed, noting both the strengths and weaknesses of available scholarship. My discussions look to reframe the scholarly material already published on my topics, to show how they are already *about* fandom, though they may not use that terminology; in this way, I work to draw previously ignored fangirls into the spotlight. In the second half of each chapter, my original research and close readings demonstrate how applying a literary fan studies frame can help us recontextualize traditions of both women's writing and fanfiction—especially where these overlap.

Second, I restricted my research to the United States. Fan cultures in the United States originally coalesced at the turn of the twentieth century around a set of American media products aimed at a national audience. The terms "fan," short for "fanatic," and the related "fandom" were first used in the 1880s to describe sports aficionados who followed the increasingly popular, recently professionalized game of baseball.[5] As the terms "fan" and "fandom" spread via print media, they were adopted by the burgeoning film industry as a marketing and publicity tactic (see chapter 2). By the 1910s, early film publicity magazines like *Photoplay* had become instrumental in defining and disseminating the idea of the fan, a consumer/spectator who built her identity around her love for the cinema and its stars. Fan cultures continued to spread through the 1920s. By the 1940s—the decade when the term "fanfiction" was finally coined, albeit with a slightly different definition than the one we use today—movie studios, radio stations, and publishers had come to rely on fan mail and other forms of interaction as market research. Though the cultural products of the early twentieth century often crossed national borders, I have mostly limited myself to writers, texts, and fans from the United States. These fan cultures have something to tell us about Americanness, I argue, especially when they intersect with things like American racial politics or the United States' entrance into World War II.

Third, I researched authors, fans, and communities who were either not white, not male, or not writing or reading science fiction. This led me to the work of women regionalists, a Black Arts poet, and the people who read love pulps and "middlebrow" magazines.[6] I purposefully chose to close-read these writers' texts together, regardless of their professional status, enduring popularity, or canonical stature, because, as I discuss below, fan studies productively troubles the supposed hierarchical distinctions between amateur and professional, unpublished and published, reader and writer. This nonhierarchical way of engaging cultural productions is, to me, one of the most exciting things that fan studies can offer to literary scholars. At the same time, I take seriously Rebecca Wanzo's and Rukmini Pande's respective calls to engage with race alongside gender in accounts of fan cultures past and present; thus, my choices of writers and fan communities are intended to tease out some of the complexities of American media fandom's multiracial origins.[7]

As a result of these choices, the chapters that follow tell a different—albeit still partial—story of American media fandom's beginnings. My hope is that this story will prove interesting to both fan studies scholars and literary scholars. I intend this book as an intervention into the currently spotty terrain of literary fan studies, one that looks to make connections across generations and to entice more fan scholars and literature scholars to excavate the history of literary fandom specifically. Its brevity should be taken as a provocation: this book is not a definitive history but my own "call to action."

Participatory Cultures, Gift Economies, and Transformative Works

I am indebted to fan studies and popular culture scholars for their theoretical work on the literary and social practices that constitute what we call "fandom." Three ways of thinking about media fandom are crucial to this work: theories of participatory cultures, gift economies, and transformative works. Working in conjunction, these three concepts have helped me to develop the terminology for fanworks I use throughout this book.

Since the 1980s, theories of popular and participatory cultures have gained prominence, working to refute the panicky screeds of writers like Theodor Adorno and Max Horkheimer. Their 1944 indictment of popular culture argued forcefully that film, radio, and magazines are the identical products of an industry designed to turn subjects into passive receivers of "an ideology to legitimize the trash they intentionally produce" (95). But, as John Fiske points out in his 1989 book *Understanding Popular Culture*, "the fears of the mass culture theorists" were overblown and excessively simplistic (23). Fiske reminds us that "popular culture is not consumption, it is culture—the active process of generating and circulating meanings and pleasures within a social system" (23). To understand popular culture, then, we must reject the image of people as "the masses, an aggregation of alienated, one-dimensional persons whose only consciousness is false, whose only relationship to the system that enslaves them is one of unwitting (if not willing) dupes" (Fiske 23–24). Instead, Fiske argues, theorists must see people—not industries—as the "active agents" in the process of culture-making: "All the culture industries can do is produce a repertoire of texts or cultural resources for the various formations of the people to use or reject in the ongoing process of producing their popular culture" (24). Borrowing from French scholar Michel de Certeau, Fiske asserts, "Popular culture is the art of making do with what the system provides" (25). Such "making do" is not a surrender but rather a form of "guerilla warfare" carried out against "the powerful [who] are cumbersome, unimaginative, and overorganized" by "the weak [who] are creative, nimble, and flexible" (Fiske 32). For Fiske, as for Certeau, these guerilla tactics—including loitering in the mall, shoplifting, and "wigging" (using company time or resources for one's own purposes)—insist upon the power of the people to define their own lives in relation to seemingly totalizing systems of consumer capitalism.

Certeau is also central to Henry Jenkins's 1992 book *Textual Poachers: Television Fans and Participatory Culture,* which has come to define the subfield of fan studies. In the book, Jenkins sets out to map a subculture self-identified as "media fandom," made up of textual consumers and producers who appropriate and transform the media properties they love. Jenkins was among the first scholars to reject "media-fostered stereotypes of fans as cultural dupes, social misfits, and mindless consumers," and instead perceive "fans as active producers and manipulators of meanings" (23). Writing against the work of Adorno and Horkheimer, as well as Pierre Bourdieu, Jenkins draws instead on Certeau's theoretical model of active reading as "poaching." In this model, fans are the "poachers" sneaking into someone else's texts to perform "an impertinent raid on the literary preserve that takes away only those things that are useful or pleasurable to the reader" (Jenkins 24). However, Jenkins is careful to note that he disagrees with Certeau's strict separation between readers and writers, emphasizing instead how fans comfortably move back and forth between the two positions (45).

Since the 1990s, scholars of participatory cultures have worked to complicate Certeau's "poaching" model in productive ways, often by studying the cultural products that creative readers have themselves made. Ellen Gruber Garvey, for instance, looks to scrapbooking, the creative practices of cutting and pasting that readers used to at once preserve and transform the ephemeral but voluminous products of nineteenth-century print culture. Garvey suggests that the "poaching" metaphor could be replaced by a metaphor of "gleaning," which scrapbook makers themselves used to describe their work (224). Mike Chasar similarly views twentieth-century poetry scrapbooking as a form of participatory culture that resists the poaching metaphor. "Far from feeling like trespassers," Chasar writes, "many American readers believed that they in fact had a perfect right to the poems they were collecting" (53). Because Americans at the turn of the twentieth century resisted copyright laws, "poems were to some extent unpoachable" (Chasar 54). Unlike a poacher who kills someone else's animal, scrapbookers and other cultural participants do not remove a text from circulation. For Garvey, they "glean" the excess from abundant fields of printed materials (224); for Chasar, poaching only becomes possible once a poem has been clipped from the commons and "privatized" in the pages of a scrapbook (55). Following Jenkins, Garvey, and Chasar, I work throughout these chapters to find more accurate ways of describing the practices and creations of fans. I have resisted using "poaching" and "gleaning" because they do not arise from self-identified Western media fans, and because their metaphoric connotations are loaded in ways that I find problematic.

Fans themselves have a sophisticated theoretical understanding of and language for their work, and so I have instead shaped my discussions around their concepts and terms. Many of these have been developed out of legal necessity. When Chasar argues that early twentieth-century poetry scrapbookers believed "that no one owned [the poems] (copyright holders included), and that they comprised instead a cultural commons" (53), he touches upon a crucial—and often antagonistic—relationship between fans and copyright holders. The development of US copyright law has influenced fandom significantly, forcing fans, under threat of litigation, to articulate their values and theorize their work in opposition to the ideas of intellectual property that make copyright possible. For this reason, fans have developed a gift economy, outside of capitalist logic, protected by (often unspoken) rules about exchange. Take, for example, how fanfiction is treated by contemporary internet fandom. A fan writes a fanfiction story (fanfic or fic), borrowing and building on characters and other elements from an existing, usually copyrighted media property. She posts this story to the internet for free, likely to an archive or social media site that does not charge either poster or reader for its use.[8] In return, readers are expected to leave positive feedback on the fic, in the form of either comments or "likes." In this way, writer and reader participate in a circulation of texts (stories and comments) that engender good feelings between members of the fandom community.[9] Any breakdown of this process, on the part of either the fanfic writer or readers, is considered a breach of community values.[10] Furthermore, the gift economy helps fans to distinguish their work from the copyrighted commodities of which they make use: as Lewis Hyde notes, we know a gift from a commodity because the former "establishes a feeling-bond" whereas the latter does not (72).[11] Thus fans are active participants in an alternative, capital-free (or capital-light) network that privileges community and good feelings; though the above example is contemporary, the chapters that follow argue that we can see the fannish gift economy at work as early as the 1890s.

In addition to bonding the community, the gift economy helps fans avoid legal challenges by copyright holders, many of whom are the "powerful" and "unimaginative" corporations Fiske describes. But merely abstaining from profits is not always enough to protect fans from being sued. Hoping to protect themselves from such possible lawsuits, contemporary fans have also adopted the language of Fair Use to signify the protected status of their creations.[12] Fanfiction and other fan creations are known as "transformative works," arguing in advance of any legal challenge that the fan creator has sufficiently transformed the commercial source material so as to parody or critique it.[13]

Though this use of "transformative" to mark a category of media production is relatively recent, I find the term useful as a description of the work performed by fans on media texts. Even more than "poaching" or "gleaning," the act of "transforming" a text speaks to the effort and intention of Western media fans. They are not simply taking, nor even just rewriting; they are purposefully using a text to talk back to the culture that produced it, while at the same time making that text speak to their own lives, experiences, and desires. For this reason, I agree with Abigail De Kosnik's rejection of the terms "derivative" and "appropriative" for describing fanworks, and with her location of the fanfiction tradition within a longer lineage of "archontic literature"—that is, "those works that generate variations that explicitly announce themselves as variations" (65). De Kosnik begins her short prehistory of fanfiction in the seventeenth century with a trio of responses to Sir Philip Sidney's *The Countess of Pembroke's Arcadia* written by women (67), and she traces this developing tradition through nineteenth-century transformations of Lewis Carroll and Shakespeare, finally locating "its most productive period over the last eighty years, with the explosion of postcolonial and ethnic American literature" (69). Her summation of fanfiction's lineage helps us see the exclusions built into fandom's white male–privileging creation myth:

> Since at least the early seventeenth century, archontic literature has been a compelling choice of genre for writers who belong to "cultures of the subordinate," including women, colonial subjects, and ethnic minorities. This body of work, this long tradition of archontic literature, is the heritage of contemporary zine and Internet fan fiction.
>
> Fan fiction, too, is the literature of the subordinate, because most fanfic authors are women responding to media products that, for the

most part, are characterized by an underrepresentation of women. (De Kosnik 71)

Though I have limited myself to fan cultures that developed during and after the term "fan" was coined and began to spread, I build on De Kosnik's insistence that fanworks, especially fanfiction, have been the expressions of women and other marginalized groups against a dominant culture that ignored or actively harmed them, not just since the internet posts of the 1990s or even the zines of the 1960s. I also find "transformative" useful because, as De Kosnik notes, it links the work of fans to Julia Kristeva's theory of intertextuality.[14] Fanworks and fan cultures engage this quality of transformation purposefully and, in doing so, distinguish themselves from works that are merely "influenced" by their predecessors (as in Harold Bloom's famous formulation).

Additionally, to speak of "transforming" a text avoids the anachronisms inherent in metaphors like "remixing" or even "collaging." Finally, the prefix "trans" has particular appeal for me, because it signals both "change" and "crossing," and because it carries connotations of queerness that inflect Western media fandom, both now and in the past.

Queer/Trans-Formations

Media fandom is a queer place. That is, media fandom is a place where fans— mostly women and gender nonconforming individuals—explore nonheteronormative sexuality, experiment with taboos, and reshape literary and media texts to demarginalize multiple forms of marginalization.[15] When I discovered *Buffy the Vampire Slayer* fandom in 1998, "slash"—fanfiction pairing same-sex characters in romantic or erotic scenarios—was almost thirty years old. Like *Star Trek* fans in the late 1960s, *BtVS* fans dared to reimagine the show with queer relationships front and center.[16] Since then, "kink memes" and "A/B/O" fic have become commonplace in media fandom.[17] Fans regularly imagine how stories would change if their characters were trans, or asexual, or polyamorous, or nonwhite, or disabled, or neurodivergent. The vocabularies of these identities, perhaps considered "jargon" by outsiders, are widely adopted and deployed without fanfare. As Ika Willis signals with an epigraph, Western media fandom does the work that Eve Kosofsky Sedgwick writes about: "to keep faith with vividly remembered promises made to ourselves in childhood: promises to make invisible possibilities and desires visible; to make the tacit things explicit; to smuggle queer representation in where it must be smuggled and, with the relative freedom of adulthood, to challenge queer-eradicating impulses frontally where they are to be so challenged" (Sedgwick 3, qtd. in Willis 154). Western media fandom defines itself as a community around the very same work: to make visible and explicit, to smuggle, and to challenge. To return to rossetti's words from this introduction's epigraph, fandom's specific set of practices—their ways of engaging with texts—are dedicated to playing in the spaces between, where all those invisible possibilities live. Sedgwick as well succinctly expresses the forces of eradication against which fandom ranges itself: in media, the long history of denying queer experience and punishing queer characters.[18]

Though this book explores fan cultures that predate Kirk/Spock slash, I have been specifically attuned to queerness wherever it arises. In the following chapters, queer love, queer relationships, and queer pleasure form some of the threads that I have followed from 1890 to 1950. But I want to be clear that I am not necessarily writing about gays or lesbians, nor gay and lesbian culture. Rather, I use the term "queer" to mark an approach to culture that rejects heteronormative gender and sexual roles, and that embraces non-normativity as a social and political position. The queerness of American media fandom has less to do with narrow categories of sexual identity than with a much broader way of being at the margins of society.[19]

Of course, fan cultures are not the only places to find literary queerness in the early twentieth century. Since Annamarie Jagose coined the term "queer theory" in 1996, scholars have produced exceptional work recovering and theorizing queer texts, queer authors, queer forms, and queer aesthetics. Much of this work is siloed by being tied to genre or movement; for example, scholars have variously claimed queerness as a distinct force in modernism, regionalism, and genre fiction. Benjamin Kahan, for instance, connects queerness to modernism by exploring "the sexually transgressive and gender deviant energies that help fuel modernism's desire to thwart normative aesthetics, knowledges, geographies, and temporalities" (348). Likewise, Judith Fetterley and Marjorie Pryse have mined regional fiction for its queerness, arguing that "if we wish, we can think of regionalist fiction in its entirety as a version of Celia's Thanksgiving dinner [in Rose Terry Cooke's story "How Celia Changed Her Mind"] dedicated to welcoming and reproducing queers" (321). Still others have examined the ways that queerness historically sat uneasily in the major literary movements. For Elizabeth English, writers of lesbian modernism in the United Kingdom needed "a third trajectory . . . a viable alternative to both realism and modernism, the literal and dissimulative" (16). And so, she argues, lesbian writers turned to genre fiction in 1930s, hiding subversive sexuality in "the frivolous, pleasurable text" that was potentially less likely to be censored (8).

Despite English's arguments that queer content can be found all over mass-market texts like genre fiction, the literary history of queerness has tended to remain anchored to specific urban centers (e.g., New York City) and celebrity authors (e.g., Virginia Woolf, Djuna Barnes, Gertrude Stein); as with the fan cultures I explore, this tendency has directed attention away from those outside these places and spotlights. Like Kahan's queer modernism, fan cultures "imagine queerness to be utterly pervasive" (353), "have as much to do with gender and sex as sexuality" (355), and "are passed from hand to hand" (356). I suggest that fannish engagements with homosocial communities (as in the women's clubs [see chapter 1] and the romance pulp's letter columns [see chapter 2]), same-sex arousal (as in Gene Stratton-Porter's essay for her women's club [see chapter 1]), and cross-gender identification (again in the pulps and in the fan mail to Marjorie Kinnan Rawlings [see chapter 3]) illuminate another aspect of the lineage I trace: the women who "invented" slash fanfiction were, in fact, following in the footsteps of their queer predecessors.

Saying Yes

In the chapters that follow, I build a literary genealogy of three interrelated fan practices that help to illuminate fan cultures of the early twentieth century: proto- and pseudo-fan communities, fan magazine letter columns, and fan mail. Each of these three practices has left behind texts and other historic artifacts, allowing me to close-read the work of fans and professional authors alike. In this way, I resist the separation of writer and reader that Jenkins felt hindered Certeau's work and that fans themselves disprove by moving frequently between the two positions.

Though I have tried to be rigorous in my historical accuracy, and though my chapters proceed in a roughly chronological fashion, this is not a work of strict literary history. My story about the early days of American media fandom doubles back on itself more than once. Additionally, I have included endnotes connecting and comparing early twentieth-century media fandom to early twenty-first-century media fandom. These endnotes are meant as a reminder that our current fan cultures have historical precedents. I hope that they will spark pleasurable moments of recognition in my fan studies audience and intrigue my literary audience into wanting to explore further.

My first chapter analyzes women's clubs as sites of interrelated fandom and literary training. Though many fan studies histories credit science fiction fandom with organizing early fan clubs and holding the first fan conventions, this chapter points out that the club and convention format long predated the science fiction clubs of the 1930s. It traces the lineage of women's social reform and literary clubs, reading them as proto-fan communities. The women's club movement, which spread across the United States in the nineteenth century, shared literary practices like communal reading, writing essays, giving oral performances, and creating printed texts like programs, yearbooks, and newspapers. Like later fan communities, clubwomen practiced critiquing and transforming shared media texts in intimate social settings. Clubs took the place of higher education for many women, especially working-class and African American women, giving them instead a private space to train as authors and critics.

The case studies of this chapter connect the club work of Gene Stratton-Porter, a white regional novelist and naturalist, with Gwendolyn Brooks, a Black Arts poet. Stratton-Porter founded a women's club in Geneva, Indiana, in 1893, and used this club to train herself to write. Comparing her surviving club essay, on Walt Whitman, with her later published novels, this chapter argues that the homosocial intimacy of her women's club helped to define Stratton-Porter's regional style, which emphasized embodied emotional experience and the sexual thrill of being in nature. Once a celebrity and regular bestseller but since largely forgotten outside Indiana, Stratton-Porter has received renewed scholarly interest in recent years, as critics have returned to environmental fiction in the face of escalating climate change and extinction fears. But scholars have yet to connect her regional fiction to her women's club work. This chapter ties together recent readings of regionalist fiction as feminist and queer with Stratton-Porter's early proto-fan community club work, reading both as expressions of the intimate aesthetics of the women's club movement.

I then turn to the work of Gwendolyn Brooks, the Pulitzer Prize–winning poet who trained in the Chicago Poet's Class under the tutelage of Inez Cunningham Stark. Brooks is a powerful transitional figure in twentieth-century literature, bridging midcentury modernism and the Black Arts movement of the 1960s and 1970s. Her work also demonstrates how literary communities of interest and practice used transformative tactics to reshape popular literary culture in their own image. Her second book, *Annie Allen*, participates in a long history of women rewriting poetic tradition for their own purposes, while also prefiguring postmodern transformative literature.[20] This case study analyzes *Annie Allen* as a literary club–influenced transformation of midcentury modernism, in which Brooks sought to rewrite both the heroic epics of antiquity and their modernist postwar progenies. Brooks's mock-heroic poetry celebrates Blackness through its "soft aesthetic," and in doing so anticipates contemporary fandom critiques of the pervasive whiteness of popular media. Finally, this chapter suggests how we may read these women writers as part of a larger tradition of transformative women's writing produced in intimate communities to varying ends.

In the second chapter, I examine literary, fan, and pulp magazines— including the *Saturday Review of Literature, Motion Picture Story Magazine,* and *Amazing Stories*—to demonstrate how thoroughly the identity of the "fan" saturated the literary marketplace in the decades between Gene Stratton-Porter's and Gwendolyn Brooks's club experiences. Resisting the fan studies myth that fandom originated in the letter columns of science fiction pulps, this chapter sketches the spread of "fan" and "fandom" as terms used to define sports, film, and book lovers in all kinds of early twentieth-century periodicals. After presenting an alternate history of the birth of "fandom" in American print media, I examine the literary fan community addressed by William Rose Benét's "Phoenix Nest" column in the *Saturday Review of Literature*. In the pages of this "middlebrow" magazine, we find an enthusiastic engagement with the transformative textual practices of fandom, and evidence that the vaunted pulp *Amazing Stories* was not as welcome in the 1940s science fiction fan community as some historians have claimed. This chapter pairs analysis of *Amazing Stories'* interactive science fiction "Shaver Mystery" with the almost century-long tradition of adaptation and transformation that novelist and screenwriter Anita Loos kicked off in 1925 with the debut of her modernist transmedia icon Lorelei Lee in the pages of *Harper's Bazaar*. Both, I argue, can be understood as precursors to contemporary fanfiction, and both were made possible by creative engagement with the form and the community of the early twentieth-century periodical press.

My third chapter moves from letters reprinted in magazines to primary documents, examining early twentieth-century fan mail as a form that likewise foreshadowed fanfiction. I begin by reading across several published studies of fan mail (all of which focus on a single author's preserved collection of letters) to find their common tropes. This comparative reading suggests that fan mail was a form with its own conventions, which fans used to build their letters to a wide variety of artists, writers, and celebrities. Then, I turn to a box of almost two hundred fan letters saved by Marjorie Kinnan Rawlings from 1936 to 1945, written by wounded World War II soldiers, teenage tuberculosis patients, and even Malcolm X's future biographer, Alex Haley. This chapter reinterprets Rawlings's career as a regional novelist through these fan letters, suggesting that Rawlings and her fans participated in a joint project to circulate pleasure—often a particularly queer pleasure—as a means of resisting the emotional pain and spiritual hunger they felt during World War II. A brief postlude follows Rawlings fandom into the present day, as readers and tourists gather at her Florida homestead, now a state historic site, to re-create her recipes and live briefly in her world. Here literary fan culture is being reinterpreted by park rangers and docents in 1930s period dress who gossip and tell tall tales about "Marjorie," a larger-than-life character just like the southern moonshiners in her books. They have preserved Rawlings's home and furnishings, rebuilt her kitchen garden exactly as she described it, keep chickens and ducks as she did, and regularly make bread, jams, and preserves on her original wood-burning stove. Rawlings's literary legacy has become an interactive domestic exhibition that adapts her 1930s regionalism to speak to an array of twenty-first-century interests, including the rise of modern homesteading and the local and sustainable food movement.

Finally, my conclusion addresses Nella Larsen's 1930 transformative short story "Sanctuary" to illuminate what we lose when we lack an understanding of the literary and historical foundations of fan culture and its radically transformative projects. Upon publication, Larsen was accused of plagiarizing "Sanctuary" from British writer Sheila Kaye-Smith. But by interpreting the story instead as an early twentieth-century example of what fans now call "race-bending," I demonstrate the historical sweep of the project to reframe white narratives around the experiences of people of color. By connecting Larsen's work to the other transformative literary practices examined in this book, the conclusion suggests the kind of reclamation work possible when we develop our understanding of the intersections between fan cultures and literature in their historical contexts.

Though I initially came to regionalism because I was looking for the literary genre that most directly contrasted white male science fiction writing, I have found it to be a tremendously productive object of inquiry that, in many ways, parallels contemporary female fan communities. American literary regionalism, once dismissively termed the "local color" movement, flourished in the late nineteenth century. Its texts were usually short stories and novels set outside the urban centers of the United States and focusing on small communities, their rituals, and their ways of life. Many of the best-known regionalists were women, including Harriet Beecher Stowe, Sarah Orne Jewett, and Kate Chopin; the genre has been defined as something of a haven for writers of color, especially women such as Alice Dunbar Nelson, Zitkala-Sa, and Sui Sin Far, whose work might otherwise be lost among white male–dominated genres like realism and naturalism. As scholars such as Judith Fetterley and Marjorie Pryse, Kate McCullough, and Stephanie Foote have recently argued, American women regionalists often worked to resist the dominant culture of the country by focusing on societal outsiders, by modeling positive community relations, and by suggesting the beauty and wisdom of the "queer" and otherwise non-normative. Though these women wrote professionally and therefore were not participating in a gift economy, their concerns seem to me to mirror the queer concerns of contemporary Western media fans.

Because regional fiction tended to be "realistic," the genre's continuation into the twentieth century has been overshadowed by more surrealistic and experimental modernist texts. When scholars like John Duvall argue that early twentieth-century regionalist fiction can be understood as part of the larger modernist project to grapple with modernization, they speak to a long-standing divide between the two genres. This divide has worked to privilege modernism, which is seen as masculine, challenging, and forward-thinking, over regionalism, which is seen as feminine, simplistic, and nostalgic. The hierarchical model of early twentieth-century literature thus works to separate genres into points on a cultural pyramid, where "highbrow" modernism lords over "mass culture" products like popular magazines, which printed many regional stories, as well as movies and the pulps.[21] Even attempts to define a middle ground—literally termed "middlebrow"—reassert the phrenological model of cultural distinction that is inherently both classist and racist.[22]

Throughout this book, my arguments are shaped by an implicit acknowl-edgment that the hierarchy of cultural distinction is, at best, artificial. At worst, it represents a purposeful rewriting of literary history to exaggerate the schol-arly and aesthetic value of literature coded as masculine, serious, and difficult. In other words, it is not enough for me to suggest we can find value in "low-brow," "middlebrow," or "mass culture" texts; I am for discarding the entire hierarchy. Thus, my discussions of regionalism and modernism in the following chapters deliberately ransack the scholarly conversations surrounding these literary genres for what I find useful, while resisting attempts to value one genre over another. When, for example, I argue in chapter 3 that Marjorie Kinnan Rawlings's work continued the tradition of women regionalists into the 1940s, I am not arguing that she cannot be considered a modernist writer nor that we should realign our hierarchy to value regionalism over midcentury American modernism. Rather, I am working to describe the mission of her work and to place it within the context of a larger body of literature with similar concerns.

Ultimately, I am uninterested in the exclusionary work of defining and rede-fining literary genres, just as I am uninterested in upholding hierarchical distinc-tions between authors and fan writers. My time participating in and studying fan communities has taught me that the boundaries of cultural distinction break down far more often than they hold. What follows, then, is a deliberately wide-ranging and nonlinear examination of literature and literary fan cultures of the early twentieth century—one that, contra Marianne Moore, attempts to say yes to the figure of the "fan" far more often than it says no.

ONE

Intimacy and Transformation in Literary Fan Communities

So when the women come together, let them put their tedious self-hood off. Let the joy of high and large communion efface the folds and wrinkles which cramp and disfigure their spiritual faces. Thus let them sit together, and if they forget to resume the heavy garment when they go out again, it will be all the better for their soul-health.

—JULIA WARD HOWE, "How Can Women Best Associate?," 1874

one of my favorite things about fandom is that the exchange of intellectual and creative property is a legitimate form of gift giving. like "i'm so enchanted by you, i love you, let me tell you a story"

—CERSEISCROWN, blog post, 2014

When William S. Baring-Gould set out to introduce the readers of *Harper's Magazine* to science fiction fandom in 1946, he began with friendship:

> The heavy-set young man with the shock of black hair pounded on the table and called for order. "Five years is a long time between drinks," boomed Sam Moscowitz of Newark, New Jersey. "But now that the boys are back and a still frightened world is trying to set itself straight, it's time for the fellows who knew it all the time—the science fiction fans—to reaffirm their fellowship. That is what we are doing here today."
>
> "Here" was Slovak Sokol Hall on the outskirts of Newark. The day was Sunday, March 6, 1946. Present were 107 eastern science fiction readers, editors, authors, and artists from as far north as Providence, as far south as Philadelphia. The occasion was their first postwar convention. (283)

Baring-Gould does not name the fan convention he describes, but he notes its similarity to other fan conventions held across the country, from New York to Denver to Los Angeles (287). The specifics are less important than the form: the semi-public gathering place, the "fellowship" between "readers, editors, authors, and artists" signified by "drinks" and conversation, and above all, the name for the practice, "convention." Since the first World Science Fiction Convention (Worldcon), held in New York City over the weekend of July 4, 1939, conventions have been seen as both a fandom tradition and innovation (Coppa 43). The first Worldcon drew two hundred participants; according to *Time* magazine, they "gathered in a small Manhattan hall . . . for three days of speeches, pseudo-scientific movies and discussion of stories with their authors" ("The Press: Amazing! Astounding!" 34).[1] Worldcon has been credited with defining a fandom infrastructure that continues to this day.

But as with so many fandom traditions, predecessors abound. Literature scholars may notice that a science fiction fan convention sounds almost identical to an academic convention: interested parties with particular expertise gather in a designated location to listen to keynote talks, discuss common texts, and maybe even screen related films. The Modern Language Association held its first annual convention in New York City in 1883; by 1939, the convention was regularly drawing more than one thousand participants (MLA Convention Statistics).

In its self-mythologizing, science fiction fandom has neglected to document the practices and institutions after which it modeled its structures. Accounts of early science fiction fan conventions, like Baring-Gould's and the *Time* article cited above, often stress the conventions' relationship to the pulp magazines of the era, while paying little attention to the cultural history of the meetings themselves. But these practices did not spring up from nowhere. Though a full history of the "convention" as general form and practice is beyond my scope, I do want to spend a moment considering some of the US predecessors to the science fiction fan convention. Before the MLA began holding its annual meeting, many conventions brought together men of power in politics or the church in order to make decisions.[2] Abolitionist societies as early as 1793 held conventions that gathered delegates from regional groups ("Convention, N."); political parties followed suit, with the regularly scheduled Democratic National Convention beginning in 1832 and the Republican National Convention in 1856. Throughout the late eighteenth and nineteenth centuries, the convention served as a space to gather representatives of a society or party.

Most of these conventions were attended exclusively or primarily by men—including the early science fiction fan conventions. But this is not to say that women did not convene their own versions of semi-public group meetings during which they could discuss topics of mutual interest, affirm their fellowship, and address social issues. Women abolitionists joined societies and attended conventions such as the World Anti-Slavery Convention, held in London in 1840. Frustrated by the male attendees' treatment of women at that convention, Elizabeth Cady Stanton and Lucretia Mott returned to the United States and organized the 1848 Seneca Falls Convention, where attendees signed a "Declaration of Sentiments" that called for a range of women's rights, including the right to vote (National Women's History Museum). First-wave feminism was born in a convention culture.

The abolition and suffrage movements were part of a larger societal interest in social reform, self-improvement, and mutual education that permeated the United States in the nineteenth century. National conventions were their largest and most public meetings, but these movements and groups built their foundations on smaller local "clubs," where members could gather more regularly and intimately. Long before Benjamin Franklin became president of the Pennsylvania Abolition Society, he gathered a group of friends and created the Junto Club, a social circle "for mutual improvement" that required members to produce original writing (Franklin 53). In histories of white and African American women's clubs, scholars note the interrelated goals and practices of abolitionist and suffrage societies, the Lyceum movement, Chautauqua schools, and various study, Bible, and book clubs (Gere and Roop 1–2; E. Long 477; Knupfer 108–13). These clubs and schools had strong literary components, attracting speakers like Henry David Thoreau and Mark Twain (in addition to political figures from Abraham Lincoln to Frederick Douglass to Susan B. Anthony), while also generating their own published texts in the form of magazines, newspapers, yearbooks, and study guides (Gere 8).

It is the lineage of these clubs in which I am interested. Most scholarly discussions of women's clubs acknowledge their predecessors and their widespread influence in the decades around the turn of the twentieth century. The women's clubs that formed after the Civil War "transformed the club tradition, weaving women's clubs into the fabric of nearly every American city, town, and village" (Gere and Roop 2). And yet, most of these accounts agree that the women's club movement ended in the 1920s. Anne Ruggles Gere and Anne

Meis Knupfer end their respective studies of women's clubs in 1920, and Knupfer is careful to note that she does not want to suggest the work of these clubs is "being 'carried on'" (137). Elizabeth Long extends her discussion of women's book clubs to 1940 but suggests that they were relieved of their necessity due to educational reforms (489–90). Long also argues that second-wave feminism "weakened the connection between literature and social reform" that had spurred on the women's club movement (490). But we know that women continued to share texts via fan clubs, from the Deanna Durbin Fan Club founded in 1937 by four teenaged girls, which published its own mimeographed newsletter (Scheiner 82), to the *Star Trek* fans who circulated zines full of erotic fanfiction beginning in the late 1960s (Lichtenberg), to the millions of fans currently posting stories and essays to internet communities like Tumblr, Wattpad, and the Archive of Our Own.

A simple "what if" question animates this chapter: Instead of viewing women's literary clubs as a sociocultural phenomenon that arose in the late 1800s until spontaneously dissolving in the 1920s (or 1940s), what if we saw these clubs as part of a lineage, stretching from women's abolitionist groups through women's clubs, through movie and science fiction fan clubs, into our present internet fandom landscape, and thus continuing in a shifting but unbroken line for hundreds of years? By reinterpreting women's clubs, specifically literary clubs, in this way, it might be possible to counter the "forgetting" that Gere asserts has rendered the "cultural work of women's clubs . . . largely invisible" (16). Though the process of "forgetting" sounds passive, Gere notes that it took significant work, in the form of "reductive and distorted images of clubwomen," to "erase their cultural work from the public memory" (256). Similarly, such erasure has made it possible for historians of fandom to ignore or "forget" the female fan communities that predated *Star Trek,* Worldcon, and science fiction fan clubs. By insisting on a broader lineage, this chapter argues that these acts of public erasure are interrelated; the same process that "distorted, trivialized, and even vilified" clubwomen (Gere 16) has continued to erase the cultural work of female fans to this day.[3]

To connect women's clubs to fan communities, this chapter reads their activities as part of that lineage. First, drawing on the wealth of scholarship already written on the women's club movement, I recontextualize their practices as forming the basis of what I call "proto-fandom." Then I use two case studies to demonstrate how this recontextualization can help us to connect the work of women writers who might otherwise never be mentioned together: Gene Stratton-Porter, an early twentieth-century white regional novelist and naturalist whose tremendously popular books are now almost forgotten, and Gwendolyn Brooks, the mid-twentieth-century African American poet who won the Pulitzer Prize in 1950 and whose fame endures. Both women participated in literary clubs that I will characterize as proto-fan or pseudo-fan communities; both were fundamentally shaped by those experiences, and both in turn left their marks on American literature.

Women's clubs were a cultural force around the turn of the twentieth century. Though we may see their forebears in the literary and self-improvement societies where Benjamin Franklin (Junto Club, 1720s) and Harriet Beecher Stowe (Semi-Colon Club, 1830s) honed their crafts, the homosocial literary spaces known as women's clubs became a national phenomenon in the decades after the Civil War. Clubs existed in major cities, small towns, and new settlements; they gathered not only middle-class Protestant white women but also working-class, Mormon, Jewish, African American, and American Indian women, mostly into segregated groups (Gere 3, 274n13). Large clubs could boast several hundred members (Gere 4); small clubs might gather no more than ten. Many clubs participated in larger organizing bodies, like the General Federation of Women's Clubs, which in 1914 claimed 1.6 million members (Gere and Roop 2). Surveying membership documents and other archives, Anne Ruggles Gere asserts that "well over two million women participated in the club movement" (5). Though not all clubs preserved and shared their documents with archives, I have seen club artifacts in libraries and collections in Athens, Georgia; Asheville, North Carolina; Chicago, Illinois; and Geneva, Indiana; scholars have written about primary documents from Texas, Ohio, Pennsylvania, and Utah.

Studies of the women's club movement demonstrate that, despite the far-flung locations of these clubs, their literary activities tended to look the same. Clubs emphasized reading, writing, and performance in a supportive social setting. Clubwomen gathered in members' homes or local meeting spaces to discuss literature, politics, art, and other topics about which they read and wrote. Discussions might be informal, but many were responses to formal papers given by club members. The Saturday Morning Club founded by Julia Ward Howe in 1871, for example, initially alternated discussions with lectures given by prominent figures—including Ralph Waldo Emerson and Bronson Alcott—but the club quickly replaced open discussion with the reading of members' papers (Gere and Roop 3). Many clubs defined their programs in advance, assigning topics, hostesses, and presenters to each week of the club season, which followed the school year (E. Long 480).

Printed texts, including programs, newspapers, and magazines, made it possible for clubwomen to share their work in ways that mirrored the contemporaneous expansion of print capitalism and prefigured networked fan communities of the late twentieth century. Clubs shared texts in networks both informal and formal. Informally, clubwomen circulated papers, constitutions, bylaws, and programs among each other; formally, federations and organizing bodies "established centralized offices that in part served as a clearinghouse for club texts" and created publications where clubwomen could publish their texts (Gere 8). Newspapers like the *Woman's Era* published and publicized the work of African American clubs and clubwomen, uniting "geographically dispersed readers" in an imagined community that centered "around the importance of literary activity as a means of self-improvement and affirmation" (McHenry 499). Every national club organization had at least one such publication (Gere 8–9). Clubwomen also worked in and across networks to mount "a public exhibit of club yearbooks, study guides, outlines of methods, portraits of officers, and photographs of clubhouses" at the 1893 World's Columbian Exposition in Chicago (Gere 8). Club newspaper *Far and Near* counseled working-class women on the economic logistics of visiting the Exposition and printed articles describing its sights for those who could not attend in person (Gere 157). Print also allowed those women who were systematically excluded from the Exposition to speak back: Ida B. Wells printed and distributed a broadside entitled "The Reason Why the Colored American Is Not in the World's Columbian Exposition" (Gere 155).

Documents like those exhibited at the World's Columbian Exposition demonstrate that clubwomen were committed to organizational structures that "signaled the seriousness of their endeavor" (E. Long 479). Clubs could and did replace college, not only for middle-class white women (E. Long 478) but also for working-class white and middle-class African American women who were further excluded from higher education (Gere 215–16; McHenry 495). Club rules, mission statements, and parliamentary proceedings were a way for women to assert authority over their own educations and attempt to refute critiques and challenges from men.[4] Outward-facing documents like programs

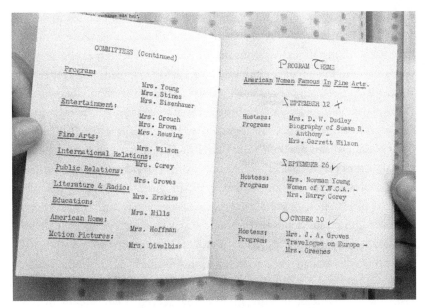

FIG. 1. Program of the Lanier Literary Club, 1950. Lanier Literary Club Scrapbooks, 1937–1993, MS158 NC Collection, Special Collections at Pack Memorial Library, Asheville, NC, 27. Photograph by the author, 2016.

emphasized the seriousness of the topics studied. As Elizabeth Long has noted, white clubwomen sought to use literary high culture to "confer cultural authority" upon themselves (478). Many clubs convened around the celebration of a distinguished literary figure: for example, for the Friday Club of Jackson, Mississippi, that figure was Emerson (Gere and Roop 4); several clubs across the country focused on Shakespeare (E. Long 479); and the Lanier Literary Club of Asheville, North Carolina, chose Sidney Lanier but supplemented the club year with diverse topics, including "American Women Famous in Fine Arts" (see fig. 1).

But clubwomen tempered the gravity of their organizational structures with communal joy, setting themselves apart from higher education by embracing fun. Women's clubs emphasized the playful aspects of their literary work, as do fan communities from the 1960s to today.[5] Clubs engaged in literary impersonation, parody, and performance that undercut the "seriousness" of their project by challenging the boundaries of "high" culture. Even as early as the 1830s, Harriet Beecher Stowe prepared for the Semi-Colon Club parodical essays that took on the voices of Samuel Johnson and Joseph Butler. In a letter, Stowe highlights the stylistic absurdities she used to channel these writers: "I have been stilting about in [Johnson's] style so long that it is a relief to me to come down to the job of common English. . . . My first piece was a letter from Bishop Butler, written in his outrageous style of parentheses and foggification" (Stowe, qtd. in Tonkovich 157). Stowe doesn't just imitate; she teases.[6] The Emerson-inspired Friday Club appropriated Emerson, as well as "A Visit from Saint Nicholas" and the Bible (Gere and Roop 14). Even club records became the subject of playful parody, as minutes from the Friday Club demonstrate: "Shall I allow myself to be carried away by the poetic fancies and melodious measure of a Carlton, or imitate the quaint humorous style of a Robb, steal the deep wisdom & philosophy of a Gibson, or making their best my own, fuse the whole into one gigantic and glorious production, or thus cast a suspicion on the originality of their matter and style, since mine must necessarily be the Epitome of what is best in all?" (Zelie Emerson, qtd. in Gere and Roop 15). Having been tasked with producing meeting minutes that served as entertainment when read aloud, the Friday Club's appointed record keepers became the subject of playful literary analysis (Gere and Roop 9). Zelie Emerson (no relation, I presume) elevates her fellow club members to author status, identifying them only by their last names and stylistic tendencies, like the great men whose books they read and discussed. She muses as to which style she should "imitate" or "steal," and teases that her literary prowess is such that, should she decide to "fuse" all previous styles together, her appropriation would be so skillful that members would suspect the earlier texts of having been appropriations. Literary styles, for these women, are "productions" that can be analyzed, interpreted, imitated, and rearranged—and these sophisticated skills are comfortably employed for laughs. Rather than treating texts as inviolable sacred objects, Stowe, Zelie Emerson, and their club peers take pleasure in appropriating, mimicking, and rewriting them—performing the same kinds of "impertinent raids on the literary preserve" that Henry Jenkins described in his seminal 1992 work on television fans, *Textual Poachers* (24).

Despite the national mechanisms for sharing club documents, groups also worked to protect their members, effectively establishing bounded spheres in which women felt safe to share work that was at turns serious, silly, and subversive. As Gere and Roop argue, "within the space created by clubs, women subverted the ideology of authorship and appropriated texts with a spirit of playfulness" (10). The idea of "space" here is key. Because clubs met in private homes or semi-private meeting rooms, the women could be relatively assured that their performances and discussions were protected from outsiders.[7] Social contracts between club members worked to prevent inappropriate in-group judgements. Clubs adopted Mary Stewart's 1904 "Collect for Club Women" as their motto, the first line of which declared, "Keep us, oh God, from pettiness" (Lanier Literary Club Scrapbooks).

Some clubs went so far as to create physical archives of texts that were closed or restricted from view. The Saturday Morning Club housed their private archives in a green trunk which members needed special permission to open (Gere and Roop 6–7). The green trunk re-creates the private drawing room, with clubwomen's texts taking the places of their bodies and voices. In both spaces, women are protected and thus (more) free to play.[8]

Scholars of white and African American clubwomen emphasize the affective bonds made possible in the same-sex spaces of women's clubs, in terms that often mirror fan studies scholars' descriptions of contemporary fandom. Clubwomen were more than acquaintances or study partners; they developed close relationships fostered by shared emotional experiences with literature. Anne Ruggles Gere notes that clubs "consciously fostered intimacy among members" by meeting in each other's homes, eating and drinking together, and working to minimize dissent (45–47). The language of this intimacy was recorded in club documents and mirrored in club newspapers (Gere 46, 50). Peer support was especially important to African American clubwomen, who faced challenges in acquiring literacy that white women did not. Black women benefited from "the intellectual relationships and the atmosphere of sympathetic female peers found in collaborative literary groups. . . . [They] relied on the combination of intellectual challenge and emotional sustenance for their developing talents" (McHenry 501). Some clubs purposefully eschewed hierarchy in their organizational strategies, preferring instead to rotate duties so that all members could gain leadership experience (Gere and Roop 5). Traditions like this one gave clubwomen "a deeply felt sense of solidarity" and led one woman to call her club "'a democracy of brains,' because status had so little meaning in their discussions" (E. Long 486).[9] Likewise, fan studies scholars describe contemporary online fandom as a "queer female space" and emphasize the sophisticated analytical work in which female fans engage (Lothian, Busse, and Reid 103, 109). Like Zelie Emerson pondering the stylistic tendencies of her fellow clubwomen, this analytical work focuses on fans' shared texts as well as on themselves and their identities.

The same-sex literary intimacy of clubwomen and fans is a powerful tool for transformation, as researchers of both groups repeatedly note. For Elizabeth Long, white women's clubs engendered a sense of "sisterhood" and made possible "the transformation of identity" that gave "an exhilarating sense of the powers and possibilities of womankind" (485). Elizabeth McHenry ascribes a similar power to African American women's clubs; especially for the mother-daughter team who published the *Woman's Era,* "reading and association with print were more than inspirational: they were transforming" (499). Through reading and club discussions, Black women could take on a set of masculine-coded skills that merged with, but did not disrupt, their feminine identities (McHenry 499). Anne Ruggles Gere argues that club work transformed not only the women who engaged in it but also the cultural and social formations of the worlds they inhabited. Gere begins her book-length study of women's clubs with a chapter on "the liking, love, and care that animated the literary practices of clubwomen, lending their reading and writing transformative power" (14). She characterizes women's clubs as "warmly supportive environments" that encouraged participants to believe "that their own production and consumption of texts could change material circumstances" and to articulate those beliefs (Gere 53). In each of these accounts, the intimate work of literary play makes possible conceptual and material changes for the women who engage in it, for their communities, and for their descendants. These changes—from increased literacy and personal confidence in individual women, to the creation of hundreds of libraries in communities across the country (E. Long 488), to constitutional amendments providing for the abolition of slavery, for temperance, and for white women's suffrage—worked together to reshape the United States during the club movement. Such transformative changes cannot be easily disentangled from one another.

For contemporary fandom, the "transformative" quality of their work also has legal significance: given the strength of copyright law in the United States, fans who create and post fanworks to the internet have adopted the term "transformative" to signal the protected status of their creations under the legal doctrine of Fair Use. By using the term, fans and their advocates (such as the Organization for Transformative Works) are arguing in advance of any legal challenge that their creations sufficiently pass the Fair Use test as interpreted by the Supreme Court.[10] While this construal of the transformative is less sweeping—it refers to texts, not social formations—it is still founded in a commitment to literary appropriation, parody, and play that contemporary fandom shares with turn-of-the-twentieth-century women's clubs.

It is possible that the cultural and media studies approach to fandom has itself transformed the conversation about active and social reading and writing practices, including those of clubwomen. Elizabeth Long consciously writes against an older interpretation of women's clubs as "engaged in a rather passive activity" (482). Gere and Roop's work on collaborative writing emphasizes a playful and subversive approach to learning within the club framework that reads as nearly identical to analyses of television fandom. Though their article does not cite them, it is hard to miss the influence of Michel de Certeau and Henry Jenkins. The literary play Gere and Roop describe fits easily into the rubric of "textual poaching" that Jenkins borrows from Certeau and extends. Jenkins writes that "fans actively assert their mastery over the mass-produced texts which provide the raw materials for their own cultural productions and the basis for their social interactions. In the process, fans cease to be simply an audience for popular texts; instead, they become active participants in the construction and circulation of textual meanings" (23–24). The fan groups Jenkins studied for *Textual Poachers* were mostly women (1); with the benefit of a wider perspective, we can see that their active reading practices, social interactions, and transformative textual productions were prefigured in the women's literary clubs of the late nineteenth and early twentieth centuries.

Accounts that end the women's club movement in the 1920s or 1940s present their literary work as both exceptional and unsustainable. They privilege a narrative in which women's clubs were defeated by college professors (Gere) and second-wave feminists (E. Long), and in doing so, contradict their own claims to the "transformative" cultural work clubwomen performed. In these accounts, women's clubs are a historical blip. I argue that we can connect women's literary club work with their contributions to the wider cultural landscape, seeing their textual practices beyond the narrow margins of their own communities. Clubwomen could and did impact literary culture and the marketplace, but accounts of both women's clubs and fan communities tend to overemphasize their members' amateur status. Most of the two million or more women who participated in the women's club movement never became nationally—or even regionally—celebrated writers. Not many were Harriet Beecher Stowe.

But women's club members did become popular, even famous, writers. They topped bestseller lists, directed acclaimed museums, won Pulitzer Prizes and Guggenheim Fellowships, and at least one opened her own film studio. In the sections that follow, I discuss two such writers—Gene Stratton-Porter and Gwendolyn Brooks—with an eye toward understanding how their literary club work shaped their writing, which in turn shaped American literature itself.

The Wednesday Club: Intimate Regionalism

Before she became a celebrated naturalist and best-selling regional novelist, Gene Stratton-Porter was born Geneva Grace Stratton in 1863, on her family's farm outside of Lagro, Indiana. She married pharmacist Charles Darwin Porter in 1886, and the couple had one child, Jeannette, who grew up to write a biography of her famous mother, entitled *Life and Letters of Gene Stratton-Porter* (1928). According to this biography, Stratton-Porter—called "Gene" by her husband and family—moved to Geneva, Indiana, in 1889 and began participating in the social life of the small town (Meehan 87–88). Stratton-Porter was not yet the naturalist, photographer, and author she is remembered as; rather, she was a bored wife who tried her hand at violin, embroidery, and china painting "to occupy her spare time" (Meehan 88). The first publication bearing Stratton-Porter's name was still eleven years away.[11] But, as biographer Judith Reick Long has demonstrated, those eleven years were spent engaged in a variety of cultural pursuits through which Gene Stratton-Porter trained herself to write, take photographs, and study nature, despite never having finished high school. These pursuits were shaped by the social education trends of the time, including the women's club movement.

Grief, as well as boredom, motivated Stratton-Porter to write. Mark Stratton, her father, died after a stroke in January 1890. Stratton-Porter later wrote that the time after her father's death was "a constant struggle to find an outlet for the tumult in my being" (*Homing* 44). First, she turned to music; then she turned to writing (J. R. Long 124). In 1892, Stratton-Porter seems to have submitted a manuscript, titled "The Strike at Shane's," to a contest run by the American Humane Education Society of Boston, Massachusetts (J. R. Long 124). The Society was offering "three $200 prizes to anyone who could write a story with as much appeal as *Black Beauty*," which they had published to much success (J. R. Long 124).[12] "The Strike at Shane's" was not one of the three winning entries, but the society published it anonymously in 1893; their president, George Angell, died in 1909 without having revealed who wrote the book (J. R. Long 126). But Judith Reick Long's biography argues compellingly that Stratton-Porter indeed wrote it, citing "its story line, its characterizations, a grammatical error found also in an early Stratton-Porter letter, as well as a certain peculiar phrase found also in one of her early works" (126).[13]

Also in 1893, Gene Stratton-Porter and her husband attended the World's Columbian Exposition in Chicago, where a national network of clubwomen had mounted an exhibition of club materials. Both Bertrand F. Richards and Judith Reick Long note that the Exposition inspired the Porters to build a large cabin in Geneva (Richards 29–30; J. R. Long 131–32), and Long notes that Stratton-Porter liked the rustic Forestry Building (131).[14] Neither mentions whether Stratton-Porter visited the Women's Pavilion and saw the women's club exhibit or the large library of books written by women.

We do know, however, that Stratton-Porter organized a women's literary club of her own in Geneva almost immediately thereafter and used the weekly meetings to practice her writing skills. The Wednesday Club was in full swing by May 1894, when it was first written up in the *Geneva Herald*. "Perhaps not many in the city are aware that we have a flourishing Ladies Club," the newspaper column reads. "The club was originated by Mrs. Beall and Mrs. [Gene Stratton-] Porter and after many meetings and much effort has arrived at the dignity of a full-blown woman's club with constitution and bylaws" ("The Wednesday Club," May 18). Though very few club records appear to exist today, this brief description demonstrates that Stratton-Porter's club was indeed part of the women's club movement discussed above. It was named for the day of the week they met, a standard club convention, and it evinced the same organizational seriousness, with its constitution and bylaws, of other clubs. One week, Gene Stratton-Porter read a letter from the president of another club on the topic of federation ("The Wednesday Club," June 15). The newspaper reports that Geneva's clubwomen were "much interested in the discussion of programs and the federation" ("The Wednesday Club," June 15), but it is unclear if the club decided to join the umbrella organization. The club also produced printed programs laying out the predetermined schedule for the fall to spring season, as other clubs did, and it encouraged members to participate in the playful manner noted of other clubs above. The newspaper write-ups praise the "spice, wit, and wisdom" of weekly "roll call," when members affirmed their presence with literary quotations and aphorisms fitting the topic of the week ("The Wednesday Club," May 18, October 19).

The club focused on literature—specifically American literature during its first season—and it required women to present a paper to be initiated into the club. The column notes the club's work was rigorous: only those "willing to give their Wednesday afternoon and several hours a week to the hardest sort of literary work" could inquire about membership requirements with Stratton-Porter, who served as secretary ("The Wednesday Club," May 18). Members presented papers on and read excerpts from literary stalwarts Washington Irving, Edgar Allen Poe, James Fenimore Cooper, Henry Wadsworth Longfellow, Henry David Thoreau, Ralph Waldo Emerson, William Dean Howells, William Jennings Bryant, and Walt Whitman. But they also wrote about and discussed women writers like Louisa May Alcott, Emma Lazarus, Margaret Fuller, Sarah Orne Jewett, Julia Ward Howe, Constance Fenimore Woolson, and Harriet Beecher Stowe ("The Wednesday Club," May 18). The clubwomen alternated reading papers and selections from the texts: Stratton-Porter read selections from Julia Ward Howe one week ("The Wednesday Club," May 18), and papers on Grace King and Mary Hartwell Catherwood at subsequent meetings ("The Wednesday Club," June 15, July 6). In the following season, spanning from 1894 to 1895, the Wednesday Club took the history and arts of England as their subject; according to their program, Stratton-Porter presented four papers and four sets of "questions" for the group ("Programme").

Of all her contributions to the Wednesday Club, only one essay appears to have survived: an appraisal of Walt Whitman, which Jeannette Porter Meehan published in her biography of her mother. Whitman, "the most Democratic man that ever lived" (Stratton-Porter, qtd. in Meehan 91), seems especially well-suited to the "democracy of brains" that the women's club sought to embody. But he also provided Stratton-Porter and her club with the thrill of sexual desire, experienced in a private circle of women.

Stratton-Porter's essay models the club aesthetics discussed above, a distinctive combination of Victorian "high" culture, deeply felt emotion, and experiments in literary impersonation. It begins with twinned claims to authority, based on her emotional work and her careful citations of literary masters:

> Before beginning the meat of this paper, I wish to say that I have approached my wonderful subject with fear and trembling. It has not been

a case of "fools rushing in where angels fear to tread," but slowly, steadily, with depth of emotion painful at times, I have given every available moment for three weeks to my subject and his book.

What I have to say of my own inspiration is open to your fullest criticism. When I quote Tennyson, Emerson, Thoreau, Ruskin, Dr. Johnson, D. G. Rossetti, and Conway, I consider myself as giving incontrovertible proofs of the statements I make. (Stratton-Porter, qtd. in Meehan 88)

As promised in the newspaper announcement, the work of the Wednesday Club was time-consuming and rigorous, but it was also emotional to the point of being painful. Stratton-Porter signals the seriousness of her work, and of the group's role in presenting criticisms during discussion, and yet her affective claims supplement the authority established by her references to canonical authors. Rather than fearing that emotions make her ineffective as a critic, Stratton-Porter claims them as a strength.

The essay continues with a brief précis on Whitman's life that continues this focus on emotionality. Stratton-Porter calls attention to episodes that display Whitman's empathy: his work as a Civil War nurse, the sheltering and feeding of runaway slaves, and his attendance at the funeral of a prostitute (Meehan 89, 92). She lingers over descriptions of his simple domestic life and his love of nature:

His house resembled a deserted ship cabin: a place in which to eat, sleep, and write—but not to live; the world was his home. His house had bare floors, walls, and rooms, was all cheap, poor, and common. The tapestries he loved were curtains of waving green; the carpet his feet trod with satisfaction was his beautiful *Leaves of Grass,* the handkerchief of the Lord, dropped to earth as a remembrance, worked with his initials marking it—Whose? The walls he loved, the blue dome of heaven, lit by the glorious golden sun-fire or sparkling and darkling with night stars. His pictures were stretches of sea and land, human movement and faces, every littlest part or particle of earth a picture of interest to his masterly mind. (qtd. in Meehan 89–90)

Passages like this one combine sentimental diction ("the handkerchief of the Lord," "the blue dome of heaven") with Whitman's own galloping sentence structures. Stratton-Porter channels his stacked clauses and parallelisms into her own long, accretive sentences, and later in the essay, when she quotes Whitman's poetry, her appropriation of his effusive style becomes readily apparent.[15] Like Harriet Beecher Stowe, like Zelie Emerson, Gene Stratton-Porter did not just pen a report on her subject; she took on his style, reproducing it to stage an exegesis of it.

She also embraced Whitman's sense of his physical embodiment and the sexuality that his poetry channels. Stratton-Porter equates Whitman's poetry with his body, as he did in "Whoever You Are Holding Me Now in Hand," one of the "Calamus" poems that had been part of *Leaves of Grass* since 1860. Like Whitman, she is not coy. He invites his reader to kiss his mouth and thrust him, in the form of the book, "beneath your clothing, / where I may feel the throbs of your heart or rest upon your hip" (Whitman 99–100); she channels Whitman's voice to caution her audience, "To the doubting, timid soul he warns: 'Do not touch my book. It is a man, it breathes; you are putting your hands on a bare body'" (qtd. in Meehan 93).

Indeed, Stratton-Porter's frank appraisal of Whitman's physical form seems intended to thrill the women gathered to listen to her paper:

> In his prime he stood six feet four, and weighed two hundred pounds. Physically, morally, spiritually, he was large and free. His beautiful head had a noble weight, ease, and repose. He had never known an illness and was of superb stature and symmetry without a flaw. He would be big and free and strong. His always open shirt-front disclosed a neck and chest of Godlike symmetry and white, glistening flesh. His hands and arms were large, and well formed. . . .
>
> He liked to stretch his body on the green sward in the sun with the winds of Heaven to fan him, and to be of the earth, earthy. He simply would not be confined; the world was his stage; he would travel it. His brain should scale mountain and peak; all nature, and all nations were his. (qtd. in Meehan 90–91)

She revels in these details, in his exposed chest and large hands. She gives her fellow club members a portrait of the author as sex symbol. Her Whitman is the Whitman of "Children of Adam" and "Calamus," the notoriously sexual poems that celebrate democracy as a gathering of bodies to touch and be touched by one another. Stratton-Porter basks in this side of Whitman, even when discussing "My Captain," about the assassination of Abraham Lincoln: "Yet it seems not a matter to mourn over," she writes. "It quickens the pulse; it wets the eye; it pulls the heartstrings, it quivers the flesh" (qtd. in Meehan 94). She spends particular time on the details of "Children of Adam," a grouping of poems containing "the frankest confessions of pure passion to legitimate ends ever put in print" (qtd. in Meehan 95). She teases her listeners that they will likely blush to read what is there, seeming to goad them into reading *Leaves of Grass* so they can feel the "quivers" she has described. And yet, Stratton-Porter ends her paper with a reassertion of literary authority, quoting Emerson and Thoreau, and a final argument for Whitman's proximity to the sacred. "If you believe in God," she entreats, "if you love the green grass, flowers, and trees: if you know what the leaves whisper and the waters murmur and the birds sing; if you love God's creation above man's manufacturing—read the book. If in your heart there is the throb of universal love and pity; if your hand has lain on the bare body of man and it has not frightened you, read the book. You will be better for it" (qtd. in Meehan 96–97). In this passionate endorsement, several threads come together: the intimacy and self-improvement of the women's club movement, in which women gathered privately in homosocial settings to reinterpret literary texts for their own uses; a prefiguration of the "queer female space" of online fandom, where women gather to share erotic experiences via text; Stratton-Porter's lifelong love of nature and her use of romantic tropes to convey that love; and her recourse to the language of religious morality.

Stratton-Porter did not, to my knowledge, write directly about Whitman again. But echoes of this paper can be found across her later, published works—that is, the themes and contexts expressed here remained central to Stratton-Porter's oeuvre, even as she definitively crossed from amateur to professional writer. Though several scholars note the intertextual relationships of Stratton-Porter's novels to American writers like Alcott, Howells, Emerson, Thoreau, and Whitman,[16] none explicitly link Stratton-Porter's club work to her published texts, nor do they consider how club atmosphere and aesthetics might contribute to the larger literary movement in which Stratton-Porter participated. But her club work, including her intimate and sexually charged report on Whitman, clearly influenced her novels—especially their engagement with emotionality and the bodily thrill of nature—and those texts helped define regionalism as a literary movement.

In novels like *Freckles* (1904), *A Girl of the Limberlost* (1909), and *The Harvester* (1911), Gene Stratton-Porter combines evocative descriptions of her natural surroundings with romantic and sentimental plots to produce fiction that participates in the feminist, queer, community-minded regionalism identified by Judith Fetterley and Marjorie Pryse.[17] These three books, among the most popular of Stratton-Porter's thirteen published novels, model the kind of empathic, transformative, and intertextual stories that permeated both women's clubs and regionalism. In *Freckles,* a poor Irish orphan with one hand is hired to guard the Limberlost swamp for a lumber company, falls in love with its wild beauty and rare specimens, and is rewarded for his empathy and care with marriage to a beautiful young woman he calls "the Swamp Angel." *A Girl of the Limberlost* follows Elnora, an impoverished but moral girl who pays for her own high school education by gathering moths from the Limberlost swamp and selling them to naturalists. She, too, is rewarded for her goodness with a happy marriage. The hero of *The Harvester,* an appropriation of Henry David Thoreau as literary character, makes his fortune raising medicinal herbs, marries a beautiful woman to rescue her from her abusive uncle, and saves her from illness with his herbal medicines—whereupon she finally falls in love with him. In each of the three stories, Stratton-Porter combines sentimental plot tropes with close observation of her natural world and the bodies of her characters, creating regional fiction infused with the empathy of regionalism and the intimacy of women's clubs.

Readings of these novels have tended to lean heavily on their predecessors in American literature, but they neglect to consider what the Wednesday Club, and the larger women's club movement, taught Gene Stratton-Porter to do with that literature. For example, Barbara Ryan reads *The Harvester* as a response to "romantic imagineerings" of Henry David Thoreau ("The 'Girl Business'" 185). She contrasts the novel's depiction of him with one written by Louisa May Alcott, focusing on the promise of "sexual rapture" that enthralls and motivates Stratton-Porter's version (Ryan, "The 'Girl Business'" 186). Ryan notes that sexual desire and Thoreau are usually thought not to mix: "It was Hawthorne, rather than Thoreau, who actually drew admiring eyes when he walked down a Concord road" ("The 'Girl Business'" 191). But it is Whitman whose "robust appearance" and "manly strength and force" Stratton-Porter seems to be revisiting in *The Harvester* (33, 355). It is her sexually charged club essay, performed for an intimate community of women, that is channeled when she writes about the

Harvester swimming naked: "He plunged with a splash and swam vigorously for a few minutes, his white body growing pink under the sting of the chilled water" (*The Harvester* 19–20). Trained in the Wednesday Club to play with her influences, Stratton-Porter is comfortable with—even adept at—reshaping the legacy of Thoreau to include the sexual thrill of the masculine body in nature.[18]

Anne K. Phillips argues that Stratton-Porter's novels introduced nonacademic readers to the Transcendentalism of Emerson, Thoreau, and Whitman (153), but that her version of the philosophy privileged domesticity and community above individuality. Stratton-Porter's fiction is full of "epiphanies . . . almost uniformly associated with the miracles of nature," wherein "Transcendentalism becomes a means of achieving not only personal but also social enlightenment and re-direction" (Phillips 154). Though Phillips mentions Stratton-Porter's club work, her article does not connect it to the project of her fiction. I argue that what Phillips has noticed is a combination of Transcendentalist, regionalist, and women's club ethics. Stratton-Porter brings these three movements into contact with one another in her fiction, finding the places where their missions touch or overlap.

Despite telling stand-alone stories, *Freckles, A Girl of the Limberlost,* and *The Harvester* are linked, making them a fascinating example of how Stratton-Porter's proto-fan community experience gets expressed in her work, and how those expressions anticipate the later work of female fans rewriting staid narratives for their own purposes. All three novels are set in the Limberlost swamp beside which Stratton-Porter lived, and they share between them several characters. Stratton-Porter herself appears in all three books as "The Bird Woman," a naturalist and photographer who inhabits the woods alongside the other characters.[19] The Bird Woman features most prominently in the first of these novels, *Freckles;* by the time of its publication in 1904, the novel's Bird Woman would have already been recognizable as Stratton-Porter, given her widely published photographs of and essays on birds. In the novel, she brings the Swamp Angel to the Limberlost, where Freckles meets and falls in love with her. Though Freckles is the protagonist of the novel, and the Swamp Angel his love interest, the Bird Woman is the catalyst who makes the love story possible. Her role in the novel represents and comments on Stratton-Porter's role as writer, drawing attention to the constructed nature of the love story, as something that must be plotted and prompted by a force outside the lovers themselves.

In *Freckles,* Stratton-Porter demonstrates her interest in appropriating and playing with literary conventions, especially those of sentimental and adventure fiction. The novel ends with a common sentimental trope: Freckles is discovered to be the lost son of an Irish lord and thus deemed worthy of marrying the Swamp Angel (Stratton-Porter, *Freckles* 158–61).[20] And yet the journey toward this cliché ending reveals Stratton-Porter's interest in otherness and empathy, and her willingness to subvert the traditional gender roles of popular fiction. Like other regionalist stories, *Freckles* explores marginalization, disability, and queerness; like her club writing, the novel does so by bringing its readers into an intimate relationship with the bodily experience of its characters, especially Freckles himself. Though the novel has been called "wholesome" (J. R. Long 178), this focus on embodiment gives it the same sense of sexual thrill that permeated her Whitman essay.

The novel's third-person narration begins closely focused on Freckles, the one-handed Irish orphan who has left Chicago to find work in rural Indiana. He stumbles into a lumber camp in the Limberlost swamp and is given work guarding the lumber company's land by the Scottish company boss, McLean. In these first chapters, Freckles must become oriented to his new job and unfamiliar natural surroundings. At the same time, the reader becomes oriented to Freckles, his physical and emotional trauma, and the depth of his feelings. Though Freckles matter-of-factly describes being beaten, crippled, and left for dead as a newborn (Stratton-Porter, *Freckles* 5), the narrator represents his emotional experience as overwhelming his body. He feels "homeless friendlessness [sweep] over him in a sickening wave" (1); like a Regency heroine, he blushes, turns white, and draws "quivering breath" (2). His "hungry heart" reaches for companionship (3, 12). Stratton-Porter's narrator relates Freckles's emotional experience in sentimental diction that makes the reader keenly aware of what is going on with his body.[21]

Stratton-Porter establishes Freckles's worthiness as a romantic hero through his early experiences in the swamp, but her version of heroism eschews masculine virility in favor of empathy and intimate care. Despite Freckles's disability, McLean hires him to walk the seven-mile perimeter of the lumber company's stand, checking and repairing the fences and preventing poachers from stealing the valuable timber. At first he is terrified of the wide-open unknown, the loud animal cries, and the marsh-grass that seems to defy the wind (8). Stratton-Porter personifies the forest as female: it is the body of a wild, wary woman that Freckles must navigate with care. Upon discovering some damaged fence wires,

Freckles "was compelled to plunge knee deep into the black swamp-muck to restring them, [and] he became so ill from fear and nervousness that he scarcely could control his shaking hand to do the work" (9). As night closes in, "the Limberlost stirred gently, then shook herself, growled, and awoke around him" (9). Stratton-Porter's sexually charged language invites us to read this as a loss of virginity—but it is Freckles, not the female forest, who nervously experiences physical intimacy for the first time. When he eventually finds his way out of the trees, "a shuddering sob burst in the boy's dry throat," but he hides his fear; no one around him guesses "the innermost, exquisite torture" he feels (10).

As Freckles becomes comfortable in the swamp, he begins to feel empathy for the animals seeking mates and to "instinctively [protect] the weak and helpless" creatures (10). After spending the winter feeding birds and other small animals, Freckles learns to love the forest, instead of fearing her: "He had been with her in her hour of desolation, when stripped bare and deserted, she stood shivering, as if herself afraid" (16). The wary, wild forest has become a scared woman, naked and in need of protection; in caring for her, Freckles is contrasted with the book's villains, a gang of poachers and thieves who want to steal her valuable timber.

So Freckles learns to care for the forest as a woman, to nurture and protect her even when she is "stripped bare" and vulnerable. Our romantic hero is a compassionate lover. Yet, when the Bird Woman and the Swamp Angel enter the story, neither woman is the human embodiment of the Limberlost that we might expect. Instead, Stratton-Porter reverses the sentimental story's traditional gender roles: Freckles becomes the damsel-in-distress who is kidnapped by the gang and must be rescued by his female companions, both of whom are proficient with firearms. When Freckles discovers the poachers sawing down a valuable tree, they capture and tie him up, planning to kill him (96). The Swamp Angel happens upon them, and though Freckles thinks he must save her, the narrator explains tartly, "the Angel was capable of saving herself" (99). She pretends to believe the gang are lumber company workers, flirts to gain their trust, and then leaves to alert the McLean and the lumber men of Freckles's capture (100–103). When she returns, with the men in tow, the Bird Woman has the thieves pinned down at gunpoint; the Angel finds Freckles "gagged and bound" and bleeding, and she rushes to free him (108–9). In a playful and purposeful reversal of the romantic cliché, two fearless women ride in to defeat the villains and save the imperiled hero.

In the end, *Freckles* does not sustain the playful subversiveness of this rescue scene. Though willing to reverse the gender roles of her characters, Stratton-Porter is ultimately unwilling to rewrite issues of class in the same way. For Freckles to marry the Swamp Angel, whose father is rich, he must be revealed as noble by birth. Still, the novel's conclusion retains some of its community-centered regionalist ethic: instead of returning to Ireland to claim his lordship and wealth, Freckles chooses attending college in Michigan and then returning to work at the lumber company with McLean (171). In the last moments of the novel, Freckles conflates the Limberlost with the Angel: "I have her and the swamp so confused in me mind I never can be separating them. When I look at her, I see blue sky, the sun rifting through the leaves and pink and red flowers; and when I look at the Limberlost I see a pink face with blue eyes, gold hair, and red lips, and, it's the truth, sir, they're mixed till they're one to me!" (172). Even in its conventionality, this ending suggests one final subversion: if the Angel and the Swamp are one, then Freckles has already consummated their marriage.[22]

Publicly, Gene Stratton-Porter downplayed the sexual suggestiveness of her works. She called the love story of *Freckles* "a slight romance as a sugar coating" ("My Life" 13) running through and adding interest to the nature book she wanted to write. Her daughter wrote that "Mother was always pleased that [*Freckles*] helped the boys" (Meehan 117). But, read against her only surviving club essay, novels like *Freckles* and *The Harvester* seem designed to please and excite the community of middle-class white women who might gather in a sitting room or parlor to contemplate the bodies of men, "large," "free," and "bare" as nature made them.

The Chicago Poet's Class: Transformative Midcentury Modernism

A veteran of both the women's club movement and Chicago's modernist art scene, Inez Cunningham Stark convened the Chicago Poet's Class at the Southside Community Arts Center in 1941. Born Inez Travers in 1888, the wealthy white socialite spent her teen years on Chicago's Gold Coast covering women's clubs for the *Chicago Tribune*. Her lengthy columns, which appeared irregularly from 1914 until her first marriage in 1916, had so much material that the city had to be split into sections: Downtown, Southside, North Side, West Side, Suburban (Travers 3). Inez wrote up literary meetings and philanthropic activities, lectures about architecture and John Galsworthy, bridge parties and reciprocity days.[23] In 1936, now remarried and using the name Inez Cunningham Stark, she became director of the Renaissance Society, a small museum of contemporary art on the campus of the University of Chicago. Under Inez's direction, the Renaissance Society embraced modernisms European and American, visual, aural, and literary. She exhibited the work of Marc Chagall, Wassily Kandinsky, and Paul Klee; she brought composer Sergei Prokofiev to debut new music; and she mounted an exhibition of modernist writers' manuscripts and letters by mining the archives of *Poetry* magazine, where she had both served as a submissions editor and published a few poems (Olson 50, 54).

But Inez was also interested in supporting the work of African American artists and writers, especially those in the nearby neighborhood of Bronzeville. She showed the work of Black painter Charles Sebree and mounted a group show entitled *Paintings and Sculpture by American Negro Artists* (Olson 50). Though she left the Renaissance Society in 1941, her relationship to both modernism and Bronzeville continued, in the form of the Chicago Poet's Class.

The class was not a women's club. It was not a fan club. It was closer to a university writing workshop, and yet it flourished in the years before such programs became widespread,[24] and it was organized in the basement of a small community arts center in a Black neighborhood notoriously segregated from the university campus next door. Still, I argue that we can interpret the Chicago Poet's Class as functioning like these groups: the class occupies the interstices of the women's literary club movement, the fan clubs of the era, postwar writing workshops, and, like the Wednesday Club, it prefigures contemporary online fandom spaces built around textual transformation and play.

Sadly, the class has been relegated to the footnotes of literary history—and likely would be forgotten completely were it not for Gwendolyn Brooks's subsequent poetic success and fame. The few brief accounts of the class forefront the ways in which it operated less like a university classroom and more like a literary club, emphasizing social bonds over learning outcomes. Brooks wrote about the class in her 1972 autobiography, *Report from Part One*. She begins the account with Inez, casting her as an "elegant 'rebel'" who defied Chicago high society by refusing to entertain its outright racism (Brooks, *Report* 65). In a scant three and a half pages, Brooks emphasizes the sociality of the class and Inez's friendly feedback. Inez, Brooks wrote, "did not care to be regarded as a teacher, but as a friend who loved poetry and respected our interest in it" (66).

In her role as "friend," Inez brought "books from her own beloved library, to be freely loaned to any member of the class who wanted them"; she bought her "students" subscriptions to *Poetry* magazine; she read poems aloud and then sat back and let the class erupt in "a burst of excitement" (66). In nonhierarchical fashion, members "diligently learned from and taught each other"; they also established a fellowship prize in honor of Edward Bland, a member of the class killed in World War II (67). Another history notes that Inez encouraged class members to enter poetry contests (Bone and Courage 219), one of which Brooks won. Other attendees likewise emphasize the intimacy and care with which Inez facilitated the group. John Carlis remembers the class thusly: "We became friends—I mean, everyone in her class. Most of the people in her class became good friends" (qtd. in Najar 316).

Carlis also elaborates on the material studied in the class, a mix of modernists ranging from William Butler Yeats to Langston Hughes to Vachel Lindsay (qtd. in Najar 316). Brooks remembers studying Robert Hillyer's *First Principles of Verse*, which focuses on diction, meter, and form and recommends reading Yeats and Lindsay, as well as T. S. Eliot, W. H. Auden, Emily Dickinson, Robert Frost, and William Rose and Stephen Vincent Benét (Hillyer 154).[25] Unfortunately, few other records of the Chicago Poet's Class exist, making it difficult to know what other poets or what specific poems were read and discussed. Still, these few examples provide interesting insight into how the class operated and what effect it had on Brooks.

The Chicago Poet's Class engaged with problematic material and reshaped it for their own purposes—a tactic that self-identified fan communities since at least the 1960s have also employed in their transformative works. Henry Jenkins points to such work in television fandom, in a description that resonates with my reading of the Chicago Poet's Class: "The fans' response typically involves not simply fascination or adoration but also frustration and antagonism, and it is the combination of the two responses which motivates their active engagement with the media. Because popular narratives often fail to satisfy, fans must struggle with them, to try to articulate to themselves and others unrealized possibilities within the original works. Because the texts continue to fascinate, fans cannot dismiss them from their attention but rather must try to find ways to salvage them for their interests" (24). As Lubna Najar has documented, Inez played the class recordings of Vachel Lindsay, the "white popular modernist" whose poetry W. E. B. Du Bois criticized for its racism (316–17). Najar wonders what potentially "uncomfortable discussions" resulted from listening to Lindsay's poetry and concludes that such discomfort "may have been precisely the moment of opportunity for recasting the racism of modernism" (317). Najar demonstrates this work through the poetry of Margaret Danner Cunningham, reading her poem "Garnishing the Aviary" as evidence of how the Chicago Poet's Class "refashioned the commitments of the [modernist] tradition in their own image" (319–20). Najar's account of the "productive" recasting of modernist primitivism sounds essentially identical to the work of the television fan communities Jenkins studied. Cunningham, Brooks, and the other poets of the Chicago class used their frustration with popular modernism, especially its racist primitivism, to create their own modernism, salvaging what they could from the tradition and making it speak to their own identities and experiences.[26]

The recent scholarly focus on the Chicago Poet's Class has helped critics better understand Gwendolyn Brooks's early poetry, especially its midcentury engagement with modernism. As others have argued, the collection that most bears the stamp of the Chicago Poet's Class is *Annie Allen*. Published in 1949, this book won the Pulitzer Prize for Poetry, making Brooks the first African American writer to win that honor. In 1987, D. H. Melhem wondered "why Brooks chose mock heroic [for *Annie Allen*], unusual for a modern poem" (63), but read in light of the Chicago Poet's Class, the choice makes sense. For example, Robert Bone and Richard Courage argue that the class shaped the book, especially its "aesthetics" and turn away from the more overtly political poems of *A Street in Bronzeville* (218). More recently, Julia Bloch reads *Annie Allen* alongside long poems by midcentury modernist writers, pointing to how its form does and does not diverge from contemporaneous poems: "Like several American poets writing in the middle of the century, Brooks used the long poem to experiment with collage, narrative, and fragmentation; Brooks's 1949 poem favors inductive assemblage over linear narrative, as is the case in contemporary works such as Williams's *Paterson* (1946–1958) or H.D.'s *Trilogy* (1944–1946)" (Bloch 441). Connecting these threads, then, I argue that *Annie Allen* differs from other midcentury modernist war poems because it emerged from the intimate collective of the Chicago Poet's Class, a pseudo-fan community where writers gathered to critique and play with shared texts, much like the women's literary clubs of the previous decades.[27]

The triptych of poems in *Annie Allen* engages in sophisticated transformative work, marrying the modernist postwar epic with the pulp archive, filtered through Brooks's neighborhood observations. The three parts represent the life of a Black woman named Annie as a series of fragmented documents: first "notes," followed by a mock epic and its "appendix" purporting to be "leaves from a loose-leaf war diary," and finally a long collection of poems whose formal coherence gradually disintegrates. In its form, then, the book represents a fictional archive: a fragmentary and incomplete collection of documents that, read together, suggest a larger story or history. As Leif Sorensen has argued, modernist poetry shared its fascination with the incomplete or mysterious archive with early twentieth-century pulp fiction, especially magazines like *Weird Tales*, the pages of which are an "intertextual archive that seems at times to continue and at others to parody modernist fascinations with ethnographic depictions of difference and intertextual efforts at consolidating a cultural tradition" (502–3). But by creating an archive of one woman's life, Brooks reaches beyond the modernist and pulp fascinations with antiquarianism and ethnography; her book recalls the green trunk of the Friday Club, where documents of women's lives were stored, as well as Abigail De Kosnik's theorization of fanfiction as a form of "archontic literature," discussed in my introduction.

Annie Allen is as much about death as it is about the life of Annie, but Brooks toys with our expectations of whose dead body will appear. Thus, "the ballad of late Annie" in "Notes from the Childhood and Girlhood" is about Annie late in the day, not dead: "Late Annie in her bower lay, / Though the sun was up and spinning" (Brooks, *Annie Allen* 34). Lazing in her backyard "bower," Annie thinks about the unsuitability of men for marriage; the second refrain of "proud late Annie" signals as well the death of her girlhood and her childish ideas about men.

Coming between "Notes on the Childhood and the Girlhood" and "The Womanhood," the mock epic "The Anniad" illustrates that death with a "soft aesthetic" that makes it feel inevitable instead of shocking or even tragic (49). In the poem, Brooks rewrites Greek and Roman heroic verse via the literary high modernism of H.D., and of T. S. Eliot and Ezra Pound, whom, Bone and Courage note, Brooks read between 1934 and 1945 (217). The poem's title is obviously a play on Virgil's "The Aeneid," calling to mind that poem's intertextual relationship to *The Iliad* of Homer. But Brooks transforms the epic into a celebration of "smallness" (*Annie Allen* 47) in forty-three stanzas about Annie falling in love with a "tan man" who leaves to fight in World War II, returns frustrated and unfaithful, and then dies, leaving Annie "to dismiss / Memories of his kick and kiss" (48). Brooks shrinks the form into short lines and sentence fragments that occlude the story. This is not the epic narrative of Virgil; Brooks makes the action difficult to follow, filling her stanzas with imperatives, gerunds, and missing subjects:

Think of sweet and chocolate,
Left to folly or to fate,
Whom the higher gods forgot,
Whom the lower gods berate;
Physical and underfed,
Fancying on the featherbed
What was never and is not. (38)

The love affair at the center of "The Anniad" is full of such negations, of "what was never and is not." Annie is an anti-Helen, for whom "no ravishment enrages. / No dominion is defied" (39). She opposes Helen physically as well: she is "underfed," and unlike the glaring whiteness of H.D.'s beloved Greek statuary, she is "unembroidered brown" with "black and boisterous hair" (39). Brooks thus challenges the antiquarian preoccupation with white beauty by emphasizing Annie's dark coloring and hair.

While contemporaneous poems such as Una Marson's "Kinky Hair Blues" depict the impossibility of celebrating Blackness in the face of white beauty standards, "The Anniad" uses its softness to sanctify its Black characters. Annie is sweet and chocolate in the stanza above; the "godhead glitters" on the brow of Annie's "man of tan" (39); and when he "leads her to a lowly room," the poem is unambiguous about the holy quality of their lovemaking:

Which she makes a chapel of.
Where she genuflects to love.
All the prayerbooks in her eyes
Open soft as sacrifice
Or the dolour of a dove.
Tender candles ray by ray
Warm and gratify the gray. (40)

Brooks's phonetics emphasize the "soft" and "tender" qualities of this stanza. Breathy sibilants appear in every line, while open vowels are paired with gentle fricatives ("soft," "of," "love," "dove"). The effect highlights the connection between "The Anniad" and the oral poetry of antiquity. But unlike her Greek and Roman inspirations, Brooks's narration does not follow the tan man to war. Rather, the poem speaks from Annie's remove from the battlefront: it can only imagine the "hunched hells across the sea" (41), and the tan man returns after no more than two stanzas away (42). The poem is more interested in what happens when "with his helmet's final doff / Soldier lifts his power off" (42); when, in other words, he returns from the relative empowerment of World War II, where Black Americans could fight and die for their country, only to find himself disempowered by a racist nation once again.

Driven by his war experience to desire "nothing meek," the tan man repudiates Annie's softness and pursues "bad honey" in the form of other, wilder lovers (43–44). Still, Annie is the hero at the center of Brooks's epic: she "seeks for solaces" in the passing seasons, in friends, in jewels and books and perfume (44–47), and when the tan man dies, she is older but not broken. She can

Adjust the posies at her ear,
Quaff an extra pint of beer,
Cross her legs upon the stool,
Slit her eyes and find her fool. (48)

Brooks deflates the grand tragedy of the epic: not only does Annie live beyond her lover's death, but she goes on to a "Womanhood" full of children and diner booths and the continued grind of "prejudice" barely sweetened by "politeness" (66).

Annie Allen continues the work of A Street in Bronzeville, making a poetics out of the regular lives of African Americans. But it also furthers this project by retelling the modernist war epic, centering an anti-Helen and reshaping poetic form to fit her life. Brooks uses the modernist fragmentation of linearity, of narrative, and of metatextual artifacts to suggest that Black lives have long been marred by such breaks—and that, rather than destroying their lives, these breaks are merely to be lived through. Like Margaret Danner Cunningham's revision of modernist primitivism discussed above, Brooks does not abandon modernism's Eurocentric engagement with ancient Greece and Rome, nor its solipsistic ahistoricity. Instead, she marshals the willingness of the Chicago Poet's Class to engage with suspect literary traditions in order to enact the transformation suggested by *Annie Allen*'s final lines: though "there are no magics or elves / Or timely godmothers to guide us," the book demonstrates Brooks's ability to "Wizard a track through our own screaming weed" (66), an ability honed in community alongside the other writers of the Chicago Poet's Class.

As these two case studies show, one basic exercise of the literary club—to practice transformative writing in a private community of like-minded friends—influenced not only "amateur" participants but also the work of professional writers. Gene Stratton-Porter drew on her club work to create sexually suggestive regionalist fiction for other white women; Gwendolyn Brooks's pseudo-fan community experience helped her define a midcentury modernism that she and her fellow Black poets could embrace with less reservation. In the fifty-five years between their experiences, these women helped shape a literary marketplace increasingly attuned to "fans" and their transformative textual practices. As chapter 2 demonstrates, when Gene Stratton-Porter opened her own film studio in 1924, film fan magazines had for years been encouraging readers to become "fans" who participated by writing letters and entering contests. And by the time Gwendolyn Brooks won the Pulitzer Prize for *Annie Allen* in 1950, "fandom" was far from niche—instead, it was regularly being discussed in the pages of popular magazines like *Time* and *Harper's*.

TWO

Fandom in the Magazines

Here end the sorrows of the race—all want and wretchedness and crime,
Where Care must seek another place—where Sin must bide another time;
Here where the heart's wiped clean and dry—where in dull breasts the flame is lit,
As young and old wait the reply—a Strike-out—or a Two-base hit?
  —GRANTLAND RICE, "At Random in Fandom," *McClure's Magazine*, 1916

I read the article in *Harper's* and I understand that "fandom" was very pleased with this picture of themselves.
  —MARY GNAEDINGER, *Saturday Review of Literature*, 1947

The proto-, pseudo-, and self-proclaimed fan communities of chapter 1 relied on their ability to gather in physical space to affirm their fellowship and practice their playful, subversive literary experiments. They gathered in sitting rooms, parlors, church meeting rooms, and hotel ballrooms. They showed up for each other, body and breath.

But they also relied on the virtual "spaces" created by circulating print materials. Magazines, newspaper columns, and printed programs helped these communities of interest and practice to publicize their work, find new members, shape US culture, and archive records of their activities for posterity. The women of Asheville's Lanier Literary Club, for example, kept scrapbooks detailing their meetings, campaigns, and achievements from 1937 to 1993—scrapbooks full to bursting with press clippings and other printed material.[1]

Circulating print material, especially periodicals, served as surrogates for the sitting rooms and meeting spaces where club members gathered. The magazines of national club federations connected far-flung clubs to one another. But they could also connect individuals—even those who could not or did not want to join in-person meetings—to a club, to a network of federated clubs, or simply to the idea of the club movement.

Fan communities continued to rely on print in circulation even as the networks of fandom grew increasingly casual and nonhierarchical. By the time Henry Jenkins and Camille Bacon-Smith published their seminal scholarly works on television fandom in 1992, membership in a community of fans did not necessarily require devoting "several hours a week to the hardest sort of literary work" as Gene Stratton-Porter's club had demanded. The organizational seriousness of the women's club movement had loosened significantly, and it continued to loosen as fandom moved off the printed page and onto the internet. And though many fans—especially those who publish thousands of words of fanfiction in fanzines or online—still spend several hours a week or more on their literary work, all that is now needed to become a member of fandom is to identify as one.

Fanzine culture exploded in the 1970s and 1980s (fig. 2). The writing, editing, printing, circulating, and reading of fanzines constituted a significant portion of fan cultures and practices, so much so that Camille Bacon-Smith begins her book *Enterprising Women* with the assertion that it is "a book about women who produce a massive body of literature, art, and criticism about their favorite television and movie characters" (3). But, as I described in my introduction, scholars like Bacon-Smith begin their investigations of fanzine culture from a flawed premise: that "media fandom began as *Star Trek* fandom" (16), and that *Star Trek* fandom adopted its fanzine practices from a small cadre of white male science fiction pulp readers of the 1930s and 1940s.

This chapter tackles that myth. In the first part, I argue that scholarly accounts of American media fandom history have obscured the relationship between early twentieth-century fandom and the literary marketplace out of which it developed. To better illustrate these connections, this section presents an alternate history of the birth of American media fandom,

FIG. 2. Fanzine button, likely created in the 1970s or 1980s. Fanlore.org.

one that takes into account the many ways that the periodical press, both literary and pulp, helped shape fans and fandom. Though literary scholarship, especially that focusing on early twentieth-century modernism, insists on the dominance of a cultural hierarchy, print culture was not strictly stratified. In the same *Saturday Review of Literature* column, for example, one could read about science fiction fandom and Edna St. Vincent Millay. The second section of this chapter turns specifically to that popular weekly magazine, reading across its issues and features to develop a case study of other literary fandom communities in the 1920s, 1930s, and 1940s. This investigation moves from the *Saturday Review* to *Harper's Bazaar,* to the science fiction pulp *Amazing Stories,* and back again to *Harper's* as it examines two very different interactive fictions built in the popular press, and what they can tell us about fandom in the magazines.

The Birth of American Media Fandom: An Alternate History

The science fiction version of fandom's origin tends to dominate discussions of media fandom and, in particular, fanfiction, despite being based on an exaggerated reality. In the foreword to *Fic: Why Fanfiction Is Taking Over the World,* Lev Grossman begins by connecting the 1966 debut of *Star Trek* with two published works of transformative literature, Jean Rhys's *Wide Sargasso Sea* and Tom Stoppard's *Rosencrantz and Guildenstern Are Dead* (xi). Anne Jamison, *Fic's* primary author, flashes back further with her "Prehistory of Fanfiction," touching on Aristotle, Chrétien de Troyes, Shakespeare, *Don Quixote,* Samuel Richardson's *Clarissa,* and George Eliot's *Middlemarch* in a playfully anachronistic retelling of literary history as fandom trajectory (26–36). Her irreverent anachronisms are useful, illuminating rather than obscuring connections between intertextuality, adaptation, and fan history. But that playfulness is quickly supplanted by the supposedly more factual version of the "Birth of Media Fandom," in which Jamison asserts, "At first, fandom culture and its zines . . . were almost entirely male-dominated" (75). She reinforces this claim with an essay by librarian and science fiction scholar Andy Sawyer that examines 1950s and 1960s British fanzines and fanfiction to argue that fandom was born in the pages of the science fiction magazines— particularly the US pulp *Amazing Stories,* with its letter column that "made fandom possible" (80). Sawyer's fandom origin story echoes the one told by Bacon-Smith, Coppa, and others. It stresses the "radical decision" of *Amazing*

Stories editor Hugo Gernsback to include that vaunted letter column that "enabled fans to start communicating with each other" (A. Spencer 94–95).

This story isn't exactly false. Yes, Hugo Gernsback included a letter column in his science fiction pulp magazine *Amazing Stories,* beginning with volume 1, issue 10 ("Correspondence," January 1927)—but letter columns had existed since at least the eighteenth century.[2] Yes, Gernsback's letter column eventually adopted the practice of printing the full addresses of correspondents—but it did so at the suggestion of a reader who wrote, in October 1927, that arguments would be easier to pursue if readers could contact one another directly (Gernsback, "Correspondence," October 1927: 713). And yes, it was in the pages of the *Amazing Stories* letter column that several readers banded together to form a "Correspondence Club" that eventually hosted Worldcon, the first science fiction fan convention—but the club was originally created "for the betterment of science," not the shared enjoyment of science fiction (Gernsback, "Correspondence," August 1927: 515). And anyway, as chapter 1 demonstrated, by the time Worldcon began in 1939, women had been gathering in proto-fan communities and holding conventions for almost one hundred years.

So Sawyer's story isn't exactly true either. It presents a history in which science fiction magazine readers and fans are disconnected from the larger networks of print culture in which they participated. Like the science fiction tales Gernsback published, the story of the origin of media fandom has a basis in factual reality. But this reality has been exaggerated into myth—self-consciously styled by early science fiction fandom participants whose versions emphasized their own involvement—creating a narrative that leaves out whole swaths of important history while also neglecting issues of interactivity in print culture, "fan" and "fandom" terminology, access to and safety in clubs and groups, interest in reading and writing, and alternative models of educational communities.

Looking beyond the science fiction pulps, it is possible to trace another version of the spread of "fan" identity and "fandom" as community.[3] In this version, *Amazing Stories'* community of readers was enabled by an already richly interactive media culture whose print aspects included corporate advertisements as well as personal and classified ads, contests, letter columns, and fan mail. These elements were important features of nearly all magazines published in the early twentieth century, from intellectual monthlies like *Harper's* and *Scribner's,* to popular "middlebrow" magazines like the *Saturday Evening Post,* to the massive industry of pulps that included not just *Amazing Stories* and science fiction but also dozens of magazines specializing in romance, Westerns, mysteries, horror stories, and more. Taking *Amazing Stories* as one element among many in the shifting relationship between the literary marketplace and consumers, the sketch that follows presents a fuller, though by no means comprehensive, picture of the early decades of American media fandom.

It would be difficult to overestimate the amount to which wide-sweeping changes in media contributed to the development of what we now call fandom. As Carl Kaestle and Janice Radway argue in "A Framework for the History of Publishing and Reading in the United States, 1880–1940," the period's "communication revolution," which included major advances in technology and dissemination such as the telephone, commercial radio broadcasting, lower-cost paper for magazines and newspapers, half-tone lithograph reproduction, wire services, and newspaper syndication, enabled Americans in far-flung locations to share reading and listening material like never before (9–13). "The revolution in print, auditory, and visual communication," they note, "strengthened the possibilities for a national popular culture" (13). But even as national corporations gave rise to corporate capitalism and US nationalism, the population centers of America became increasingly diverse, due to both immigration and the migration of southern African Americans to the cities of the North. Conflicts between corporate consolidation and diverse populations "led to the creation of alternate, diverse, locally generated bodies of knowledge situated within evolving subcultures and countercultures that helped people to make sense of these charged interactions" (Kaestle and Radway 15). The loose association of communities we now call "fandom" were part of this development, flourishing alongside the corporate consolidation of media and storytelling to which they emphatically spoke back, and expressing themselves in a variety of print locations.

Furthermore, these subcultural bodies of knowledge did not operate in isolation. Rather, as Margaret Beetham argues: "Though each journal might constitute a particular community of readers, there was a great deal of overlap and borrowing. And, of course, readers entered into this circulation of ideas and images. It was, and still is, one of the characteristics of the periodical press that it invited readers to become writers—most frequently through letter pages and competitions. To describe the periodical as an 'interactive' form is to deploy anachronism but the form did invite reader participation well beyond any interior change of consciousness or silent participation in the 'we' of the reading

The Motion Picture Fan
By La Touche Hancock

He's a spunky little fellow, without a
  trace of yellow,
He knows his motion picture A. B. C.
He rivals all the sages, and accurately
  gauges
The films that will be pleasing to
  a "T".

He's very free with strictures, on in-
  appropriate pictures.
On every mechanism he's *au fait*,
He can talk about the locus, of the
  fluctuating focus,
And let you know the minute it's
  O. K.

Should he discourse on shutters, weigh
  every word he utters,
You'll find he won't make much of
  a mistake.
His original disclosures, on powder
  and exposures,
Are anything, believe me, but a fake.

So on ad infinitum, you'll find there's
  not an item,
On which he will not have his little
  say,
He's business-like, and handy, in fact,
  he's quite a dandy,
This hero of the motion picture day!

FIG. 3. "The Motion Picture Fan," by La Touche Hancock. *Motion Picture Story Magazine* 1.5 (June 1911): 93.

community" (235). Though Beetham is describing British suffragette periodicals of the 1880s and 1890s, her assertions are relevant to print culture across
the Atlantic in the following decades. Periodicals relied on reader interaction
in ways that heavily influenced fandom, as I discuss below. But they also interacted with the larger literary industry: "periodicals were never self-contained
entities. Endemic in the form were addresses to other publications, whether
other serials or books" (Beetham 235). This networked interactive print culture
set the stage for the birth of fandom at the turn of the twentieth century.

As I noted in my introduction, the term "fan" first appeared in the late 1880s
and originally referred to enthusiasts who followed the emerging sport of
baseball. The periodical press enabled readers to follow their teams in text,
and to feel that they were part of a community of fans, without needing to
visit the ballpark. Here, as in all examples of textually constructed fandoms,
we see proof of Benedict Anderson's assertion that "print-capitalism . . . made
it possible for rapidly growing numbers of people to think about themselves,
and to relate themselves to others, in profoundly new ways" (36). After being
coined in the sports pages, the word "fan" then began appearing in early film
magazines, signifying a person who follows motion pictures the way a baseball
fan follows his team.

In a poem from the June 1911 issue of *Motion Picture Story Magazine* (fig. 3),
"The Motion Picture Fan" is described as a young man who demonstrates his

superior knowledge of the film industry: he can judge good movies and expound on the technical details of the filmmaking process. The poem's final stanza suggests this portrait might be more than a little satirical; the dandyish fan, it seems, simply cannot keep from having "his little say" on everything related to motion pictures.

Although this poem pokes fun at the feminized, know-it-all film fan, the film magazines soon realized that such devoted interest made fans the ideal consumers—both of films and of the magazines that promoted and even stood in for them. Early film magazines featured advertisements for other periodicals, especially those that appealed to what we might call the fannish sensibility. In 1911 *Motion Picture Story Magazine* ran an advertisement for the *New York Dramatic Mirror* that proclaimed the paper "indispensable" for the "moving picture fan" (November 1911: 639), and an advertisement for the *Strand Magazine*'s "146 Pages of Reading" including Arthur Conan Doyle's "The Adventure of the Red Circle," which the ad declared in large text was a Sherlock Holmes story (April 1911: 396).[4] These appeals to fans were not isolated incidents but rather the editorial strategy under which the magazine functioned. As Kathryn Fuller observes, it was around this time that *Motion Picture Story Magazine* became "a lively, interactive colloquium for the sharing of movie fans' knowledge and creative interests" (137). And only three years later, the November 1914 issue of *Photoplay* includes a reference to "dyed-in-the-wool fans" who possess comprehensive knowledge of motion pictures—not just the stars but the production companies and their film series (20; see fig. 4)—but this time, written in a tone of approbation.

Photoplay also advances the possibility that fans can become professionals working in the film industry—in other words, that they can use their specialized knowledge to become even more active participants and be granted bona fide insider status. A "Thumbnail Biography" of scenario (script) editor Richard V. Spencer begins with his declaration: "I became interested in motion pictures early in 1909. . . . Of course I had been a fan long before that" (168). Though not all fans would, could, or wanted to become film professionals, Spencer's casual assurance of his fan status demonstrates how important the identity was to early film magazines.

Once discursively defined, fans could be marketed to, not just as consumers but also as budding experts and hopeful professionals-to-be. *Photoplay*'s advertisement section reinforces this multivalent aspirational matrix.[5] In it, readers

MARY FULLER

as every dyed-in-the-wool fan knows, is the famous Edison leading woman, star of the "Mary" series and heroine of the "Dolly of the Dailies" pictures, who recently left Edisonville to become a Universal star. She used to imagine that she would become an opera star, and spent several years having her voice trained. Then at seventeen she went on the stage, and from that into the world of photoplay, where she scored a tremendous triumph.

Photo by Bradley, New York

FIG. 4. Promotional portrait of Mary Fuller. The caption begins, "Mary Fuller, as every dyed-in-the-wool fan knows, is the famous Edison leading woman." *Photoplay*, November 1914: 20.

find ads for specialized products like the Fox Literary Keyboard, intended specifically "for photoplay writers" (*Photoplay*, November 1914: 157), as well as books and magazines that teach how to write scenarios that will sell (165). Film fans who aspire to write photoplays are encouraged to enter a contest for new motion picture plots and receive yet another book on "How to Write Photoplays" (186–87), while "amateur photographers" can mail away for "2 Camera Books Free!!" (176). Fans without professional aspirations are offered movie star–branded perfumes (183), collectors' photographs (167, 179), and stamps (174), encouraging fans to collect not only knowledge but also consumer goods.

Advertisers had come to assume that consumers aspired to be fans, and the film industry would continue to lead the charge in promoting interactivity between fans and companies via contests, advertisements, opinions polls, and letter columns (see Orgeron; and Whitehead). But it is also important to acknowledge that early film magazines like *Photoplay* and *Motion Picture Story Magazine* were primarily composed of narrative texts—of stories—interspersed with film stills and publicity images. In other words, these magazines appealed to the new market of film fans by capitalizing on the already-established conventions of literary periodicals like *Scribner's* in printing long stories ("novelettes"), short stories, and serials. That same November 1914 *Photoplay* boldly announces "Another Jesse Lasky Novelette" on its cover, suggesting that the inclusion of a long narrative story was a large part of the magazine's appeal.[6] Fan interactivity and the sharing of "stories" went hand in hand; Kathryn Fuller observes that as *Motion Picture Story Magazine* moved away from interactive content, they also removed the word "story" from the title (145).

Once there were fans, there was "fandom," and again, the periodical press used literary forms to explicate and situate this growing yet amorphous community. The June 1916 issue of *McClure's Magazine* features baseball poems and sketches headlined "At Random in Fandom" (13; see fig. 5). Among these poems are the lines that opened this chapter:

> Here end the sorrows of the race—all want and wretchedness and crime,
> Where Care must seek another place—where Sin must bide another time;
> Here where the heart's wiped clean and dry—where in dull breasts the
>   flame is lit,
> As young and old wait the reply—a Strike-out—or a Two-base hit? (13)

At Random in Fandom

Sketches by Arthur William Brown   *Verses by* Grantland Rice

Here end the sorrows of the race — all want and wretchedness and crime,
Where Care must seek another place — where Sin must hide another time;

Here where the heart's wiped clean and dry — where in dull
breasts the flame is lit,
As young and old await the reply — a Strike-out — or a
Two-base Hit?

TYRUS RAYMOND COBB
Take seven parts of hurricane and eight of
dynamite;
Add fourteen parts of flame and flash and
twenty parts of fight;
Toss in another twelve for speed and raw
nerve on the job.
And if it breaks the ball game up you'll
know the answer's COBB.

WALTER JOHNSON
We know that Matty's Fadeaway comes
drifting by like Fate;
We know how Alexander's curve revolves
across the plate;
But what has Walter Johnson got? No living
player knows,
For no one ever sees the ball that Walter
Johnson throws.

THE COACHER
"Get in the game — head up, old scout."
The Coacher's call swings to a shout;
So at Life's base the voice of fame —
"Get in the game — Get in the game."

THE VETERAN
What has he left of the name and fame
That came to him from the good old game.
The game that his soul had learned to love?
A faded dream — and a worn-out glove.

THE UMPIRE
An Umpire died — and went below,
To where hell's hottest blazes glow,
"O, what rare bliss," he called in mirth,
"Compared to what I caught on earth."

AFTER THE GAME
Since Batting Eyes or proper breed
Are trained to go for Curves and Speed,
The player jumps his day's fatigue,
To sign up with the Chicken League.

ARTHUR WILLIAM BROWN —

FIG. 5. Grantland Rice, "At Random in Fandom," *McClure's Magazine*, June 1916: 13.

Grantland Rice's mock-heroic verses may not be enduring works of great poetry, but neither do they ridicule fans' affective engagement with baseball. Rather, like much of Rice's celebrated sportswriting, they work to elevate the sport and its fans to their own heroic level, mixing earnest emotional expressions and heightened language with sports slang.[7] The turn from the elevated language of wretchedness and Sin to the game-day vocabulary of strikeouts and base hits generates humorous friction—it may provoke laughter—but the joke includes fans. It is meant for them; it invites them to see themselves as simultaneously serious and joyful, literary and fashionable. And lest we doubt *McClure's* literary pedigree, or its imbrication with popular media of its day, this page of baseball poems is followed by an illustrated story by future Pulitzer Prize–winning author Edna Ferber, here touted as the author of a successful play starring Ethel Barrymore (14).[8]

The idea of the "fan" did not stay confined to the worlds of sports and film, and given the multiple links between sports coverage, film magazines, and literary periodicals, this spread seems inevitable. As Margaret Beetham remarks, media like the periodical press "make for leaky boundaries" (231). As early as the 1910s, the "fan" identity was used to market literature to readers. "Fan" came to partially replace the clunkier "book-lover" in places like the October 1917 letter column of *Argosy*, where the editorial staff used it to describe a letter-writer who likes an author's stories ("The Log-Book" 765). By the early 1920s, advertisements in publishing industry magazines like *Publishers' Weekly* and *Bookseller and Stationer* used "book fans" as shorthand for passionate consumers of the book form. The advertising copy in *Publishers' Weekly*, encouraging publishers to buy ad space in the *Chicago Daily News*, even notes the marked difference between "book-fans" and "the *most casual of readers*" (1882, original emphasis). This delineation suggests that the concept of the devoted consumer *as fan* had moved beyond the film and sports industries, and was thoroughly established in the literary marketplace.

At the same time, pulp magazines were coming into their own. Pulps, like their literary-intellectual and film fan magazine counterparts, published a variety of short stories, serials, and "novelettes" in a mix designed to attract readers who wanted complete narratives but also to bring them back each week or month to finish that longer story. Like other magazines, they encouraged interactivity by holding story contests, printing letter columns, and encouraging readers to think of themselves as a community.[9] *Love Story Magazine*, a popular love pulp that debuted in 1921, featured not one but two departments where readers could interact with editorial staff and each other by writing in. "The Friend in Need" was an advice column that promised its primarily female correspondents, "Your letters will be regarded confidentially [sic] and signatures will be withheld," and that letters that could not be answered in the magazine would be answered by mail (148). The other department, "The Friendliest Corner," worked within these same gendered privacy concerns to connect readers with each other, in what looks surprisingly like contemporary internet fandom "friending memes."[10] Subtitled "Miss Morris will help you to make friends," "The Friendliest Corner" printed brief correspondent biographies that listed details like age, interests, occupation, and physical appearance (fig. 6). Interested readers could then write in and have their letters forwarded to the friend they chose. The magazine actively worked to promote a sense of community that extended beyond singular readers and the editorial department: "Miss Mary Morris . . . will see to it that you will be able to make friends with other readers, though thousands of miles may separate you" (Morris, "The Friendliest Corner," May 2, 1929: 143). However, it also cautions that only 'appropriate' matches would be made: "It must be understood that Miss Morris will undertake to exchange letters only between men and men, boys and boys, women and women, girls and girls" (Morris, "The Friendliest Corner," May 2, 1929: 143). Age and gender determine and limit suitable friendships, encouraging homosocial relationships or requiring writers to textually perform another identity.

It is impossible to know if "The Friendliest Corner" succeeded at fostering friendships between readers. Nor can we know for certain if those readers who wrote in represented themselves faithfully, or if they adopted a different gender or age in order to solicit letters that would "match." Nor, indeed, can we know if the department even sent on the letters it received, or if it simply kept the enclosed forwarding postage. But the popularity of the idea itself is evidenced by the roughly five pages the department took up each week, in which *Love Story Magazine* readers from Ohio to Nova Scotia sought to connect with others who had the same taste in reading material—before *Amazing Stories* even began publishing its vaunted letter column where fandom supposedly "began."

Pulps tended to be separated by genre in form, but not necessarily in audience or creator. At pulps' height in the 1920s and 1930s, readers could choose from multiple titles containing only mysteries, romance, science fiction, Westerns, or sports stories. But genre crossovers were popular as well, leading to

The Friendliest Corner

By MARY MORRIS

Miss Morris will help you to make
friends

Miss Mary Morris, who conducts this department, will see to it that you will be able to make friends with other readers, though thousands of miles may separate you. It must be understood that Miss Morris will undertake to exchange letters only between men and men, boys and boys, women and women, girls and girls. Please sign your name and address when writing. Be sure to inclose forwarding postage when sending letters through The Friendliest Corner. In case of change of address, be sure to notify this Corner, so that mail can be forwarded.

Address Miss Mary Morris, "Love Story Magazine," 79 Seventh Avenue, New York, N. Y.

JUDE OF FLORIDA is a chum, a sport, and a student. She is also very lonesome, and if any one would care to know why—well, they will have to write to her. She will answer all letters immediately.

DEAR MISS MORRIS: I am a girl, twenty years old, married, and am a brunette. I am easy on the eye, a chum, a sport, and a student. I am very lonesome, and if you would like to know why, you will have to write to me. Will exchange photos and answer every letter immediately.
JUDE OF FLORIDA.

Even if Dixie Kid goes broke buying stamps, he will answer all letters sent to him.

DEAR MISS MORRIS: Come on, boys, write to a nice boy from Dixie. I promise every one that answers my letter a lasting friendship and heaps of peppy letters. I would like to hear from fellows between sixteen and twenty-one years of age.
Remember, I'll answer every single letter I get, even if I go broke buying stamps.
THE DIXIE KID.

Waiting of Rochester is married and has a baby girl.

DEAR MISS MORRIS: I would like to make Pen Pals with every one from everywhere. I am nineteen, married, and have a baby girl of eighteen months.
Will answer every letter and exchange snapshots. WAITING OF ROCHESTER.

This boy is bubbling over with life, pep, and the joy of living.

DEAR MISS MORRIS: I'm bubbling over with life, pep, and the joy of living. Would like several young chaps to be my Pen Pals, and then I'll be completely satisfied.
I'm twenty-three, five feet seven inches tall, and have dark-brown hair and eyes. Fond of sports, music, dancing, and most everything.
Come on, boys, make it snappy; you've simply got to write to me.
SENOR CYCLONE.

Hungry Heart is a lover of music and literature.

DEAR MISS MORRIS: I am a middle-aged lady, and I get lonesome for companionship. I love music, literature, and all beautiful

FIG. 6. A letter column from 1929 promises to help readers make friends with each other, resembling contemporary internet-based "friending memes." Mary Morris, "The Friendliest Corner," *Love Story Magazine* 64.4 (August 24, 1929): 142.

romantic Westerns, mystery science fiction, and sports romances. These various genre-themed magazines were largely published by the same handful of companies, known as "fiction factories," and written by a surprisingly small pool of professional pulp writers, who worked across genres at will but often under pseudonyms. As Lee Server explains, publishers were "ever mindful of consumer trends . . . [and] turned every popular story into an instant genre, commissioning countless variations on a successful character type, setting, or plot twist" (18). Literature scholars might characterize this outpouring of fiction as cheap and forgettable (and they do—see Dinan 44; Nolan 65; and Sorensen 501), but for this fan studies scholar, it is hard not to also see in it anticipations of our contemporary, thriving fanfiction culture, in which anonymous or pseudonymous authors turn out hundreds of thousands of words a year, in easily available stories conveniently sorted by genre, trope, and type. Though there are significant differences between the fiction factories responsible for commercial pulp magazines and the fanfiction community—not least of which are the ability and desire to earn money for writing—Lee Server's celebration of pulp stories as "thriving on unconstrained creativity, held accountable to few standards of logic, believability, or 'good taste'" (9) reads like an anticipation, in many respects, of fanfiction today.

In the early twentieth-century period of media integration, few cultural texts stood on their own. Newsstands displayed a range of magazines, which in turn advertised other magazines, books, and films, and wrote about sports, theater, and radio. Indeed, many magazines, including the pulps, had ties to other forms of popular media, especially radio. *Love Story Magazine* had a radio show featuring fifteen-minute radio drama adaptations of their stories. *Amazing Stories* owed its existence to the popularity of a short story Hugo Gernsback wrote and published in his magazine *Modern Electronics* (Server 118), and the science fiction pulp was cobranded with the call letters of Gernsback's radio station, WRNY. Listeners with an affinity for radio became known as "fans" too, and they sent massive amounts of fan mail to the personalities and shows they heard over the airwaves. A 1931 magazine notes, "Myrt and Marge, William Wrigley's radio ladies, are receiving about 800 fan mail letters each day" (*Sales Management* 396). Some of these radio shows, like *Myrt and Marge,* were scripted radio dramas; others featured readings of prose and poetry or discussed popular literature of the time. Mike Chasar has written extensively about "radio poetry programs [that] produced a huge amount of material in terms of broadcast hours, fan letters that circulated millions of poems and editorial commentary on those poems, new reports and features, and print spin-off or tie-in products that took highly visible magazine and book formats" (20).[11] Chasar notes particularly the ways that "listeners responded to, or even preempted, what they perceived to be a corporate commodification of their poetry by spelling out the terms of their participation and ongoing listenership in relation to the logic of gift exchanges" (21). Beginning in the late 1920s, with the debut of commercial radio networks, and continuing through the 1930s and 1940s, the letters of these radio fans are a fascinating counterpoint to the myth of media fandom's singular emergence in the pages of *Amazing Stories*.

So the periodical press and other media outlets worked from the 1880s through the 1930s and 1940s to discursively construct "fans" and "fandom" via advertising and interactive content meant to unite readers in communities of interest and practice, bonded together by their emotional responses to narratives and by their participation in a set of specific activities. Having an affective relationship with literature was hardly new.[12] But having a streamlined, specific language for that relationship, as well as an identity that encompasses particular practices (of collection, mastery, and textual response) was new, and it changed the way the media talked about and to passionate readers. Fans and media worked together (and sometimes at cross-purposes) to construct reading as both interactive and communal—and this working together was not just something that happened in *Amazing Stories*. Rather, it was built into the very structure of the periodical press and the other forms of integrated media on the rise in the early twentieth century. As Sean Latham and Robert Scholes argue, "periodicals . . . are by their nature collaborative objects, assembled in complex interactions between editors, authors, advertisers, sales agents, and even readers" (529). The same can be said, to some extent, of radio, film, professional sports, and literature—in other words, of the broad range of American media out of which fandom was born.

Though I have focused on the textual traces of fandom in corporate and commercial media, I do not mean to suggest that fandom was created by a top-down process in which corporate media created identities and dictated terms. Rather, as I've tried to make clear, the creation of fandom as group identity, practice, and model of community depended on the interactions between media creators and consumers at all levels of the culture industry hierarchy.[13] The periodical press serves as a rich archive of US media fandom's history because it has been collected and preserved, and because its model of interactivity could, in many ways, sidestep copyright laws that have made publishing fanfiction difficult, if not impossible, for more than one hundred years.

This alternate version of the birth of American media fandom opens up a vast field of potential fan studies research. Case studies of early fandom history can be explored in context, for both the similarities and the differences of each burgeoning fan community. To that end, I now turn to another letter column—one that worked to gather and unite a fandom before and after its much-mythologized *Amazing Stories* counterpart, and even interacted with that community of early science fiction fans in interesting and unexpected ways.

Literary Fandom's Virtual Meeting Spaces

The *Saturday Review of Literature* debuted in 1924, when the editorial staff of the *Literary Review* section of the *New York Evening Post* split from that paper. This staff included a few major figures of 1920s "middlebrow" publishing, including Henry Seidel Canby, Amy Loveman, Christopher Morley, and William Rose Benét. Though these names are obscure now, throughout the 1920s, 1930s, and 1940s they signaled quality middle-class literary values. Canby taught at Yale; Loveman served on the reading committee for the Book-of-the-Month Club; Morley helped found the Baker Street Irregulars and was also an early judge for the Book-of-the-Month Club; Benét was family friends with celebrated modernist poet Marianne Moore, and he won the 1942 Pulitzer Prize for poetry. Their magazine sought to mediate between several points on the cultural hierarchy of the era, embracing and promoting a sophisticated-yet-fun mix of academic rigor, pulpy mass entertainment, and "highbrow" art. In its first ten years, the *Review* published American and British literary figures such as Edith Wharton, Lytton Strachey, George Santayana, Louis Untermeyer, James Weldon Johnson, John Buchan, Edwin Arlington Robinson, Robert Frost, Amy Lowell, Edna St. Vincent Millay, Conrad Aiken, Edith Sitwell, Langston Hughes, T. S. Eliot, Aldous Huxley, Lord Dunsany, Vincent Starrett, and Willa Cather, among many others.

Volume 1, issue 1, begins with a mission statement by Henry Seidel Canby that establishes the *Review* in the role of cultural mediator, as a fulcrum between intellectual overseriousness and uncritical enthusiasm. Of the art of literary criticism, Canby writes: "The half hearted intellectual afraid of his enthusiasm, is as much of a charge upon criticism as the entranced sentimentalist. One suffers from too little love to give and the other from too little sense in loving" (1). Given love's crucial role in the magazine, it is no surprise that its pages were, from this first issue, a gathering place for the burgeoning fannish sensibility in literature. Thus, alongside war poetry, book reviews, and a reading-themed advice column, the first issue features an H. G. Wells pastiche that would not look out of place in a science fiction fanzine. "The Nightmare," credited to "H. Jeewells" but written by Christopher Ward, imagines Wells as a sixteen-year-old boy given to dreaming about strange future civilizations where everyone does science naked (6). Written in an absurd reproduction of British dialect, the brief story features Wells trying to explain to his family his dream of England two thousand years in the future, where "on'y them works at anythink, flower beds an' vegtibble gardens, as works fur love" (6). Wells's family scoffs at the implausibility of his dream-vision, which parodies the themes of socialism and eugenics in his early scientific romances. As the story ends, his uncle derides his dream as a nightmare that ignores hundreds of thousands of years of human nature, and begs him to "stick to wot you knows about" if he ever grows up to write a book (7).[14]

Though Ward's pastiche is critical of Wells, its set-up and punch line only succeed if the reader is familiar with Wells's work, especially his 1924 novel *The Dream*. "The Nightmare" thus functions as an inside joke between Wells's fans, who are assumed to be reading (and whose "nightmare" would be if the uncle's dour presentiment were to somehow come true). This reading is corroborated by the *Review*'s choice to print a response to "The Nightmare" in issue 3, written by a seventeen-year-old, G. Peyton Wertenbaker, who had recently published his first science fiction story in Hugo Gernsback's *Science and Invention* and would go on to write for *Amazing Stories*. In the letter, Wertenbaker praises Ward's parody as loving tribute, decries a *New York Times* review of Wells's novel written by G. K. Chesterton, and effuses that "Wells is indeed a poet, the greatest poet in the world . . . the Poet of the Dawn, the dawn of man's true glory, the dawn of absolute poetry" (54). Wertenbaker's letter demonstrates further connections between readers of the pulps and the more mainstream periodical press, and between "fans" and "authors," and amateurs and professionals. Above all, I argue, it demonstrates that few if any fannish interactions take place in a vacuum. Book lovers and fans found many places for themselves at this time, and certainly more than one publication contributed to their understanding of their identities and cultures.

The *Review* assumes its readers are "book-lovers" (August 2, 1924: 15, 23) and "fans." The word "fan" itself appears twice in the first issue: once in a back-page advertisement for a crossword puzzle book (24), and again, more importantly, in the magazine's "Phoenix Nest" feature (22). Edited by William Rose Benét, this hybrid news and letters column was a *Review* mainstay—a convivial literary social space that encouraged its readers and correspondents to think of themselves as a community united by their love of books. In other words, it was the letter column of a literature fandom.

Each week until his death in 1950, Benét wrote as equal parts literary insider and enthusiastic fan, filling the "Phoenix Nest" with loving literary parody and pastiche, news, gossip, opinions, and reader contributions. He begins his first column with a poem that gleans from William Shakespeare and John Keats, transforming their words into a teasing, Orientalist ode to the phoenix and dedication for the column itself (or "colyum," in Benét's colloquial spelling):

"Let the bird of loudest lay
On the sole Arabian tree,
Herald sad and trumpet be,
To whose sound chaste wings obey."

Thus writ Shakespeare in a poem
I but vaguely understand
Yet—because it's come to hand—
Let it serve me for a proem.

[. . .]

I met a Phoenix in the sands
(To turn to Keats, with tongue in cheek,)
Its feet were claws—it had no hands
But a whale of a beak!

[. . .]

With the which unblushing crib
I this colyum dedicate
And my pen I consecrate
From the handle to the nib

In the service of my betters
And the books that they compose.
Aid thou my initial throes,
Phoenix, patron fowl of letters! (August 2, 1924: 22)

Benét's dedicatory poem demonstrates his adeptness at mixing together literary references from a range of periods and styles—including classical mythology, Elizabethan and Romantic verse, and Jazz Age slang—and hints at both his wide-ranging literary vocabulary and his willingness to make fun of himself. Benét performs the unschooled, "middlebrow" book-lover, and this tactic serves to shape the column as a friendly, unintimidating space for all those readers who might be able to quote Shakespeare but can't quite understand his meaning.

From this first column, it is clear that Benét thought of the "Phoenix Nest" page as a virtual representation of a physical space that would gather together a community of readers. He roams "the vast silence of this fantastical desert," his mock-heroic diction turning the pages of the *Review* into a fanciful place where "an occasional Chimaera may stroll our way, attracted by the rattle of our Underwood," and the phoenix cries out "From among the dates—publishers' dates" (22). Benét's column is full of such puns and juxtapositions, which, like Ward's parody of Wells, hinge on readers' knowledge and mastery of literary forms and figures. But, unlike the 1911 poem "The Motion Picture Fan" quoted above, Benét, Ward, and the *Saturday Review of Literature* approach the fan community as insiders—laughing with, not at, fans.

Having thus established this gathering space for his imagined community, Benét fills the remainder of the page with an allusive stream of literary notes and musings that ranges between Carl Van Vechten, Arthur Rackham, Edith Wharton, Douglas Fairbanks in the silent film *The Thief of Bagdad,* Paul Robeson in Eugene O'Neill's *All God's Chillun Got Wings,* Ring Lardner, Mark Twain, *The Dial,* Rebecca West, and on and on. Benét begs to know who is publishing E. R. Eddison's high fantasy novel *The Worm Ouroboros* in America, as he has been dying to read it; he then declares, "we register here and now as a thorough [E. M.] Forster fan," before concluding the column as "the Arabian sun has set on our perfect week" (22). The virtual space of his column has transformed into the time between issues of the magazine, subtly inviting readers to reconvene in the next column, next week.

Benét's friendly editorial "we" and his ready claiming of the identity of "fan" made his "Phoenix Nest" a lively virtual salon to which literary fans of all kinds could gain entrance. Benét welcomes all (or at least, all who can feel at home in his Orientalist fantasy), and he never shies from his own fan status: in addition to Forster, Benét readily admits himself a "fan" of H. C. Bailey, a detective novelist whose main character "comes nearest to the dream of all good detective-story readers—the dream of the lamp lit again in Baker Street, the fog settling down outside and Watson smoking his pipe by the fire when the knock comes on the door" (December 2, 1933: 309). In the 1940s, in between discussions of "Great Authors" like Shakespeare or John Milton and contemporary luminaries like Booth Tarkington and Henry Miller, Benét published a series of correspondence from the National Fantasy Fan Federation, remarking on just how many literary "big shots" were part of "fandom" (October 28, 1944: 32).[15] In a 1945 column, he follows a discussion of Algernon Charles Swinburne with the answer to a reader's inquiry about science fiction fandom terminology, and includes the National Fantasy Fan Federation's recruitment address (February 3, 1945: 28). A 1947 column finds an ongoing debate about America's favorite poet (suggestions include Conrad Aiken, Edna St. Vincent Millay, and Robert Frost) bracketing a letter from pulp magazine editor Mary Gnaedinger, who writes: "I was interested in the discussion of [William S.] Baring-Gould's article in *Harper's* ["Little Superman, What Now?"] which you ran in The Phoenix Nest for October 26. I read the article in *Harper's* and I understand that 'fandom' was very pleased with this picture of themselves" (January 4, 1947: 32). That Benét chose to print her letter clearly shows overlap between the various fan communities his column hosted—readers of American poetry, the pulps, and the *Review*. Indeed, Benét's regular habit of printing pastiche or parody poems—written by himself and his readers and correspondents—suggests that the practices of those overlapping circles of fans had more in common than not. That is to say, no matter the genre or form, literature fans of the era expressed themselves in the same way many fans do today: by crafting their own transformative creative works.

But Benét's column also suggests the limits of goodwill surrounding fan creativity, and his printing of Gnaedinger's laudatory letter further dispels the fan studies myth about the primacy of *Amazing Stories*. Baring-Gould's 1946 article, of which Gnaedinger felt fandom approved, presents a fascinating look at post–World War II science fiction fandom, including *Amazing Stories'* fall from grace under the editorial guidance of Raymond A. Palmer. Baring-Gould notes that the once-vaunted pulp now has "a place at the very bottom of the list" of American science fiction magazines (285). He attributes this fall primarily to Palmer's decision to devote much of the magazine to "The Shaver Mystery," a series of articles, purporting to be factual, about a race of evil men with telepathic powers living underneath the major cities of the world:

> Palmer's most successful bid for new readers has been "that mystery known by the name of the man who started it all, The Shaver Mystery." Briefly, a writer who signs himself Richard S. Shaver has written articles for *Amazing* in which he maintains that beneath New York, London, Paris, Berlin and virtually every other world capital, lies a network of caverns, the home of a race called the *deros* (or *deroes*). . . .
>
> Palmer seems anxious to give the impression that he himself is firmly convinced of the existence of Shaver's deros, for he has made a number of unequivocal statements in his capacity as editor, such as that "*there are caves in Tibet and they are full of deros who make life a hell for mankind outside Tibet as well as inside*." (Baring-Gould 286, original emphasis)

Baring-Gould faults crass commercialism for the prevalence of "The Shaver Mystery," but as his account reveals, Palmer's "bid for new readers" is made still more insulting by his insistence that the stories are real. The sin is, in effect, the dual betrayals of the fannish gift economy: Palmer has violated unspoken fandom principles by being too blatantly commercial *and* by attempting to disguise his sales gambit in a way that only further exposes how gullible he thought his readers were.

Read generously, "The Shaver Mystery" could be seen as a fascinating experiment in interactive storytelling: an example of an Alternate Reality Game (ARG) that precedes the implementation of early ARGs by fifty years.[16] Because it was set in the "real world," "The Shaver Mystery" encouraged readers to take up the fiction themselves; *Amazing Stories* already had a lively letter column to host reader contributions, and Palmer rewarded readers by not only printing their letters but also reshaping the magazine so as to emphasize them:

> Palmer has launched several departments in *Amazing Stories* to keep his readers "informed on the developments in the greatest 'hunt' by science fiction fans in history for what may be the most important of truths," and he welcomes contributions. He gets them, too—even though "many believe they are risking their lives by writing to us." These people, says Palmer, have two things in common: "First, they do not know whether or not they are reincarnated from a previous existence, members of an ancient race . . . sent here in human form, or what. But they do know they are heading for a definite purpose which has to do with whatever is going on [in this *dero* business]. Second, they have spent their lives so far in perfecting themselves in certain trades and professions which do not overlap. . . . And indications are that when all these people are united they will make an organization which not only will have an expert on every subject, trade, and profession, but that their pooled knowledge will be far IN ADVANCE OF ANYTHING THAT HAS BEEN DEVELOPED ON EARTH TO THE PRESENT DAY! Thus, we urge every reader who has such convictions . . . to write to your editor, WHO IS ONE OF THOSE PEOPLE!" (Baring-Gould 286, original emphasis)

If we read "The Shaver Mystery" as an ARG, then Palmer is the "puppet-master" working behind the scenes to create a thrilling gameplay experience for his readers. Members of this imagined community are both united in their participation and singled out as fantastically special—reincarnated beings or "members of an ancient race"—and assured that their lives, their trades, and their individual bodies of knowledge are crucial for the success of the game. In other words, "The Shaver Mystery" gave participants a chance to play science fiction characters based on themselves but endowed with purpose and direction; the game provided the thrill of fantasy, a validation of readers' mundane lives, and a chance to practice writing science fiction narratives and find out if they were good enough to get published.

But Baring-Gould refuses to see "The Shaver Mystery" as a game. Instead, he frets that readers were unable to distinguish fiction from their day-to-day experiences, and he quotes several Shaver letters with disturbingly violent content:

The letter writers on the whole take themselves and *Amazing Stories* very seriously. J. B. of Chicago, whose firm has developed "a very small two-place helicopter that will land in a twenty-five-foot circle on any terrain whatever" proposes "to investigate the caverns [of the deros] by air, armed not with a pencil, a notebook, and a scientific attitude, but with a flame thrower, a submachine gun, and a scientific attitude. Believe me," he concludes, "I can secure these weapons—I know some people. I realize that this is strictly illegal, but such things are sometimes necessary."

Writes Ex-Captain A. C.: "(After) my last combat mission on May 26 ... I and Captain —— left Srinagar and went back to Rudok and then through the Khesa Pass to the northern foothills of the Kabakoram. We found what we were looking for. We knew what we were searching for. For heaven's sake, drop the whole thing! You are playing with dynamite. My companion and I fought our way out of a cave with submachine guns. I have two nine-inch scars on my left arm that came from wounds given me in the cave when was I fifty feet from a moving object of any kind. . . . My friend had a hole the size of a dime in his right bicep. It was seared inside. How we don't know. But we both believe we know more about the Shaver mystery than any other pair. . . . Don't print our names. We are not cowards, but we are not crazy." (Baring-Gould 286–87)

Baring-Gould reproduces these letters without much in the way of interpretation or commentary. But he chose them from among the many pages devoted to correspondence regarding "The Shaver Mystery." Again, they share a dedication to the fiction of the conspiracy and their representation of fantasy violence. Baring-Gould's choice to quote these letters, as evidence of readers' too-serious engagement with science fiction, suggests a distaste for conspiracy and violence in the wake of World War II. Though his article never mentions Hitler, or Nazism, or even Judaism, it is hard not to read his critique of *Amazing Stories* as a warning about the parallels of "The Shaver Mystery" to the global anti-Semitic conspiracies that had set the stage for the concentration camps of the 1930s and 1940s. And Baring-Gould is clear that he is not the only one who finds "The Shaver Mystery" distasteful: he cites fan magazine *Fantasy Commentator*, which plainly calls *Amazing Stories'* readers and correspondents "crackpots" (286). Although some fan studies scholars have praised *Amazing Stories,* science fiction fans of the 1940s did not necessarily hold the magazine in similar esteem.

Pulp magazine features like "The Shaver Mystery" and "The Friendliest Corner" suggest how compelling periodical press interactivity could be, and how difficult these texts are to analyze and judge. Printed and read with little context, these letters may pose more questions than they answer. Just as we cannot know how many "Friendliest Corner" participants were subverting the gender and age strictures of that column, we cannot know how seriously to take the men who wrote of hunting *deros* with submachine guns: Did they believe the conspiracy, or find it a useful fiction for white supremacist recruitment? Or were they self-consciously crafting their own stories as contributions to—or even commentary on—the thrilling science fiction tales that filled *Amazing Stories?*

Some questions are unanswerable, and the above may be one of them. Nevertheless, our sense of fandom history is enriched by attending more fully to the complexities, even the mysteries, of the relationships between fans and periodicals in the early twentieth century, especially when those relationships help us better see the white exclusionary foundation of some fannish spaces. But, to reiterate an earlier argument made in this chapter, it is also important to remember that *Amazing Stories* and the other science fiction pulps were not the only places where fans interacted with textual representations of people both real and fictional.

Lorelei Lee: Anita Loos's Modernist Transmedia Icon

More than twenty years before *Harper's* published W. S. Baring-Gould's feature on science fiction fandom, the women's edition of the magazine launched another kind of interactive fiction: an ever-expanding tale of an irrepressible blonde duping gullible men for personal gain. The blonde in question, Lorelei Lee, is the narrator of Anita Loos's 1925 novel *Gentlemen Prefer Blondes.* Subtitled *The Intimate Diary of a Professional Lady,* the book is a wild romp through the glitzy, cosmopolitan world of the Jazz Age. In absurdist prose replete with misspellings and malaprops, Lorelei unfolds the story of her journey from business college in Little Rock, Arkansas, to Hollywood stardom—with stops in New York, London, Paris, and Vienna. Along the way, Lorelei tricks several men out of money and jewels, is acquitted for a murder she definitely committed, flummoxes Sigmund Freud, and finally traps a film censor in a marriage that bankrolls her own sexually charged acting career.

Blondes began as a magazine sketch for *Harper's Bazaar,* but it quickly became a novel, a stage play, a film, a comic strip, a radio play, and a stage musical. Loos published a sequel and several further stories about Lorelei and slyly referenced the book in many of her subsequent writing projects. Lorelei went on to appear in the 1953 film adaptation of *Gentlemen Prefer Blondes* starring Marilyn Monroe, but she also worked her way, unauthorized, into all kinds of popular texts, from Dorothy Sayers's 1932 mystery novel, *Have His Carcase,* to a Robert Heinlein science fiction series. This pervasive intertextuality was made possible by Anita Loos's own engagement in the interactive fan culture of the twentieth century. Lorelei exemplifies what I call the "modernist transmedia icon": a textual and visual representation that crossed easily between genres, forms, and so-called "brow levels." Lorelei demonstrates the interconnectedness of media in the modernist era, and she is an avatar for the pleasurable "work" of early twentieth-century interactivity, much of which was performed by women.

Like a lot of participatory media of the early twentieth century, Lorelei's ubiquity has faded almost entirely from our view. If we think of her now, we think of Monroe. We think of Hollywood, of popular culture; we don't think of a modernist novel that sounds like Gertrude Stein and was praised by Edith Wharton, James Joyce, and William Faulkner.[17] The subsequent devaluing of Lorelei—and of Loos as an author—illustrates the cultural hierarchies we impose on modernism, as well as the systematic erasure of female cultural labor. The literary history of interactivity has not yet been told; missing from the story are the women who answered the call to engage with and transform early twentieth-century media, and in doing so, found agency, authority, and sometimes even an income. In this section, I want to surface a few of the textual connections and transformations Anita Loos took part in, as a way of resituating her work in a tradition of women's transformative writing.

To reiterate what I argue above, the early film industry and its related print media were intensely interactive—in other words, they helped marshal communities of interest and practice who prolonged their engagement with the products of the culture industry through creative interventions. Film fan magazines—most aimed at female readers—encouraged amateur writers to submit scenarios via contests and other calls to action. In this way, "fans" of the movies were brought into the chain of cultural production. Anita Loos got her start in cinema by simply mailing scenarios to studios to see if they would be bought. That was in 1911; by 1924 Loos herself was being advertised as an expert who could teach film fans "How to Write Photoplays," with the attendant assumption that of course they would want to.[18]

Gentlemen Prefer Blondes began as a brief sketch. Loos claims that H. L. Mencken told her to publish it in Harper's, where it would get "lost among the ads" ("Biography" xli). But far from getting lost, Blondes began interacting with and commenting on the print culture that surrounded it. In the novel's first chapter—the original sketch that ran in Harper's Bazaar—an admirer gives Lorelei a set of Joseph Conrad's Collected Works as a present:

> Well I forgot to mention that the English gentleman who writes novels seems to have taken quite an interest in me, as soon as he found out I was literary. I mean he has called up every day and I went to tea twice with him. So he has sent me a whole complete set of books for my birthday by a gentleman called Mr. Conrad. They all seem to be about ocean travel although I have not had time to more than glance through them. I have always liked novels about ocean travel ever since I posed for Mr. Christie for the front cover of a novel about ocean travel by McGrath because I always say that a girl never really looks as well as she does on board a steamship, or even a yacht. (Gentlemen Prefer Blondes 8)

Magazines such as the Saturday Review of Literature advertised this "whole complete set" of Conrad's novels in 1924—meaning it was possible, while browsing the magazine stand, to read Doubleday, Page & Co.'s advertising copy and then read about Lorelei receiving the books as a birthday present. Loos makes a satire of this up-to-the-moment engagement with the real literary marketplace. When Lorelei misreads Conrad's literary work as being about "ocean travel," she is building on the advertisement's representation of the novels as "tales of love . . . tales of adventure . . . tales of romance" (104).[19] And when Lorelei conflates "high" literature about ocean travel with her own modeling work, she reminds readers that print culture was neither more nor less vacuous than other forms of image-centered publicity.

Loos frequently uses humor to comment on the supposed shallowness of Lorelei's labor, and in many ways prefigures Walter Benjamin's critique of art in the age of mechanical reproduction. Lorelei's background as an actress and a typist means that the text is engaged with mechanical reproduction on a thematic level; as Laura Frost notes about the typewriter and the cinema, "both are American, individuality-flattering technologies that traffic in copies" (303). With these two jobs, Lorelei has been involved firsthand in suspect industries of endless replicability—as, of course, had screenwriter Loos. Lorelei, then, is the fictional figure that allows Loos to transform her own work into the subject of her satire, both within *Blondes* and in subsequent projects.

In 1932, for example, Loos was tasked with cleaning up the screenplay for *Red-Headed Woman*, a Jean Harlow film about a social-climbing typewriter girl who sets her sights on the wealthy son of her boss, which was being adapted from a novel by Katherine Brush. Loos took over the film's script from F. Scott Fitzgerald, a writer of the modernist canon whose 1925 novel *The Great Gatsby* has since overshadowed *Blondes*. The story that Loos recounts in her autobiography *Kiss Hollywood Good-By* stages an evocative argument between Fitzgerald's work and her own commercialized product: "It seemed that several of [Irving Thalberg's] staff authors had written scripts for *Red-Headed Woman*, but they had only emphasized the fact that it was a pretty banal soap opera. The latest filmplay was by Scott Fitzgerald. 'Scott tried to turn the silly book into a tone poem!' Irving said. 'So I want you to make fun of its sex element just as you did in *Gentlemen Prefer Blondes*'" (*Kiss* 33–34). In Loos's tale, Thalberg positions Fitzgerald's artistic skill against both Brush's "silly book" and Loos's ability to turn the serious subject of sex into a joke. What secures a manly literary reputation doesn't sell a picture. Though Fitzgerald's tendency toward abstract seriousness wasn't useful in this case, these formal qualities have aligned him with modernism; Loos, on the other hand, excels in humor and the transformation of the banal, making her successful in the mass market.

As in this anecdote, Loos was never far from Lorelei Lee or *Gentlemen Prefer Blondes*. She relentlessly worked and reworked her "professional lady," including in the "Biography of a Book" that purports to tell *Blondes'* origin story. Loos added this introduction to the novel in 1963, and it continues to accompany recent editions, effectively framing the book for contemporary readers. The story of the "Biography" is simple enough: Loos says she was inspired to write the novel when she witnessed a group of men fawning over a statuesque blonde on a train from New York to Los Angeles. The men, her Hollywood coworkers, ignored Loos entirely, causing her to surmise that the blonde possessed some strange power of attraction simply by virtue of her hair color. But the "Biography" conceals more than it reveals, re-presenting the text through several different genres, styles, and cultures, with the seeming aim of downplaying Loos's own artistry, even while reveling in the pleasure of transformative textual practices.

Loos in the preface is physically slight (weighing "about ninety pounds" [xxxvii]), childish in her behavior ("my slant on life was that of a child of ten" [xxxviii]), and most importantly, absolutely not a "real novelist" (xxxviii). As part of Loos's "small" pose, she repeatedly treats rereadings of *Blondes* with sly sarcasm or dismissal: "In fact, if one examines the plot of *Gentlemen Prefer Blondes*, it is almost as gloomy as a novel by Dostoievski. When the book reached Russia, this was recognized, and it was embraced by Soviet authorities as evidence of the exploitation of helpless female blondes by predatory magnates of the Capitalistic System. The Russians, with their native love of grief, stripped *Gentlemen Prefer Blondes* of all its fun and the plot which they uncovered was dire. It concerns early rape of its idiot heroine" ("Biography" xxxix). Loos goes on to recount the plot of the novel from the "Russian" point of view, and she connects it again to her devalued placement in the literary hierarchy. With such material, she explains, "any real novelist such as Sherwood Anderson, Dreiser, Faulkner or Hemingway probably would have curdled his readers' blood with massive indignation" ("Biography" xxxix). This effect is unrealized in Loos's text, which keeps in "all its fun." At the same time, Loos makes fun of Russian cultural preoccupations and their transformed version of the book.[20]

In another recasting of *Blondes*' emotional impact, William Empson adapts a line of the novel for a tragic poem about societal gender roles. Paired with lines like "Gentlemen prefer bound feet and the wasp waist," the poem's refrain, "A girl can't go on laughing all the time," takes on an increasingly dire tone with each repetition (Empson, qtd. in *Kiss* 201). Loos plays dumb with its intent; she writes: "That poem confuses me; either it doesn't quite make sense or I'm fearful that, with study, Empson will make too much sense and at this late age I'll suddenly turn into a weeper" (*Kiss* 201). These artistically serious reinterpretations of *Blondes* give us another way to respond to the text as cultural product. Reframed and reimagined, the elements inherently present in the text produce a very different emotional response. But this response, the idea that Loos or her reader would "turn into a weeper," is disavowed by the novel itself. Ever the humorist, Loos dissembles by denying the tragic element she has already admitted exists in the novel.

Dissembling and downplaying are Loos's default modes—the tools of her trickster trade, so to speak. Even the veracity of "Biography" is up for debate. Penned almost forty years after Loos originally scribbled the idea for *Blondes* in a notebook, the novel's origin myth (the train, the blonde, the fawning men) bears striking resemblance to a 1943 short story by Katharine Brush, author of *Red-Headed Woman*, entitled "Lounge-Car Blonde." Published in the *New Yorker*, the story features a female narrator who encounters a similar blonde on a train ride from Chicago to Los Angeles. The "Hollywood males" on the train rush to aid the blonde with her bags while the narrator, dumbfounded, looks on. The lounge-car blonde herself was likely based at least in part on Lorelei (the narrator notes, "There wasn't a brain in her head," which sounds an awful lot like someone describing Lorelei [60]). But, I want to suggest, it is possible that Loos reincorporated the homage to her work into her own creation story for the novel. It wouldn't have been the first time Loos performed this kind of dialectic with Brush's work.

Her rewrites for the screenplay of Brush's *Red-Headed Woman* include an opening montage of star Jean Harlow. In one shot, the usually blonde Harlow examines her red hair in a mirror and asks sarcastically, "Gentlemen prefer blondes, do they?" Promotional photos for the film feature Harlow holding a prop book emblazoned with the title *Gentlemen Prefer ~~Blondes~~ Red-Heads!* In one photo of the series, Loos hovers in the background, preparing to smash a champagne bottle over Harlow's head (see fig. 7).

The usually blonde Harlow frequently took roles written by Loos. Though she never played Lorelei Lee, she did star as a strikingly similar blonde with lofty marriage ambitions in 1934's *The Girl from Missouri* (dir. Jack Conway). Loos shared screenwriting credits with her husband, John Emerson, and Howard Emmett Rogers, but the bones of the story are quintessentially Loos-ian: Eadie (Harlow) runs away from small town life to pursue her dream of marrying a rich man, accompanied by her feisty best friend, Kitty (Patsy Kelly), who tragically can't stop falling for attractive but working-class men. Like Lorelei, Eadie is prim to the point of parody; like Dorothy, Kitty is a font of bawdy wisecracks that often steal the scene. Here, though, Eadie's first catch (Lewis Stone) ends up dead by his own hand rather than hers, and the resolution finds Eadie married not to a boorish film censor but rather the young, handsome, and wealthy son (Franchot Tone) of a business magnate (Lionel Barrymore). *The Girl from Missouri* never lives up to the standard set by *Gentlemen Prefer*

FIG. 7. Promotional photograph of Jean Harlow and Anita Loos for *Red-Headed Woman*. MGM/Photofest.

Blondes; ironically, Harlow's Eadie is no Lorelei Lee in part because of the film censorship enacted by the Motion Picture Production Code, which the Motion Picture Producers and Distributors of America (MPPDA) began stringently enforcing in 1934. Still, Jean Harlow's blonde bombshell persona would inspire Marilyn Monroe, and the Motion Picture Production Code would be on its way out by the time Monroe made her iconic turn as Lorelei Lee in the 1953 musical film adaptation.[21]

With these and countless other creative transformations afoot, it is no wonder that we can find unauthorized versions of Lorelei in some rather out of the way places. While copyright laws prevented other authors (and fans) from cribbing Lorelei outright, at least one found a way around this restriction with a little creative transformation of her own. Mystery writer Dorothy L. Sayers names the "regular little gold-digger" (187) who appears briefly in her novel *Have His Carcase* "Leila Garland" but gives her Lorelei's platinum blonde hair, repetitive speech patterns, and malapropisms.[22] In addition to overusing verbal tics like "terribly," "I mean," and "I said," Leila mistakes "obelisks" for odalisques (184–85). Most tellingly, she mimics Lorelei's habit of speaking of herself as a "girl" in the third person: "What is a girl to do when a man won't confide in her? . . . I mean, a girl never knows she may not get mixed up in something unpleasant. I mean, it isn't quite nice, is it?" (183). Lorelei's cameo appearance, in the guise of Leila, lasts only a few pages, befitting the procedural structure of Sayers's mystery novel. Though *Have His Carcase* cannot accurately be called fanfiction, its temporary appropriation of another author's character shares a certain fannish sensibility, an approach to literary characters that we saw previously in the work of Gene Stratton-Porter, and that we will see again in the next chapter, from the fans writing to Marjorie Kinnan Rawlings.

Since her creation in the mid-1920s, the character of Lorelei Lee has never left our cultural consciousness. Even after Loos, Harlow, Sayers, and Monroe, she continues to pop up in places as varied as Robert Heinlein's 1973 science fiction novel *Time Enough for Love* and the 2012 NBC musical drama television series *Smash*. As a transmedia icon of the modernist era, Lorelei has crossed platforms, continents, and centuries. These are the connections and transformations that surface when we attend to the sprawling networks of twentieth-century print culture. Ignoring these connections renders invisible so much fan labor, transformative textual work, and women's creative engagement with cultural products. Lorelei's replicability—which we might now identify with Marilyn Monroe by way of Andy Warhol, but which really began with the *Harper's Bazaar* version of Lorelei—makes her a powerful representative of women's creative agency. Not only is Lorelei an archetype of glamour to which women aspire, but she is also a textual product open to interpretation, alteration, and play. Her almost century of what *Harper's Bazaar* might call "makeovers" suggests the lineage of cultural work in which early twentieth-century women were engaged.

The precursors to fanfiction writers were not only the men inventing violent infiltrations into and conspiracy-fueled theories about science fiction magazine stories. They were also the women borrowing and adapting glamorous icons of female sexuality and power for their own use. And, as chapter 3 demonstrates, they were also the teenagers, soldiers, housewives, and Book-of-the-Month Club members reaching out to the authors they admired. We turn now from magazines to mailboxes, examining the fan letters sent to authors and other public figures for what they can reveal about transformative creativity, fan communities, and the gift economy.

THREE

Fan Mail as Communal Literary Practice

Entre nous I'm not in the habit of writing fan letters and when my thoughts penetrate such ideas I get the willies. Somehow with you its different. . . . (Maybe after I finish this letter I'll wonder where O Where I obtained all my boldness.)

—MARY LOUISE AGUIRRE, in a letter to Marjorie Kinnan Rawlings, 1939

You'll probably be months getting this because I'll have to mail it to a forwarding address, but I hope you do anyway—that you'll number me among your admirers, proteges or what have you.

—ALEX HALEY, in a letter to Marjorie Kinnan Rawlings, 1944

Fan Mail as Form

By 1937, fan mail was a national crisis. At least, that's how it seemed to Bergen Evans, writing in the pages of *Scribner's Magazine* to lament the rise of the form, calling it an infantile pastime that made more trouble for film stars and radio personalities than it was worth. Evans's only somewhat tongue-in-cheek article, part of *Scribner's* regular "Life in the United States" series, opens with a declaration that the writing of fan mail, whether "abusive or adulatory," now "must occupy a considerable percentage of our national leisure" (55; fig. 8). These letters, he explains, are reliably provoked by any media appearance, whether the subject has given a radio speech, won a contest, or murdered their grandmother (Evans 55).

Evans focuses specifically on the fan mail of film stars, citing his recent opportunity "to read several thousand fan letters in Hollywood and to talk with the men who made a business of handling them" (55). These letters, usually "pathetic, stark pleas for help from the radiant demi-gods of the screen,"

Fantasia

BERGEN EVANS

I HAVE seen no reliable statistics upon the subject, but the writing of abusive or adulatory letters to people whose voices are heard over the radio or whose pictures appear in the papers or on the screen must occupy a considerable percentage of our national leisure. Imply in a radio speech that the dog is (or is not) man's best friend, and your mail box will bulge for days. Appear in the rotogravure in a bathing suit, and your correspondence will soon afford you a complete survey of abnormal psychology. If you win a contest or murder your grandmother, the post office will have to put on additional deliverymen.

To those of us who are neither beautiful nor wealthy enough to have our inanities publicly chronicled, the thought of receiving letters full of unsolicited admiration is quite alluring. Particularly around the first of the month. If in place of that somewhat nasty item from the Collection Agency, for instance, one had a few words of worship from some lovely unknown, the day would get off to a decidedly better start. A stack of laudatory epistles laid beside the coffee and bacon—that were the true epicurean breakfast!

So, at least, I had often thought until an opportunity to read several thousand fan letters in Hollywood and to talk with men who made a business of handling them taught me the sweet advantages of obscurity.

In the first place, it is expensive to receive very much fan mail. Some stars have received as high as forty thousand letters a month, each one of which must be answered, or the admirer becomes a hater. And unless my elementary arithmetic fails me, annual return postage on that many letters would be fourteen thousand, four hundred dollars. Say fifteen thousand, as a round figure, if one allows for the cheapest grade of stationery. And then you must throw in a secretary—another two thousand or so. Some of the studios handle the fan mail for the stars and manage to

[55]

FIG. 8. A 1937 article about fan mail is illustrated with a line drawing of a man and a woman in an overwhelming pile of letters. Bergen Evans, "Fantasia," *Scribner's Magazine* 101.4 (April 1937): 55.

demonstrate that "many of the writers are children in fact, but almost all are children in mind" (Evans 56–57). Evans roasts letter writers for their naïve belief in the veracity of cinema, and cynically sums up the practice thusly: "Certainly fan mail reveals the immense loneliness of modern life, the millions to whom a shadow on a screen is more familiar than any real person" (57). These "masses" are, in Evans's estimation, unable to be critical about the entertainment products they consume, and this evokes for Evans a prescient sense of danger only two years before the outbreak of World War II: "Their naïveté, their uncritical attitude, and the depth and simplicity of their emotional responses suggest what a powerful instrument of propaganda the movies might be" (57). Given the passionate simplicity of the masses, Evans dourly concludes, "it is probably fortunate for the country that the [film] industry is controlled by men who aim to amuse" (57). He does not suggest that the country is in any way fortunate for the other media that publicize winners and murderers.

Evans's short essay illuminates several issues that will be central to this chapter. For although letters of admiration had been written—to actors, to public figures, to authors—for hundreds of years (at the least), the first half of the twentieth century saw something new. Periodicals for film fans and literature lovers actively encouraged readers to take up their pens and talk back. An increasingly reliable international postal system made it more likely than ever that their letters would reach the intended recipient. And as the identity of the "fan" was gaining traction, cultural products like novels and films were indeed being used as propaganda meant to unite the far-flung residents of a massive nation—not through their politics, but through their pleasure.

This chapter examines fan mail as a distinct form, one made possible by the creation of the "fan" identity detailed in chapter 2. In the first section, I pull together a selection of published work on the fan mail of single authors, in order to analyze the tropes that appear. In the second and third sections, I explore fan mail from the archive of Marjorie Kinnan Rawlings, whose 1939 Pulitzer Prize and inclusion in the Armed Services Editions program, the Book-of-the-Month Club, and *Reader's Digest* brought her national recognition. Rawlings saved a large portion of her fan mail from about 1935 to 1946, which provides us with a compelling look into the actual texts that fan mail writers produced. Using these letters, and Rawlings's various responses to them, I argue that fan mail provided its writers a workshop space where they could hone their authorial voice.[1] Unlike uncirculated texts, letters allowed fans to submit this apprentice work to a master for approval and, ultimately, inclusion in the archive.[2]

Despite the nearly pathological tendency toward fan mail that Bergen Evans diagnosed in the late 1930s, scholarship on the period and on letter-writing more generally has been slow to turn to fan letters as objects of sustained analysis. These two gaps are likely interrelated; as Theresa Strouth Gaul and Sharon M. Harris point out, though critics in the eighteenth and nineteenth centuries were interested in the letter as a form, that interest dwindled considerably in the early to mid-twentieth century and has only seen a resurgence in the past thirty or so years (2–3). Major works like Janet Altman's *Epistolarity: Approaches to a Form* (1982) have emphasized epistolary fiction, particularly French and British novels of the long eighteenth century; scholars of American literature, like the contributors to Gaul and Harris's edited volume, have focused their attention on the antebellum period almost exclusively. Furthermore, this growing body of epistolary studies has faced challenges with reading "letters on their own terms," tending instead to treat them as indistinguishable from other forms of life-writing or as "historical documents valuable only for revealing information about famous people or events" (Gaul and Harris 2–3). The few considerations of fan letters that have appeared, while useful, often evince one or more of these shortcomings. Those focused on antebellum literature can only apply the terms "fan" and "fandom" anachronistically; articles on twentieth-century fan letters largely decline to grapple with the letter as an object and a genre.[3]

There are several challenges involved, then, in any analysis of fan letters. Anachronisms and the imprecise application of fandom terminology muddle a field that, as I argue in my introduction, needs more clarity and specificity. At the same time, the letter must be encountered as a literary object in its own right. This means analysis should be supported by the rich and diverse body of work developed by epistolary studies. The fan letter should be treated as a subgenre within the larger genre of the letter, and close attention should be given to the specifics of the forms, the latter arising out of the former. We should ask what the letter does and, then, within that framework, what the fan letter does. This chapter aims to do that.

Though built around readings of epistolary fiction, Janet Altman's work on epistolarity is crucial for our current understanding of the letter as a form with its own conventions, tendencies, and ways of making meaning. As Altman writes, "the epistle as narrative instrument can foster certain patterns of thematic emphasis, narrative action, character types, and narrative self-consciousness" (9). Her analysis of epistolary fiction's approach to mediation is particularly useful for understanding the letter as a form. Because the letter functions "as a connector between two distant points," she asserts, "the epistolary author can choose to emphasize either the distance or the bridge" (Altman 13). For Altman, this pair of options explains why so many seduction novels are told in epistolary form: "The lover who takes up his pen to write his loved one is conscious of the interrelation of presence and absence and the way in which his very medium of communication reflects both the absence and presence of his addressee" (14). This is the consciousness that Evans flatly denies in his *Scribner's* article; in his estimation of fan mail, letter writers delude themselves into feeling a presence where only absence exists. And yet, as Altman further argues, the letter is a more complex means of communication than Evans's simplistic schema allows: "the two persons who 'meet' through the letter are neither totally separated nor totally united" (Altman 43). Every letter inherently contains both positions.

Letters can simultaneously unite and separate lovers but also families and other communities. Ronald J. Zboray suggests that the mobility of antebellum Americans led them to develop their high literacy rates, as they used letters to connect themselves to distant communities and support structures (28), which were increasingly necessary given the period's "harsh realities of chronic disease, uncompensated disability, and periodic unemployment . . . which had to be borne without any government or employer systems of personal security" (29). Letters could "conquer" the time and space interposing between an individual and her community support structure; this, Zboray argues, necessarily affected how Americans read, giving them a taste for sentimental fiction, with complicated plots and large casts of characters who speak not in "naturalistic dialogue" but in "multipage soliloquies" (30). Sentimental fiction like *The Wide, Wide World* and *Uncle Tom's Cabin* thus "came to mean a great deal to their readers, for the personal letter had created an avenue of emotional release, a form of intimacy, in a society increasingly threatening the individual with isolation" (30). Zboray proposes that the characters of these novels "could become surrogates for departed kin and neighbor" (30). As such, the "mutual interaction" between American letter-writing and fiction tastes "transformed the very nature of the self, from one defined by total immersion in the community to one self-constructed in the act of writing and reading in letters the constructed selves of others and their interpretations of local conditions" (Zboray 31). Isolated Americans in need of consolation and support thus found it both in letters and in fictional texts that resembled letters. Accustomed to reading, interpreting, and feeling with artifacts of textual self-construction, the American reading public was prepared to see little difference between members of their real and imagined communities—not, as Bergen Evans suggests, because they had the minds of children, but rather because they were savvy readers and writers themselves.

It is into this reading-and-writing public, primed for the textual construction of self and community, that "fandom" as a concept and community was introduced. As I detailed in chapter 2, film fan magazines were encouraging interactive fan participation as early as 1912. Many of these interactive elements were specifically textual, often involving epistolary contact between fans and magazines, fans and studios, and fans and stars. Magazines, Marsha Orgeron notes, "awarded letter writers with publication or prizes, further solidifying the worth of active participation and affirming the value of being an engaged reader" (13). They also dedicated magazine space to explaining "What Happens to Fan Mail" (Larkin 40; Orgeron 6), assuring fan writers that their letters were valued. Furthermore, as chapter 2 demonstrated, this cycle of epistolary communication and reward extended beyond the film fan magazines. The popular press relied on contests to encourage interactivity among a wide swath of readers, not just those who followed the cinema. "Training fans to interact with both pen and pocketbook" (Orgeron 8) was not just the purview of film fan magazines or "Hollywood's corporate ideology" (Orgeron 8), but can be observed throughout the history of print culture.[4] As Courtney A. Bates reveals in her work on Willa Cather's fan mail, fan letters were sometimes published beyond the film magazines, as in the 1914 book version of S. S. McClure's autobiography, which Cather ghostwrote. Bates points out that "the autobiography exhibits how the seemingly private genre of fan letters can easily slip into the public realm, thereby popularizing both the impulse to write and the rhetorical patterns used to give that urge expression" (6.4).[5] In turn, fan mail provided feedback not just to movie studios and magazines, but even to the American Federation of the Arts, whose convention proceedings of 1934 note that the radio program *Art in America,* funded by a grant from the Carnegie Corporation, had received more fan mail than the Federation's other educational programs (Roosevelt 3).

But admiring epistles were more than just marketing materials; they served pedagogical purposes as well. Educators at the turn of the twentieth century stressed letter-writing as a skill to be practiced by all students. Authenticity was crucial: teachers were encouraged to have their students write and mail real letters. Authors and other public figures are suggested as good recipients in a textbook from 1902 (Ryan, "A Real Basis" 169); a *Manual in Elementary English* from 1922 reiterates this suggestion in a list of possible epistolary assignments: "Perhaps the teacher has read aloud a certain book which the class greatly enjoyed. . . . If the author is living, the class may write to him, telling him how much they enjoyed the book" (Hodge and Lee 20–21). The *Manual* emphasizes the importance of letter-writing as a practical skill, "because the average person after leaving school does little other writing" (Hodge and Lee

19). A 1941 study of sixth-grade letter-writing assignments shows that fan mail was the second most frequently assigned form (Smith 170). Thus, it is clear that in the first half of the twentieth century, educational discourse became keenly aware that letters of admiration were now called "fan mail"—and that this form could be used by students to hone their composition skills. While articles like Evans's stirred up anxiety, more measured voices in forums like the *Journal of Education* likewise noted that fan mail spoke to the "direct influence" of the film industry ("Belding's Page" 62). In the *Annals of the American Academy of Political and Social Science* from 1932, a sociology professor examines fan mail as evidence of the interplay between media and "the inculcation of social values" via the psychological process of identification (Willey 107).

Like Marsha Orgeron and Bergen Evans, the academic journals of the 1930s fail to look outside the nascent film industry in their appraisal of fan mail. "Fan letters," Orgeron declares, "which emerged when fans sought out stars' studio addresses from magazine editors, made the desire to emerge from spectatorial anonymity tangible" (5). Though this desire may have been made newly tangible to young film fans, scholarship like Bonnie Carr O'Neill's work on readers' letters to Fanny Fern demonstrates that epistolary expressions of admiration and identification existed long before the film industry came into being. Hollywood's genius was merely to publicize such textual productions. But as the studies mentioned below demonstrate, fan mail to film stars looked much the same as fan mail to writers and painters; it is precisely the pedagogical and identificatory functions of fan letters—that is, their uses for their writers, not their intended recipients—that unites them.

Bringing together analyses of readers' letters and fan mail from several different essays demonstrates some fascinating congruencies in form and expression. Here I want to detail some of these commonalities. They can broadly be categorized into the following tropes: apology and justification, familiarity, authority, enumeration of related fan practices, expressions of pleasure and affective responses, identification, and emulation. Though not all letters contain examples of each trope, and some may contain none of these, the similarities across the body of letters already analyzed by scholars is too notable to ignore—and it has not, to my knowledge, been discussed elsewhere in print.[6] I want to establish these tropes before turning to Rawlings's archive of fan mail, in the hope of connecting my own single-author analysis to a broader reading of fan letters, primarily though not exclusively from the first half of the twentieth century.

Many of these articles note the fragmented nature of the archives examined, and suggest that the letters saved demonstrate what the recipients valued most. Orgeron questions archival practices, asking "why certain letters were kept, saved, shared, or deposited at an archive while others were not," but notes, "These questions have rarely been addressed in the scholarship given that fan mail remains a largely neglected element of celebrity and fan history" (20n3). More recent scholars have attempted to at least suggest answers to these questions. Bates asserts that her selection of fan letters is "not a random sampling" but inherently shaped by Cather's choices: "Cather enjoyed these kinds of letters [those under analysis] enough to preserve them during her life" (1.10). Of Georgia O'Keeffe's fan mail archive, Linda M. Grasso notes, "O'Keeffe apparently valued the letters because she kept them meticulously filed" (39n9). But despite the fragmented and incomplete nature of these archives, the fan letters saved suggest a dominant form, a way of constructing "fan mail" that was commonly understood.

Fan letters often begin with an apology or a justification for writing. Fans writing to Cather "often declare themselves as fans in the opening lines of their letters"; but whereas some suggest their letters will be "a welcome pleasure," others feel certain their missives are "a trespass" (Bates 1.6). Jennifer Parchesky describes as "typical" a letter to Dorothy Canfield in which a college student announces that she has never written a fan letter and wishes that Canfield not consider this as one (253n12). Grasso's study of O'Keeffe's fan mail takes its title from one fan's assertion that "I never write to strangers, but you are no stranger to me" (26). These fan writers look to establish themselves as having a reason to write to a public figure who both is and is not known to them on a personal level. This anxiety, which writers feel they must soothe in the first lines of their letters, stems from the disconnect of the parasocial relationship that publication and celebrity necessarily creates; as Bates astutely argues, "Fan letters can assuage the disconcerting contradiction that readers are both deeply familiar with and also unknown to their favorite authors" (1.8). Orgeron notes in her analysis of Clara Bow's fan mail, "Even those correspondents who profess reluctance or feel a certain impropriety in their acts of writing often express an unusual sense of familiarity with the star" (18). While one of Bow's fans apologizes for her "impertinence," another explains that she read about Bow's health problems and felt "as if a real friend of mine, and not a movie star far beyond my reach, was lying sick" (Orgeron 18). And a fan writing to radio host

Ted Malone explains: "I liked you so well today—I just had to tell you about it. You were more like yourself" (qtd. in Chasar 109). These fans look to give concrete reasons for having written and feeling a sense of familiarity or friendship with their celebrity addressee, and often use as their justification the workings of the print or media industries that have been designed specifically to make them feel close to these famous strangers. In other words, everything about early twentieth-century media encouraged fans to feel as though they knew celebrities; their fan letters confirm this tactic's effectiveness.

These letters are often conversational, even chatty. But the casual tone of many fan letters is contrasted, though not contradicted, by their authors' assertions of authority—as, for example, in the lines quoted above, where a fan judges how "like [him]self" Ted Malone has appeared. This sense of authority comes from a constellation of related fan practices, including but not limited to reading and rereading, collecting and cherishing artifacts and texts, and even traveling in the footsteps of the celebrity or their characters. The authors of Bow's fan mail detailed "their reading habits, collections, and conversations" in order to "impress Bow with their mastery of her as a celebrity" (Orgeron 17).[7] Likewise, fans wrote to Cather of their "devoted, repeated rereadings of her texts," and Cather kept letters that "demonstrate how readers treated her books as objects worthy of repeated enjoyment and special treatment. . . . Fans describe well-used books to substantiate their claims of careful reading" (Bates 1.8; 4.9). Cather's fans also wrote to her of trips they had taken, inspired by her novels and characters (Bates 4.6), making Quebec, New Mexico, and Virginia into pilgrimage destinations. O'Keeffe's fan mail often made use of "merging and absorption metaphors" to express the depth of the fan's connection to the work, as when one fan wrote that a painting at her doctor's office "is now part of me" (Grasso 28–29).

As these examples begin to suggest, fans often work diligently in their letters to render their complex emotional responses to the celebrity and her work. O'Keeffe's fans write of her paintings giving them enjoyment, "a feeling of calmness and serenity," "perspective," and "*peace*"; another explains succinctly, "They're beautiful. I feel them" (Grasso 33–35, original emphasis). Bow's fans write that they can "truly feel with [her]" and that they "all sympathized" about her various personal problems (Orgeron 19). Cather's fans write of her characters in much the same way; they write of crying for her characters but also feeling like them (Bates 2.4, 3.2). Likewise, Gene Stratton-Porter's fan correspondents wrote to her that "your books touch . . . the deeper, more vital and real fibres of my nature" (Ryan, "A Real Basis" 167). Strikingly, fan letters and analyses of them speak repeatedly of "pleasure": the pleasure of a good book, a beautiful painting, or an enjoyable film. Often such pleasure becomes an emotional response that must be paid back (Bates 4.14), that cannot be adequately expressed via text (Bates 3.2, 4.3; Grasso 35–36), or that comes on like "a dull ache, almost a nausea" (Grasso 36).

This intensity of affect, of "feeling with," speaks to the deep kinds of identification that fan letter writers made with celebrities and their work. These letters repeatedly point out similarities between writer and recipient. Fans of Bow describe having the same hair color (Orgeron 19); fans of O'Keeffe, the same taste in shoes (Grasso 30). Often, fans marry affective identification with a more literal coclaiming of artist status. Women write to O'Keeffe that they are painters (Grasso 36), to Bow that they plan to be movie stars (Orgeron 20), and to Cather that they are writers and teachers using her work as model (Bates 3.4, 3.5, 4.12).

For fans of authors especially, the fan letter is a powerful place to practice the composition of all manner of texts. Just as students were encouraged to hone their letter-writing skills by sending correspondence to public figures, fledgling writers could and did use their letters to practice techniques of description, voice, plot, and more. Bates details multiple letters in which Cather's fan correspondents "relate their own story of a location or event on which Cather had written" (4.3), in effect practicing their storytelling skills by writing their own versions of her stories. For Bates, these letters contribute to the archontic nature of Cather's texts, as "they offer a continuation of her narratives by adding their work to hers" (4.14). Other letters quoted use "the indirectness of analogies" (Bates 3.2) to describe Cather's work to her as "a rare piece of lace woven with an intricate design" or "a buoy held under water—restrained but exerting a constant pull" (Bates 3.1). Such letters attempt to evoke Cather's own narrative voice and give it back to her, in a practice or workshop space that promises the possibility of the master responding with feedback for the student.[8]

In the same vein, Georgia O'Keeffe's fans write to ask for advice on their artistic endeavors (though Grasso does not note if they ever sent examples of their own work), and Clara Bow's letters often include scripted interactions, at least one of which reads to Orgeron as "a bit like a movie plot" (19). Orgeron credits these moments of emulation to the discourse of the film fan magazine.

But though her arguments do effectively demonstrate the similarities between fan magazine discourse and fan letters, my broader reading of scholarship on fan mail suggests that this is not a function specific to film fan magazines in and of themselves. Rather, Bonnie Carr O'Neill has noted that, as early as 1851, epistolary responses to Fanny Fern's *Olive Branch* columns "should be understood as emulating [Fern's] practice of self-identification even when they stridently oppose her views . . . or even when they claim to love her" (163). Given that "the conversational qualities of Fern's writing are consistent with conventions of letter writing" (O'Neill 163–64), her articles and her correspondents' letters mirror epistolary style back and forth through the very conversational markers mentioned above. The *Olive Branch* often published both sides of the correspondence, further demonstrating that the conversation in which fan letters participate can join the archive of the text that motivated such conversation.

Regional Voices

With this conversational frame in mind, I now turn to the work and correspondence of Marjorie Kinnan Rawlings, a novelist whose multiple accolades made her a public figure exactly at the moment that fan mail had saturated the American consciousness. By considering some of Rawlings's best-known writing alongside the fan mail that it motivated, this section suggests new ways of considering these texts and their relationship to both regionalism and fandom. Though regional literature has often been neglected or treated dismissively by scholars of the early twentieth century, the following discussion demonstrates the genre's importance to a variety of community- and nation-building endeavors undertaken in the shadow of World War II. As Stephanie Foote has argued, "regional writing is an object lesson in how national literary traditions are constructed through powerful, ideologically driven mechanisms of inclusion and exclusion" (25). These traditions, I argue, became the very propaganda that Bergen Evans fretted about in his 1937 *Scribner's* article. And yet, at least in Rawlings's work and correspondence, propaganda is tempered by a self-conscious refusal of nationalist violence and a commitment to a particularly queer sort of pleasure that circulated between Rawlings and her fans.

Marjorie Kinnan Rawlings is perhaps the perfect figure to round out the case studies and close readings in this book. Her lifelong writing career was consistently fostered by the interactivity of early twentieth-century print culture. Born in Washington, DC, in 1896, Rawlings spent her teenaged years winning writing contests held by the *Washington Post*. By the time she began college, thirteen of her stories and poems had been published in the *Post's* popular Children's Page, and she had won second place and seventy-five dollars for a story contest in *McCall's Magazine*. At the same time, she served as associate editor and then literary editor for her high school's literary magazine, which also published her work (*Uncollected Writings* 15). Rawlings continued her award-winning writing and her editorial work in college at the University of Wisconsin (*Uncollected Writings* 87–88). After graduation, she found a job writing promotional material for the YWCA and then held a few newspaper positions (*Uncollected Writings* 151), including writing a daily syndicated column in poetry form, entitled "Songs of the Housewife" (see *Poems by Marjorie Kinnan Rawlings*). In 1928, Rawlings and her then-husband Charles moved to Cross Creek, Florida, where Rawlings had purchased a homestead on seventy-five acres of land, including a commercial orange grove (fig. 9).

Inspired by her Florida Cracker neighbors,[9] and having had her autobiographical novel *Blood of My Blood* rejected for the Atlantic Prize in early 1929, Rawlings began researching and writing Florida stories in the regional mode. She sold two of these stories to *Scribner's Magazine* in 1930, effectively beginning her career as a Florida regional writer. By her death in 1953, at the age of fifty-seven, Rawlings had become a literary celebrity, known primarily though not exclusively for her Pulitzer Prize–winning novel *The Yearling*, which was adapted into a film by MGM in 1941.

But despite Rawlings's successful career and celebrity status, and though her circle of friends included now-canonical literary figures like Zora Neale Hurston, Ernest Hemingway, F. Scott Fitzgerald, Thomas Wolfe, and Carl Van Vechten, her work has been largely neglected by critics and scholars. This is as true now as it was in 1966, when Gordon E. Bigelow published the first book-length study of her work. Bigelow grapples with her exclusion from the literary canon, suggesting that Rawlings simply doesn't fit comfortably in the narrow categories by which we understand the writing of her period: "Her major themes and attitudes place her squarely in one of the mainstreams of American culture, and yet she belonged to none of the literary schools or groupings of the period in which she wrote, unless it is to the regionalists and their rediscovery of the beauty and worth of the American scene as a subject for literature"

FIG. 9. Marjorie Kinnan Rawlings's Cross Creek, Florida, homestead. Photograph by the author, 2015.

(1). But Bigelow's discomfort with placing Rawlings among the regionalists is palpable—and it is a discomfort that Rawlings shared.

A 1937 letter demonstrates Rawlings's frustration at reviewers who saw her work as merely regional: "Mr. Ransom's comment on the books was disagreeably patronizing—as he meant it to be. To say that he admired them as regional or local color novels, was to deny them all merit on any other counts. If I thought my stuff didn't have something more than local color, I'd stop writing" (*Selected Letters* 142). Rawlings took issue with what she perceived as exploitation in the work of the New Deal regionalists; in a lecture on "Regional Literature of the South," written for the Annual Luncheon of the National Council of Teachers of English in 1940, Rawlings lambastes "the futile outpourings of bad writing whose only excuse is that they are regional" (*Uncollected Writings* 273). Such stories, she asserts, are crassly commercial and stereotypical to the point of dehumanizing their supposed subjects: "Regional writing done because the author thinks it will be salable is a betrayal of the people of that region. Their speech and customs are turned inside out for the gaze of the curious. They are held up naked, not as human beings, but as literary specimens" (*Uncollected Writings* 275). Against "salable" stories, Rawlings contrasts the "honest and artistic regionalism" of "native or long-resident writers" like Ellen Glasgow, Julia Peterkin, Elizabeth Madox Roberts, and Zora Neale Hurston (*Uncollected Writings* 276–78)—but also, it is worth noting, like herself.

Regional literature's maligned status has become a critical commonplace, but the genre has recently experienced a critical renaissance, especially among feminist scholars interested in regionalism's feminist and queer potentiality. As Stephanie Foote and Kate McCullough have pointed out, regionalism provides a unique vantage point from which to examine issues of identity, community, and nation-building in American literature. For Foote, regionalism's focus on "non-normative persons" (28) enables the genre "to figure difference as both a commodity and a positive value in itself" (34). Thus, Foote notes, while scholars like Richard Brodhead have implicated regional literature in a project of imperialism (34), the genre provides its own counternarrative in the form of its non-normative writers, making value out of their authority and authenticity (36–37). Finally, for Foote, late nineteenth- and early twentieth-century regionalism "helped to establish a way of imagining communities that interrupted even as they sustained a national culture" (40).

Whatever Rawlings's or her critics' discomfort with the "regional" label, it is impossible to deny that her most successful pieces of writing are driven by closely observed details of a place (Florida) and its people (poor white Crackers and poor African Americans). Furthermore, as this chapter argues, Rawlings's work and her fan correspondence form a convincing case study for the regionalist project of interrupting and yet sustaining national culture. Rawlings has not to this point been recovered by the many scholars revitalizing regional literature studies, partly because she doesn't fit neatly into the prevailing scheme of literary categories: she's too late to be a nineteenth-century regionalist, but she doesn't belong with the 1930s New Deal regionalists either. I suggest that we should class her with the earlier women regionalists, like Sarah Orne Jewett and Kate Chopin, whose work focused on queerness and marginal identities, and stressed empathy, compassion, and reparation in community settings. Her fan mail demonstrates this connection, which periodization currently renders invisible.

The majority of Rawlings's archived fan mail was received between 1938 and 1946, roughly from the publication of her two most well-known works, *The*

Yearling (1938) and *Cross Creek* (1942) to the Cross Creek invasion-of-privacy suit brought against her by Zelma Cason and Rawlings's subsequent departure from Cross Creek. The letters are kept in their own box in the Rawlings archive at the University of Florida; by my estimation this box contains around two hundred individual pieces of correspondence. Though many letter writers mention her other books and stories (particularly 1933's *South Moon Under*), the concentration of fan mail received and saved by Rawlings during this period suggests several possibilities. First, Rawlings may have assembled these letters from a larger collection as part of the invasion-of-privacy trial evidence.[10] Second, it is possible that Rawlings both received and saved more fan mail during these eight years, the first four of which Bigelow suggests "represent a peak period in Marjorie's life, not only in terms of popular success, but in terms of writing creativity and personal happiness as well" (23). Third, it is possible that Rawlings's celebrity and her well-known small-town Florida address combined to make her significantly more accessible during this time. While a 1935 letter from Franklin Shields is addressed to Rawlings care of her publisher, later letters, like Lucille Shearwood's from 1939 (discussed below), are often simply sent to "Cross Creek" or "Hawthorne" (where the nearest post office was located). No street address is necessary.

To better understand Rawlings's fan mail—both generally, in light of the discussion above, and specifically, in the context of her individual career—it will be helpful to establish an overview of her major works and her authorial voice. As I argued more generally above, fan letter writers frequently mirrored an author's voice back to her, making the letter a workshop space where what is produced becomes a piece of a text's archive. In the following readings, I emphasize Rawlings's techniques and thematic concerns, and point to moments that resonate with fan mail tropes. I also turn to Rawlings's fan mail archive itself, giving those texts the same kind of close reading and attention. My hope here is to suggest textual connections between Rawlings's work and the fan letter as a form without necessarily asserting causality. Instead, I suggest, the matrixed interactions of the periodical press, epistolary forms, and American fiction meant that these kinds of texts overlapped in fascinating ways. In the end, I posit some ways that regionalism and fandom interacted with each other and with broader issues of Americanness in the 1930s and 1940s.

Rawlings's first Florida story appeared in *Scribner's Magazine* in February 1931, under the title "Cracker Chidlings," and it demonstrates Rawlings's early experimentation with a Florida vernacular that she would later hone. The story was subtitled "Real Tales from the Florida Interior," an assertion of authority on the topic that distinctly mirrors Rawlings's earlier newspaper writing. The piece is not a singular, sustained narrative but rather a collection of tales, framed with a brief introduction to the "uncivilized Florida interior" and the origin of "Florida Crackerdom," and then presented under subheads that further emphasize the newspaper-like quality ("Cracker Chidlings" 127). The text shifts between narrative modes rapidly, as if Rawlings is testing them out to find which will suit her best:

> Word came that Fatty Blake, snuff and tobacco salesman and Anthony's richest citizen—wealth in Anthony, as elsewhere, is relative—was having a big doin's on a certain Thursday night. The world, it appeared, was invited. Finally Fatty himself drew up in front of Adams's store to verify the advance story. Fatty was inviting two counties to his doin's, and all was free. Squirrel pilau and Brunswick stew. Fatty couldn't likker you, as he would like to do, but if you brought your own 'shine and were quiet about it, why, he'd meet you at the gate for a drink, and God bless you. "I got boys in the woods from can't to can't," Fatty said (from can't-see to can't-see, or "from dawn to dark"), "gettin' me squirrels for that pur-loo. I got me a nigger comin' to stir that pot o' rice all day long. And my wife, God bless her, is walkin' the county, gettin' what she needs for Brunswick stew, the kind her mammy made ahead o' her in Brunswick, Georgia." ("Cracker Chidlings" 127)

This passage begins in a third-person narrative voice, perhaps localized to the community, but with interjected commentary—"as elsewhere," "it appeared"—that evinces distance or observation. This voice is Rawlings-as-narrator, an outside observer setting the scene for her audience of other, farther-removed outsiders. The narration preserves the colloquial spelling of "doin's," but it is not performing a full Florida Cracker dialect yet. Fatty's arrival to the store and the story marks a transition; the spelling of "squirrel pilau" remains standard, but the sentence structure becomes colloquial, as the narrative voice begins to change over. The change is rapid, and by the next sentence, the narrative voice has adopted Fatty's dialect and his second-person direct address. "Liquor" becomes "likker," but Fatty is still "he." Rawlings then presents Fatty's voice directly, via quotations that preserve his dialect pronunciations. "Pilau" is now "pur-loo," and Fatty's peculiar phrasing must be explained twice over, in a parenthetical interjection that reminds the reader of the contrast between the narrator's voice and Fatty's.[11]

Scribner's followed "Cracker Chidlings" with an editorial note announcing that Rawlings would soon have another story in the magazine: "Mrs. Rawlings has tapped a rich vein of narrative. Her entry in the $5,000 Prize Contest, which is a story of a young man and woman of this region, will appear in an early number. Note the announcement of a new prize contest in this number, a contest for the best narratives of personal experience or observation" (134). The note doubles as both an advertisement for their prize contest and a reassurance to potential participants that entries can and do make their way into the magazine. It is interesting to note, though, the ambiguous phrasing of this announcement. Rawlings had not actually *won* the $5,000 Prize Contest. Indeed, various chronologies and biographical accounts of Rawlings's career suggest that she sold the story to *Scribner's* in the same manner as "Cracker Chidlings," though for $700 this time, instead of the mere $150 her first story brought her (Bigelow 15).

These two *Scribner's* stories brought Rawlings to the attention of Maxwell Perkins, the Scribner's & Sons editor who became famous for working with Ernest Hemingway, F. Scott Fitzgerald, and Thomas Wolfe. Rawlings began a professional relationship and correspondence with Perkins that would last until his death in 1947. Her first letter to Perkins, in response to his inquiry into whether she would like to write a novel about Florida, demonstrates two interesting points. First, as early as 1931, Rawlings already had the ideas for most of her major books. Her descriptions of the infant ideas for *South Moon Under, Golden Apples,* and *Cross Creek* are all recognizable (*Selected Letters* 43–44). Second, Rawlings received epistolary fan responses to even her first major publication. She was eager to share these with Perkins: "Out of the welter of equally indiscriminate praise and abuse that I have received, I am sending on three letters of favorable comment that may interest you as they did me, for they are from three of the comparatively rare souls who have seen the Florida I see. The comments of the elderly man from Massachusetts, who saw this Florida in his youth, I found quite touching. May I have the letters back, if you don't mind, for out of my gratitude for their genuine understanding, I want to answer them" (*Selected Letters* 44). These three letters do not appear to be held in the

Rawlings Papers at the University of Florida, neither in Box 39 nor in her general correspondence, nor do Rawlings's responses to them. But even the brief description offered here suggests ways in which these early fan letters conform to the tropes detailed above. The correspondents write to Rawlings their own versions of her story's subject matter, and Rawlings favors them because they express a congruence with her writerly vision.

None of Rawlings's writing for the next eleven years would stray far from the Florida that she saw, nor from the issues of authority and voice that defined her earliest regional writing. Her first novel, *South Moon Under*, was published by Scribner's in 1933. It is a chronicle of the Lantry family, who establish themselves in the harsh Florida scrub and turn repeatedly to moonshining when more lawful means of making money prove untenable. The novel opens with an author's note that stakes a claim for looseness and authority at the same time: "Since 'South Moon Under' is a novel and not a history—its characters, with one or two minor exceptions, entirely fictitious—the author asks the indulgence of the few Floridians who really know the Big Scrub, for the loose chronologizing of such happenings as the Big Burn, the inception of game and liquor laws, the activities of the Wilson Cypress Company, and so forth" (*South Moon Under* 2). Bigelow suggests that, at this time, Rawlings "had told herself that she would no longer write with an eye on possible sales, would no longer try to produce 'literature'" (12). But the note appended to *South Moon Under* demonstrates quite clearly that Rawlings was still concerned about her audience, or at least one small segment of it: "the few Floridians who really know the Big Scrub." Here Rawlings attempts to guard against the kind of critical ire she drew from the editor of the *Ocala Evening Star* for "Cracker Chidlings" (see Bigelow 12; and Rawlings, *Selected Letters* 38). She looks to prove that she knows the factual details of her material (the "Big Burn," liquor laws, the cypress lumber industry) with an authority that allows her to be "loose" with her chronology.

Rawlings's training as a journalist had made her finely attuned to issues of voice and authenticity. In letters to Perkins, she identifies her work along a spectrum of truthfulness: her stories are, variously, "basically true," "a 3,000-word true yarn told me by one Cracker friend," and "half fact and half fancy" (Perkins and Rawlings 41). Rawlings had a passion for the lengthy and immersive research that went into her stories. In the initial plans that she detailed to Perkins in 1931, she writes that "two of [the four planned novels] need several more years of note-taking" (Perkins and Rawlings 37), and though she feels in March 1931 that she's ready to begin "the novel of the scrub country" (Perkins and Rawlings 37) that would become *South Moon Under*, by June she writes Perkins that her readiness has progressed to a stage of further research: "My plans for a novel have advanced . . . I have arranged to go over into the scrub and live, for as long as I need to gather up the intimate, accurate details that make up the background" (Perkins and Rawlings 40). She spent several weeks of 1931 living with an "old woman and her 'shiner [moonshiner] son," returning to Cross Creek with "voluminous notes of the intimate type, for which the most prolific imagination is no substitute" (Perkins and Rawlings 44). But even after this trip, she writes Perkins, "I have to go back again to stay another couple of weeks, for I need more information about the 'shining on the river of forty or fifty years ago" (Perkins and Rawlings 45).

The combination of closely observed regional detail and imaginative story-making is apparent not only in the author's note quoted above but also in the contrast between the narrative voice and the dialect forms of the characters' speech. These two voices—the cosmopolitan narrator and the regional characters—mingle together throughout the novel. The opening passage demonstrates this effect:

> Night entered the clearing from the scrub. The low tangled growth of young oak and pine and palmetto fell suddenly black and silent, seeming to move closer in one shadowy spring. The man told himself there was nothing to fear. Yet as he walked towards his cabin, naked and new on the raw sand, darkness in this place seemed to him unfriendly.
> He thought, "Time I get me a fence raised tomorrow, maybe 'twon't seem so wild, like." (*South Moon Under* 3)

The reader is ushered into the exotic regional setting alongside the literary personification of nighttime, only to encounter an anonymous man to whose thoughts the narrator has access. But the narrative voice maintains some separation from this man. It interjects figurative language (the cabin described as a newborn) in a clause that separates his action (walking) from his perception (unfriendly darkness). The next paragraph juxtaposes these with the speech patterns of his direct thoughts, distinctly colloquial and presented in the dialect form that so consistently characterized regional writing.[12]

As a family chronicle, *South Moon Under* focuses on a succession of characters, moving through three generations of Lantrys as the story progresses. The narrative voice, which remains cosmopolitan throughout, becomes an anchor point—a constant amid the shifting focalization. It occasionally tries to justify itself, as at the opening of the second chapter, which takes Lantry's daughter Piety as the focus of the third-person limited narration:

> An hour before sunrise the girl Piety was awakened by the throaty cries of hoot-owls. The great night-birds had seldom sounded in the piney-woods. The bare pines were not to their liking. . . . Their cry was stirring, like a thick sob. It rose in a rhythmic crescendo of four major notes, subsiding in agony in a minor key.
>
> It had a pattern and a tune. It was, strangely, a dance step. A bass fiddle was playing a schottische. Piety had seen a man and woman from Virginia dance the schottische. Slowly; one-two-three-four. And then a quick running step; *one-two-three! (South Moon Under* 12–13)

The narrative voice contrasts its own cultured faculty for description with Piety's backwoods experience of the world and ways of knowing. The cries of the hoot-owls are described three times over: first atmospherically, as a "thick sob"; then figuratively, as a piece of orchestral music, with precise terminology; and finally, as folk music, described not in terms of keys and crescendos but rather as a visible string instrument, a well-known dance name, and an easily observable pattern of steps.[13] This juxtaposition demonstrates neatly the differences in the narrator's knowledge and the characters'. The narrator reaches for the cosmopolitan metaphor, whereas Piety employs words she knows to describe something she has seen.

Letters to Rawlings from editor Maxwell Perkins suggest that early drafts of the novel contained even more of this juxtaposition of voices, which Perkins counseled Rawlings to tone down significantly. In a letter from August 1932, Perkins gives extensive notes on the draft Rawlings has sent, explaining in several places that Rawlings's tendency toward narrative interjection breaks up the reader's experience of the novel. As Perkins puts it, "I think you tend to destroy the reader's illusion of being present by breaking in with exposition" (Perkins and Rawlings 55). In another place, he asks Rawlings to omit a sentence from the narrator's perspective: "such interpolated comments by the author tend to weaken the reader's illusion of . . . hearing actual dialogue" (Perkins and Rawlings 55). He encourages Rawlings to let her story speak for itself, explaining, "I think your dialogue and narrative can be trusted to do what you want without the help of comment and explanation" (Perkins and Rawlings 55). In the juxtaposition of cosmopolitan narrator and regional characters, Perkins's editorial guidance was to minimize the former and emphasize the latter.

But moments of juxtaposition still stand out. The text often uses dramatic irony to suggest the differences between kinds of knowledge, as when Piety is shown mispronouncing "zodiac" as "zondike," but knowing by heart the folk superstitions that relate astrology to the farming year (*South Moon Under* 145). Rawlings's regionalism also interacts with issues of modernization here and at other moments. The almanac, with its suggestion of national print culture, precedes the incursion into the scrub by the Murkley Cypress Company, which all but strips the area of its cypress trees, and by the federal government, which further threatens the Cracker way of life by enacting new laws about liquor and hunting.[14]

As Rawlings and Perkins's professional relationship developed, she continued to forward him fan letters she received, but only the ones that "interest[ed]" and "delighted" her, such as a missive from the president of the Wilson Cypress Co., real-life counterpart to the Murkley Cypress Company she had written about in *South Moon Under*. Rawlings enclosed this letter with a note to Perkins in March 1933, to demonstrate her own sense of herself as burgeoning literary celebrity who must deal with issues of both the marketplace and her fans. She inquires into how the book is selling, shares a story about the reaction of the family she stayed with when researching the novel, and relates that "the whole town" of Ocala, Florida, is waiting patiently to read the two library copies they possess: "Everyone tells me with great pride, 'I've got my name on the list to read your book. I can hardly wait.' I say politely, 'I do hope you'll enjoy it,' and I'm bursting, like Cabell with his letter answers, to say something such as, 'Do you think I'm a damn orchid, that I can live on air?'" (Perkins and Rawlings 103). "Cabell" is James Branch Cabell, an author and friend of Rawlings, who in 1933 published *Special Delivery*, a collection of "witheringly luminous emotional responses of Mr. Cabell to his typical fan mail" (front flap), published alongside the civil, brief letters he actually sent.

Rawlings is thinking of herself here as someone who receives "fan mail," with all the joy and frustration the designation connotes. She questions Perkins about the emotional negotiations of celebrity:

> What is one supposed to do about answering letters, anyway? I have a whole swarm about Jacob's Ladder that I never answered because it seems so futile. I tried to keep up for a while and found it almost impossible to hit a cordial but distant medium. I either sounded cold and heard later I was considered high-hat—or sounded too big-hearted and had the correspondents on my neck. You just can't be bothered with only men in Boston who send you candy. Do you think it matters in the least if you don't answer mail at all? Of course several of those I'm sending you today I shall very much want to answer, because the contact appeals to me. So send me back this batch, please. (Perkins and Rawlings 103–4)

As in asking after her sales, Rawlings is working to navigate professional authorship, hoping to use Perkins as her guide. She describes struggling with the appropriate tone for her responses, seeking a happy medium that will please her fan correspondents enough but not too much. Rawlings's questions imply that too much generosity on her part opens her up to being hounded by fans who mistake her "big-hearted" tone for a personal invitation to continue the correspondence. Rawlings would prefer only to answer letters when "the contact appeals to [her]," as with the president of the Wilson Cypress Co.[15] As none of these letters appear to survive in the archive, it is hard to know exactly what in them appealed to Rawlings.

Perkins doesn't seem to have had any advice for Rawlings in dealing with her fan mail, though he does write back to ask if Scribner's could use the story about the Big Scrub family to promote the novel (Perkins and Rawlings 104). Rawlings cautions him away from this idea. She fears exposing her research subjects and their illegal activities: "It would be a matter of actually getting a definite family in trouble with the law by identifying them too publicly with my book-characters" (Perkins and Rawlings 105). This sensitivity to legal matters and a desire to protect the identities of her regional subjects foreshadows the invasion-of-privacy trial Rawlings would be swept up in a decade later (see the end of this chapter for a discussion of the trial). Though she had no way to know it in 1933, Rawlings was right to be cautious regarding the very serious toll that her regional authenticity could take.

As it was, *South Moon Under* sold admirably even without the testimony of the scrub family for publicity. The Book-of-the-Month Club chose it as their main selection for March 1933 (Perkins and Rawlings 87), and Perkins reports to Rawlings in April 1933 that the novel was the third best-selling book in the country according to the *New York Tribune* (Perkins and Rawlings 106).

Though no fan mail from the time of *South Moon Under*'s immediate release survives in the Rawlings archive, a slightly later letter, from 1935, suggests what appealed to the novel's readers and which of their responses appealed enough to Rawlings for her to preserve. "About forty years ago I used to hunt and fish about various parts of the scrub," writes John Franklin Shields, on letterhead for his law firm in Philadelphia. The letter continues:

> I note you refer to Moss Bluff or Mossy Bluff and the killing of a particular large alligator by one of your characters near this place. This is of interest to me by reason of the fact that the largest 'gaitor I ever saw was at a place about eight miles from Moss Bluff and I estimated to be 25 or 30 feet long. I was about 50 yards from it at the time it slid into the water at a little island on the edge of a lake which we called Half Moon Lake which was east of Electra on a blind road which carried us into the sand beach on the lake at the edge of the scrub.[16]

This paragraph has more in common with *South Moon Under* than simply the Floridian flora and fauna. Its sentences, gradually lengthening with clause after clause, trace a linguistic pathway from the cosmopolitan North to the rural South that mirrors Rawlings's novel. Thus a cordially described "particularly large alligator" becomes the scrub hunter's "largest 'gaitor I ever saw," as the Philadelphia lawyer adopts the colloquial turns of phrase of his former hunting grounds.[17] Shields wants to know if his Moss Bluff is the same one Rawlings's novel describes, and also if she knows the story of Nick Myers, a Florida man who was rumored to have threatened an outsider in the same fashion as one of Rawlings's characters. He relates too that he "knew the Ocklawaha River when the original cypress was there . . . and later knew some of the Wilson Lumber Company who were the people from Palatka who took out the original cypress." The excitement of recognition and connection is palpable in Shields's letter as he explains, "Naturally I recognized, reading your book, that you thoroughly knew the localities and the people as well as being able to tell the story in an entertaining and captivating manner." Shields reaches out to Rawlings's authoritatively voiced novel with authority and firsthand experience of his own. Given that Rawlings valued the approval of those who knew Florida as she knew it, it is little wonder this letter survives when so few others from this point in her career do. Unfortunately, there is no indication as to whether she ever wrote back.

South Moon Under shares several features with Rawlings's third and most successful novel, *The Yearling*. Indeed, the latter book was born out of the former, suggested first when Charles Rawlings read a draft and told his wife, as she relates to Perkins, "Take out all the profanity. If you do this, you automatically open up a wide and continuous market for the book *among boys*, entirely distinct, an accidental by-product, from your mature appeal" (*Selected Letters* 57, original emphasis). Rawlings balked: "I remember, out of the red fog that enveloped me, remarking caustically that possibly the book could become the first of a series, 'The Rover Boys of Florida'" (*Selected Letters* 57). Charles backpedaled, explaining that he meant a boys' book in the tradition of "Huckleberry Finn, Treasure Island, and some of Kipling" (*Selected Letters* 57).

South Moon Under went to press with its profanity intact. But Perkins agreed with Charles; in October 1933, he pressed Rawlings to write a book for boys, suggesting that men would enjoy it as well (Perkins and Rawlings 126). Rawlings wrote back to caution Perkins that, were she to undertake the boys' book, she would "not consider anything but an out-and-out boy's juvenile," while also worrying that "a book [for adults] in the same general locale could only be compared with the first book [*South Moon Under*], could only be called its sequel [*sic*] or successor at best, and, at worst, would be considered an attempt to capitalize on what earlier interest there was in such characters in such a setting" (Perkins and Rawlings 127). Yet, in the same letter, she inquires, "The book being strictly a juvenile, is it legitimate to lift three or four incidents from South Moon, particularly those of the deer playing in the sink-hole in the moonlight, and the cat-hunt?" (Perkins and Rawlings 128). Rawlings's thinking about the novel seems strangely at odds here: she refuses to write a sequel or successor to *South Moon Under*, and yet she also wants to incorporate passages from the novel, as if she is thinking of crafting a juvenile adaptation of her first book. Perkins counseled her not to "lift out any of the actual words in 'South Moon Under'" but gave her the go-ahead to "retell the incidents" she had mentioned (Perkins and Rawlings 129). Perkins and Scribner's did not want Rawlings to plagiarize her own work, but they were perfectly happy to let her transform the elements of an adult novel into something more suitable for boys.

To make her "boys' book on the scrub" (Perkins and Rawlings 124), Rawlings transforms *South Moon Under*'s rough and distant Lant into the dreamy, nurturing Jody of *The Yearling* (1938). Both boys delight in the relative freedom of life in the scrub, and in the outdoor pleasures of tracking, hunting, and camping. Lant listens to old man Paine describe fire-hunting for deer "twitching in his eagerness" and "[runs] for his gun and shells" when Paine suggests they go hunting themselves, to kill the deer that has been eating their crops (*South Moon Under* 99–100); likewise, Jody is "wild to begin the hunt" for the bear that killed his mother's brood sow (*The Yearling* 31). But Jody prefers the story of the hunt to the hunt itself (*The Yearling* 69), and on another occasion, feels "sickened and sorry" to see the "mangled death" of a deer (*The Yearling* 85). And while Lant does feel connected to the deer he hunts (*South Moon Under* 106) and "sorry to have killed" a pregnant squirrel (*South Moon Under* 119), he is not identified with these female animals in the way Jody is. Indeed, *The Yearling* repeatedly casts Jody in the role of mother to the scrub animals: he nurses a raccoon with a "sugar-teat," holding it "cupped in [his] arm" like a mother with a baby (*The Yearling* 62), and later feeds his yearling deer by "[dipping] his fingers in the milk and [thrusting] them into the fawn's soft wet mouth," directing it to "do whatever I tell you . . . like as if I was your mammy" (*The Yearling* 208–9). Lant "want[s] to kill" (*South Moon Under* 106), whereas Jody wants to mother.

But perhaps the biggest change comes simply from Rawlings's choice, following Perkins's advice (Perkins and Rawlings 126), to fix Jody at an indeterminate but distinctly preadolescent age for the course of the story. Lant grows up, in *South Moon Under,* and the narrative orients the reader to his age: first fourteen, then sixteen, then nineteen years old. Jody's boyhood is lengthened until it fills the whole of *The Yearling.*[18] The novel's "innocence to experience" narrative arc is established with early foreshadowing: Penny Baxter, Jody's father, thinks to himself, "Let him kick up his heels. . . . The day'll come, he'll not even care to" (*The Yearling* 25). The story pursues this day unflaggingly, as hunts, a hurricane, and the killing of his pet deer teach Jody about the harshness of nature and death. Finally, in the book's closing line, Jody is separated from the boy he was: while he lies sleeping in his bed, "Somewhere beyond the sink-hole, past the magnolia, under the live oaks, a boy and his yearling ran side by side, and were gone forever" (*The Yearling* 509). Rawlings freezes Jody just at the transition point between childhood and adulthood, suggesting in this moment that his preadolescent self will continue to inhabit the scrub, like a ghost, forever frolicking with his yearling pet.

She also freezes the scrub in a preindustrial agrarian moment, dropping the modernization theme that was so prevalent in *South Moon Under*. By setting the book in the 1870s instead of the 1920s, Rawlings frees herself to exclude the almanac, the cypress company, and the government's invasive enclosure and bootlegging laws from *The Yearling*. Furthermore, Rawlings's third-person limited narration, so closely aligned with Jody's consciousness, does much less to suggest a cosmopolitan world outside the scrub. Though the narration does not take on the regional dialect of the characters, there is less of a clear distinction between the two voices. Thus, when Jody sees a spring bubbling up from the sand, the narrative voice uses a simple simile not outside Jody's grasp: "It was as though the banks cupped green leafy hands to hold it" (*The Yearling* 4). A rainbow is "so lovely and so various that Jody thought he would burst with looking at it," but it does not suggest anything outside his own limited experience (*The Yearling* 9). This is not to say that Rawlings eschews the kind of regionalist social commentary her earlier novel made possible through its juxtaposition of the cosmopolitan and the rural. But rather than comment on federal incursion into isolated regions and traditional communities, *The Yearling*'s social commentary hews closer to the individual.

By giving readers access to the simple yet profound consciousness of a nurturing boy-mother, Rawlings suggests the potential queerness of male adolescence,[19] presenting Jody's desire to nurture as natural and comprehensible. Though ultimately painful, Jody's experience of raising Flag is presented as pleasurable, and in the end it links him inextricably with his mother, Ora, who lost at least four children before Jody was born; with his father, whose "bowels yearned over his son" when Ora could feel only detachment (*The Yearling* 23); and with his closest friend, a disabled boy nicknamed Fodder-wing, who teaches Jody how to care for baby animals (*The Yearling* 59–62). Maternal pleasure in *The Yearling* lacks definitive gender boundaries: boys nurse baby raccoons and deer with makeshift "teats," and fathers feel labor pains. Within the novel's marginalized community of Florida Crackers, Fodder-wing and Jody represent a further remove from normativity—compassionate prepubescent males in a world of rough hunters and brawling sailors. In this way, the novel participates in the strain of regionalism that Stephanie Foote characterizes as "a genre in which marginalization itself was a positive virtue" (35). If, as Foote argues, regionalism is defined by its "[interest] in representing non-normative communities or cultures to a national audience" (30), then *The Yearling* creates value not only by giving voice to Florida Crackers but also by aligning the reader with a queer boyhood that resists the supposedly conventional masculinity of that community.

Jody and Flag resonated deeply with the reading public; *The Yearling* was a massive success that unquestionably brought the Florida scrub and its Cracker residents to national attention. Maxwell Perkins proclaimed he "never knew a book that had such universal liking" (Perkins and Rawlings 344). It became a bestseller, was released as the main Book-of-the-Month Club selection for April 1938 (Perkins and Rawlings 333), and won the 1939 Pulitzer Prize. MGM bought the film rights for thirty thousand dollars (Perkins and Rawlings 342). In a flurry, and without leaving the backwoods of Florida, Rawlings had parlayed her regional observations into national celebrity.

As after the publication of *South Moon Under,* Rawlings used her letters to Perkins as a place to reflect on her success and her readers' feedback. "I am getting the most wonderful and touching letters," she tells him in May 1938, when the book had been out for just two months (Perkins and Rawlings 346). Already, Rawlings had been struck by the similarities across such letters, and she was coming to develop a theory of fan response that cast her own work as an interactive impetus to reader creativity. She continues her letter: "Readers themselves, I think, contribute to a book. They add their own imaginations, and it is as though the writer only gave them something to work on, and they did the rest" (Perkins and Rawlings 346). Her modesty has the air of a suddenly successful writer struggling to understand why *this* work struck a chord—"the so-called 'success' seems to have nothing to do with me," Rawlings writes (Perkins and Rawlings 346)—and yet the sentiment unifies much of the fan mail Rawlings writes about and saves during the course of her career. By preserving such letters—the ones that demonstrated her readers' imaginations and active work in coauthoring their experience of the novels—Rawlings expands her own archive to include the voices of the many correspondents, professional and nonprofessional writers alike, who interacted with and transformed her books.

It is again hard to know exactly which letters Rawlings refers to above; few letters dated from March to May 1938 survive in her papers. But even the later fan letters praising *The Yearling* evince the imaginative work of her readers. As in the broad collection of fan mail analyzed in the first section of this chapter, these letters share a remarkable number of expressions—the conventions or tropes of the fan letter as a form. Across the small group,[20] multiple authors use the following tropes: they announce their discomfort with the form, make recourse to their own authority of the subject matter, speak to their intellectual and emotional experience of the novels' characters, claim kinship with Rawlings by virtue of being authors themselves, demonstrate their aesthetic sensibility, and comment on their sense of "pleasure" in reading.

In letters from January 29 and February 20, 1939, respectively, Lucille Shearwood and Jack Latham each declare that they do not usually write "fan letters," but that they felt they had to express to Rawlings how *The Yearling* made them feel. For Shearwood, that feeling is one of tremendous personal connection to the characters: "To me, it is so real and alive—I know Penny and Jody better than I know people I meet daily—and how much better I understand them. I can see Baxter's Island; hear the chirring of the squirrels—and feel intensely interested in all Ma Baxter's cooking, smelling the cornpone—marvelling at the detail in which you described the household and farm jobs." Shearwood frames her admiration of the novel's details with references to her own imagination. She personalizes her response with repeated "I" statements: "to me," "I know," "I understand," "I can see . . . hear . . . feel." Only after this litany does she reintroduce Rawlings's own work, the details of her descriptions within the novel. And though this approach to praise may seem to diminish Rawlings's own agency and act of creation, it is exactly the approach that Rawlings calls "wonderful and touching" in her letter to Perkins.

While Shearwood's enjoyment of the novel is deepened by her imaginative work, it is grounded by her partial knowledge of Florida: "I have visited at Ft. Pierce each Spring for the last two years, so I knew some of the Florida trees—but so much of the story of animals and shrubs was strange and fascinating." Meanwhile, fan correspondents like J. H. Brinson draw on incredibly specific knowledge of the Florida scrub to express their appreciation. Brinson's August 1939 letter presents Rawlings with a map of her own work, filtered through the chatty "reminiscences" of a former schoolteacher who lived in a neighboring part of Florida from 1885 to 1887. Brinson appreciates Rawlings's carefully researched regional details, writing: "I have been all along Salt Springs Run and could easily imagine myself seeing Old Slewfoot lunge into the run and swim across. Your descriptions are wonderfully authentic." Like Shearwood, Brinson values the authenticity of place in Rawlings's novel, testing it by its ability to support imaginative work.

For those intimately acquainted with the real Florida that Rawlings has adapted into her book, place becomes a character in itself: "You mention Penny driving Old Caesar accompanied by Julia to Grahamville. About ten days ago I came up with a Mr. Dillion Graham and his wife here. This place on the Ocklawaha was named for his father and we talked it over. . . . Volusia has disappeared from the map but I crossed the St. Johns there by ferry once in order to get a boat at Astor down the river. The store where Penny did his trading was operated by Gus Dillard who had a good orange grove there" (Brinson). There is a kind of pleasure in the facts themselves, and how the real world weaves together with the fictional one. Like Rawlings with her extensive research, Brinson claims authority by supplementing Rawlings's setting with his personally observed real-world details.

Beyond place, many of these fan letters draw special connections to the main characters of *The Yearling*: Jody, the young protagonist; Penny, his father; and Flag, his yearling deer. The characters come off the page for the fans who write to Rawlings. As Paul Rittenhouse hesitantly expresses, "One feels he knows the counterpart in his own life, of all the characters—I should better say each character." Even more personable and enthusiastic is May Cox: "*Penny* and *Jody* are to be *my life long* friends! And of course *Flag!*" Shearwood, Rittenhouse, and Cox all bring the characters out of the novel and locate them within their real lives.[21]

Others use Jody to make sense of their emotional response to the novel. A fan who signs only as "Ataloa" uses Jody as a standard by which to describe his reaction: "I feel just like your beloved Jody when I try to find the right words for all that wells up within; it only spills over in futile longing." This moment suggests an inexpressible depth of feeling evoked by the novel that only the novel itself can help parse.

Fan mail gave these writers somewhere to practice finding "the right words for all that wells up within," as well as to try out various identities and authorial voices. Though a letter is not as safe as a private journal or diary, it is certainly safer than a piece of writing intended for publication. In fan letters, correspondents like Shearwood and Latham could—and did—test out their identities as authors. The letter is a powerful medium for this experimentation: as Gaul and Harris point out, "Authorial selves emerge through epistolary exchange with others; the process of constructing an authorial persona does not occur in isolation but through the mechanisms of dialogue and response that letters facilitate" (10). So Latham can confide—or boast?—that, though young and unpublished, "I feel one of my short stories will click soon." Lucille Shearwood uses her letter to express a palpable dissatisfaction with her authorial self: "I have been battling with a N.Y. newspaper for the last seven years, and before that edited some weeklies—always promising myself that when I had time, I would write something noble. Right now, I have time—and what am I doing? Watering my Florida chandelier plant (2 ½ ft. tall) and writing a stinking weekly colyum." Like the fan correspondents writing to Clara Bow and Georgia O'Keeffe, Shearwood builds on a coclaimed identity—author. And at the same time, her playful spelling of "column" suggests her own attempts to render dialect for the amusement of her audience—in this case, the writer she so admires. Shearwood repeats this tactic in her final lines, this time quoting Rawlings's writing back to her in an attempt, just like Ataloa's, to express the inexpressible: "I see this letter isn't turning out the way I expected, but mine never seem to. Hit frets me, you not knowin' how I feel. I mean!" "Hit" mimics the regional voices in *The Yearling,* most especially Jody, who during the novel's emotional climax cries out to his beloved deer, "Hit's me!" (*The Yearling* 488).

Feelings are troubling for these fans; they cannot be contained, nor explained. Or, perhaps more accurately, the standardized form of fan response necessitates an understanding of feelings as difficult, even impossible, to express directly.[22] Fans like Ataloa, Latham, and Shearwood—not all of whom identify themselves as writers—use the fan letter to work out how to express their feelings in text. Even more strikingly, these fans, who are separated by geographic distance and time, use the same expressions as each other, and as other fans of other authors, artists, and actors, while at the same time incorporating Rawlings's voice and work into their letters. These fans create something new by combining standard fan mail forms with adaptations or transformations of Rawlings's style.

For fans like May Cox, Myron Milliman, and Hector Chevigny, it is easier to put words—or more specifically, a single word—to the feelings that *The Yearling* gives them. All three writers specifically use "pleasure" to describe their experience of reading the novel. Indeed, it would not be a stretch to assert that "pleasure" is the defining characteristic of the epistolary fan response to Rawlings's work, especially going forward into the World War II years. It is also a word that crops up again and again in the fan mail considered in the first section of this chapter, the fan mail received by Willa Cather and Georgia O'Keeffe. But what does "pleasure" mean?

National Pleasures

When faced with the massive corpus that fan letters represent, it is impossible to ignore this word, this one word, that appears repeatedly. On the one hand, to be a fan implicitly means to experience pleasure: to enjoy things, to be made happy by them. But on the other hand, this kind of consistency—again across distances, times, and identities—demands further interrogation. As Deidre Shauna Lynch reminds us in her book *Loving Literature: A Cultural History*, reading for emotional pleasure did not come naturally to the English-speaking world. Multiple "redefinitions of literary experience—and of the interior spaces of the mind and home" were needed (Lynch 5). As early as 1810—at least seventy years before the development of the "fan" as a named identity—literature was being recognized by the emotional connections that readers could make to it. Lynch explores British literature of the late eighteenth and nineteenth centuries, arguing that "individuals needed to *learn* to develop and to legitimate their own private, individuated relationships with that abstraction, the canon, the 'literature' that had, in the wake of copyright decisions of the late eighteenth century, come to constitute Britons' public domain" (12, original emphasis). Only by developing personal relationships with literature could readers come to love it.

The learned relationship of loving reader to beloved text was not limited to Britain in the nineteenth century. As Janice Radway explores in *A Feeling for Books*, American literature of the early to mid-twentieth century was likewise shaped by the notion that reading for leisure was reading for pleasure. In tracing the history of the Book-of-the-Month Club, Radway self-consciously invokes the at-times "suspect pleasures" of "middlebrow" reading (37). Radway seizes on pleasure as a marker of the Book-of-the-Month Club reading experience following her encounter with a 1983 article about the Club's history by Al Silverman, entitled "The Fragile Pleasure." Throughout *A Feeling for Books*, the word itself marks an alternate reading experience to that of reading for instruction, or improvement, or intellectual challenge, an experience shaped by the Book-of-the-Month Club's selections and popularity. Analyzing the readers' reports the Club used to make its selections, Radway "conclude[s] that literary writing was judged a failure at the Book-of-the-Month Club when the editors thought that the labor it required of the reader would not pay off in terms of engagement or pleasure" (71). The readers' reports tacitly demonstrated to Radway that a selection should provide the reader with "some sort of pleasure or reward . . . not the cognitive pleasure of solving a difficult puzzle or following the trail of a difficult argument. Nor was it the pleasure of achieving critical and analytical distance in one's familiar world. Rather, this pleasure appeared to be more emotional and absorbing; it seemed to have something to do with the affective delights of transport, travel, and vicarious social interaction" (72). Though Radway primarily reads and references readers' reports from the early 1980s, there is a clear and obvious link between the pleasurable "feeling of immersion, [the] sense of boundaries dissolved" that Radway identifies (114) and Marjorie Kinnan Rawlings's fan mail, with its emphasis on geographical and emotional immersion.

Rawlings herself had three books chosen and released by the Book-of-the-Month Club: her first and third novels, *South Moon Under* and *The Yearling*, which elicited so much of her early fan mail, as well as *Cross Creek*. In this memoir about the joys and challenges of life on her Florida homestead, Rawlings depicts herself as a newcomer to the tightly knit and surprisingly integrated rural town of Cross Creek, a "Yankee" who has nevertheless found her spiritual home in the weird South. She describes being initiated into the "queer" community by its African American matriarch, Martha Mickens, and affirms her commitment to her adopted home as a "commitment to shared sorrow, even as to shared joy" (17).

Cross Creek was published by Scribner's in 1942, after more than ten years of saving material, drafting sketches, and working to find what biographer Gordon Bigelow describes as "a structural scheme and a tone which would hold such diverse elements together" (39). Rawlings's letters to editor Max Perkins suggest that she initially felt the book to be too episodic and "conversational" (Perkins and Rawlings 464). At Perkins's suggestion, Rawlings connected the episodes and incidents of the memoir like "a single piece of string with knots in it, the knots being the episodes, but each connected with the other by the incidents" (Perkins and Rawlings 470). Rawlings still worried that *Cross Creek* would miss its mark, but by the time she began revising it in 1941, she knew what she wanted it to accomplish: "No one knows better than I that it is a *queer* book. If we can get it right, I would hope that its effect on readers would be to take them into a totally strange world, and that they should feel a certain delight and enchantment in the strangeness" (Perkins and Rawlings 499, original emphasis). Perkins, for his part, felt the memoir offered something vital to a United States mired in World War II. "'Cross Creek' may be queer, but it is lovely, and it is human," he wrote to Rawlings. "It is a great pleasure to read such a book in such times" (Perkins and Rawlings 499).

What did it mean, in the late 1930s and 1940s United States, to feel pleasure when reading? With that question in mind, I turn to *Cross Creek*, Rawlings's final Florida book, reading it in concert with its fan mail to better understand what was at stake in the practice of reading for pleasure during this time. What are the pleasures of *Cross Creek*, and of Rawlings's work more generally? And why, during the Second World War, did these particular pleasures become so popular with the American reading public, as Perkins predicted they would? What did they provide that Americans needed?

True to Perkins's prediction, *Cross Creek* was an enormously popular book: propelled by the Book-of-the-Month Club selection, it became a major bestseller and was, in December 1943, her second book to be printed in an Armed Services Edition. With such wide distribution, the memoir found a passionate audience who once more reached out to Rawlings in letters. It was also Rawlings's most interactive text, one that built on her early magazine work and the epistolary relationships she had developed with a variety of fans.

Rawlings's *Cross Creek* fan mail suggests that her inclusion in the Book-of-the-Month Club aligned her specifically with the so-called "middlebrow" readers to whose pleasure the Club catered. Thus, when Alexandra Apostolides writes to Rawlings in 1943, begging, "Will you please believe me utterly when I declare to you that you and Undset are, in my opinion, the two greatest women writers I have ever, ever, ever come across?" she is constructing herself as a Club subscriber, with all the attendant connotations about literary taste and pleasure mapped by Radway. Sigrid Undset, the Norwegian novelist and 1928 Nobel Prize winner, would have been known to a reader from San Francisco through her 1,100-page historical epic *Kristin Lavransdatter*, released in America as a Book-of-the-Month Club selection in 1929 and still being offered as a free Book-of-the-Month Club gift in 1937.

Yet Apostolides also writes to establish her literary tastes and authority beyond the Club. Her letter continues: "Honestly I mean this; you both walk along the path of Tolstoi, and pass even him in some ways. And I worship Tolstoi!" Like another fan letter's reference to Brahms, like the multiple letter writers who ask Rawlings if she knows the work of philosopher Henry George, and like the correspondent who wishes Harriet Beecher Stowe's ghost could receive copies of Rawlings's books, Apostolides's letter maps her particular network of cultural knowledge, creating a position of readerly authority from which to judge. The letter is a chance to test the fan's own powers of literary criticism—not only defining her personal canon but also drawing out the book's most important features and the fan's ability to recognize those features.

For Apostolides, as for R. H. Battle, those important and pleasing features of the memoir often involve not the comedy of the book but its sadness—its "shared sorrow" and its sense, as Battle writes, of things "passing." Apostolides characterizes *Cross Creek* as "a eulogy on the real greatness of America's people" and notes that "through the book, likewise, runs a slender thread of loneliness (and what individual is not lonely oftentimes?); but that, too, is precious." The immersive pleasure of the reading experience could and did include sensations that we normally characterize as negative, and fans mirrored this experience back to Rawlings in their letters, often quoting or approximating quotations of Rawlings's work back to her. Battle wonders whether Rawlings "got as much pleasure out of writing one sentence [about seasons passing] as I did reading it," copying out the sentence for her, while Apostolides misquotes a passage at the end of the memoir's introductory chapter. In the passage, Rawlings counters the urban bias that suggests the loneliness of her rural home cannot be enjoyable:

> For myself, the Creek satisfies a thing that had gone hungry and un-
> fed since childhood days. I am often lonely. Who is not? But I should
> be lonelier in the heart of a city. And as Tom says, "So much happens
> here." I walk at sunset, east along the road. There are no houses in that
> direction, except the abandoned one where the wild plums grow, which
> will bloom in springtime. . . .
> Folk call the road lonely, because there is not human traffic and hu-
> man stirring. Because I have walked it so many times and seen such a
> tumult of life there, it seems to me one of the most populous highways
> of my acquaintance. I have walked it in ecstasy, and in joy it is beloved.

Every pine tree, every gallberry bush, every passion vine, every gore rus-
tling in the underbrush, is vibrant. I have walked it in trouble, and the
wind in the trees beside me is easing. I have walked it in despair, and the
red of the sunset is my own blood dissolving into the night's darkness.
For all such things were on earth before us, and will survive after us, and
it is given to us to join ourselves with them and to be comforted. (*Cross
Creek* 13–14)

The narrative voice of *Cross Creek* seems to address a hidden listener, a
"you" to whom Rawlings elegiacally reveals her "I," as in the passage above.[23]
This technique gives an undeniable element of epistolarity to *Cross Creek*,
though it is not an epistolary text. Janet Altman defines epistolarity as "the
use of the letter's formal properties to create meaning"; it is "primarily a frame
for reading" that "can only be argued by an act of interpretation" (4). Rawlings's memoir lacks the formal frame elements—a named recipient, a date,
a signature—that usually mark a text comprised of letters, and yet it shares
many of the "ways of making meaning" that Altman analyzes (4). The book
is structured as a series of episodes, roughly grouped together by theme but
with little sense of placement in time—like stories being related to a far-off
correspondent as the author remembers them. Indeed, *Cross Creek* strikingly
resembles Altman's characterization of the epistolary romance, "a slow-motion
affair" that "entails an increased emphasis on psychological nuance and the
details of everyday life" (Altman 21). As in the passage above, Rawlings marries
her emotional life to the regular occurrences of the natural world, situating the
spectrum of human emotions within Cross Creek, the "strange world" that is
yet somehow accessible and welcoming.

To achieve this effect, Rawlings begins the memoir first by locating the
community as though on a map, and then by locating herself within Cross
Creek: it is "a bend in a country road, by land, and the flowing of Lochloosa
Lake into Orange Lake, by water. We are four miles west of the small village
of Island Grove, nine miles east of a turpentine still and on the other sides we
do not count distance at all, for the two lakes and the broad marshes create
an infinite space between us and the horizon" (*Cross Creek* 9). This careful
mapping mirrors J. H. Brinson's 1939 letter discussed above. Though I do not
want to suggest that she drew on that letter as inspiration, I argue that the
pleasures of mapping, of re-creating place with words, are held in common by

Rawlings and Brinson. The wonderful specificity of place-names, distances, and directions speaks to "the desire for the real" that Stephanie Foote argues regionalism worked to mediate (36). Rawlings's descriptions of Cross Creek's place on the map are highly accurate—and yet, they are also tinged with the mythic. Juxtaposed with the four miles west and the nine miles east are the other "sides," stretching infinitely toward the horizon.

Rawlings invites the reader to inhabit this real and yet more-than-real space with her. In an act of enclosure that mirrors the opening of *South Moon Under*, Rawlings frames her memoir with an approach: after viewing Cross Creek as on a map, the reader approaches it from the road, before finally stepping onto Rawlings's farm and closing the gate behind her:

> Yet the four miles to the Creek are stirring, like the bleak, portentous beginning of a good tale. The road curves sharply, the vegetation thickens, and around the bend masses into dense hammock. The hammock breaks, is pushed back on either side of the road, and set down in its brooding heart is the orange grove.
>
> Any grove or wood is a fine thing to see. But the magic here, strangely, is not apparent from the road. It is necessary to leave the impersonal highway, to step inside the rusty gate and close it behind. By this, an act of faith is committed, through which one accepts blindly the communion cup of beauty. One is now inside the grove, out of one world and in the mysterious heart of another. (*Cross Creek* 15)

Rawlings welcomes her reader into a place that is both real (four miles from Island Grove, on the other side of a rusty gate) and sacramental (a good tale, an act of faith, the communion cup of beauty). The "mysterious heart" of this world becomes a metaphor for the mysterious heart of Rawlings herself, and her reader as well. With this lyrical prologue, she creates a place for her fans to connect with her emotionally as they did with her earlier fictional characters. This "strange world" is a space in which to grapple with emotionality.

My argument extends the assertions of Judith Fetterley and Marjorie Pryse, who characterize regionalist fiction as a "form of 'emotional tutorial' that provides its readers with the opportunity to do the emotional and cognitive work of developing their capacity for empathy" (348).[24] Like the regionalist texts they analyze, Rawlings's memoir accomplishes this by "emphasizing its own relationship with readers; … by challenging individuation as the desired model of emotional development; and by proposing instead a model of separating while staying connected" (Fetterley and Pryse 348–49). Rawlings sets herself apart in Cross Creek, but she also opens her separate space to her community of readers, encouraging them to take "the communion cup of beauty" and join her. Furthermore, whereas Fetterley and Pryse suggest that the "effects" of regionalist models of empathy "may be difficult to determine outside of the classroom" (342), Rawlings's fan mail archive provides us with hundreds of pages of examples.

Indeed, the intense emotional content of the *Cross Creek* fan letters mirrors Rawlings's elegiac self-disclosure. In turn, these letters demonstrate how emotional experience becomes spiritual sustenance, "feeding" readers in a time of rationing, deprivation, and war. Thus, like the self-aware fans quoted in the first part of this chapter, Mollie Atkinson apologizes for reaching out, giving as justifications both her own emotional turmoil—"I get so overwrought and frustrated here"—and the one-way intimacy that the memoir has made possible. Many fans write to say they feel similarly, that "after reading 'Cross Creek,' somehow you don't seem like a stranger" (Atkinson). Some, like Atkinson, write to Rawlings after World War II to thank her for taking them "right away from the anxieties of war." Others, like Louis Dollarhide and Mary Louise Aguirre, write from hospitals where they read *Cross Creek* and felt it spoke to them in their convalescence.

The former letters, sent by the young soldier Dollarhide to Rawlings in the winter of 1943, are especially compelling. Three of his letters exist in the archive; a fourth letter, sent seven months prior, is mentioned but does not appear to survive. From "flat on my back in the hospital," Dollarhide reaches out to Rawlings in page after page of fine, straight script that reads like his direct response to, or even version of, *Cross Creek*. His letter from January 1 begins *in medias res*, detailing Dollarhide's movements around the Gulf Port Air Force base, where he is recovering: "Dear Miss Rawlings: Last night when I walked from the study hall about 18:30, the roar of the propeller up at test blocks was almost deafening. … The air was crisp and cold, and stung my face as I walked from the warm room. With no moon to obscure them, the myriad stars appeared as distant friends." The geography of the base and the nature surrounding it are mapped as carefully as Rawlings's Florida farm in her memoir, with which Dollarhide is intimately familiar. *Cross Creek* invites this intimacy, or at least the illusion of it, and Rawlings's publicity works to extend that feeling. Thus, on February 20, Dollarhide writes: "Looking through a back issue of the *Saturday Evening Post* yesterday, I found the article showing you in the surroundings of Cross Creek and St. Augustine; and studying the pictures with particular interest, I felt, as I am sure most of your admiring readers did, that I had rounded a corner and come face to face with a friend. The pleasure of the surprise broke for awhile the monotony of this daily grind of continued hospitalization." Dollarhide positions himself as one among many—fully aware of the article's wide circulation—and yet he personalizes his relationship to Rawlings. She appears, like January's stars, as a distant friend.

Dollarhide's feeling of friendship was not entirely one-sided. For, as we learn in this letter, Rawlings did write back to him on at least one occasion. In the touching final lines of the February letter, Dollarhide reminds Rawlings of their shared bond:

> About seven months ago, Mrs. Rawlings, in a fit of despair and loneliness, as one fumbling in darkness, I wrote you a letter. You answered it, and in a moment, gave me light and hope. That light and that hope have remained with me, teaching me the value of the moment, the charm of minutiae which heretofore had gone unnoticed, the beauty one can find even in harshness.
>
> Thank you again for lending an ear—though I must admit my intrusion is something like the neighbor's radio.

Bergen Evans thought fan mail signaled our loneliness. But what if fan mail could assuage loneliness? And what if, in some way, however small, it did?

Sixteen-year-old Mary Louise Aguirre begins with the common disavowal of herself as a fan. In a charming letter from September 1942, the teenaged tuberculosis patient confesses, "Entre nous I'm not in the habit of writing fan letters and when my thoughts penetrate such ideas I get the willies." But, she continues, "Somehow with you its [*sic*] different." Aguirre praises *Cross Creek* and declares her "ambition to be a writer." She practices combining Rawlings's cosmopolitan narrative voice with regional African American dialect channeled through Rawlings's characters: "I've been disillusioned about people's ways so many times I've failed to realize there are such *fine* species of *fine* humans as in [^the] creek—I've always had such high ideals [^(still do)] of Life and as I grow they always seem to be shattered in one way or another—But when I read 'Cross Creek,' Martha seemed to whisper 'Honey, they iz still fine things in life even if all the people don't practise 'em.'" Like Alexandra Apostolides, Aguirre's version of *Cross Creek* is not a perfect re-creation. Martha Mickens's trademark pet name "Sugar" becomes "Honey," and her dialect is clumsily transliterated. And yet, Aguirre's imaginative addition to Rawlings's work—her own vision of Martha speaking directly to her—accurately captures the central importance of Martha as a figure of comfort and emotional stability, a fixed point at the center of a world increasingly "shattered" by modernity.

For if there is a thread to be found between each of the disparate narratives of *Cross Creek,* it is Martha Mickens, the African American heart of the community whom Rawlings purposefully sought to "interw[eave] into the episodes" throughout (*Selected Letters* 209). Though Carolyn Jones suggests that Martha is the "most disruptive Africanist presence in *Cross Creek*" (226), Rawlings's partly fictionalized portrayal of Martha gives the community a spiritual center and guardian—not a disruption but a comfort that resonated with white and Black readers alike.

Rawlings, initially an outsider in the insulated community of Cross Creek, relies on Martha to bring her into the fold. Martha has the power of naming, and of initiating one into the community: "It was when old Martha, who had set up the Brices as Old Boss and Old Miss, referred to me one day as Young Miss, that it was understood by all of us that I was here to stay" (*Cross Creek* 13). Rawlings casts Martha as a priestess of initiations, of birth and death, and even as an actual goddess: "When old Martha Mickens shall march at last through the walls of Jericho, shouting her Primitive Baptist hymns, a dark rock at the core of Creek life will have been shattered to bits. She is nurse to any of us, black or white, who fall ill. She is midwife and layer out of the dead. She is the only one who gives advice to all of us impartially. She is a dusky Fate, spinning away at the threads of our Creek existence" (*Cross Creek* 25). As a mythic figure, Martha functions as go-between for the two populations of Cross Creek—white and African American—who would otherwise be segregated. She moves easily between the two groups, and she cannot be placed in time. Rawlings describes her as a kind of apparition whose age is indeterminate: "Martha welcomed me with old-fashioned formality. She came walking toward me in the grove one bright sunny December day. I turned to watch her magnificent carriage. It was erect, with a long free graceful stride. It was impossible to tell her age. She walked like a very young woman and walks so to this day. She is getting on to seventy, yet glimpsing her down the road she might be a girl" (*Cross Creek* 27). Graceful, almost ageless, and impartial, Martha is also the keeper of historical knowledge for the community. As she did with poor-white Piety in *South Moon Under*, Rawlings uses regional dialect to juxtapose the supposed ignorance and deep wisdom inherent in Martha's rural Black identity. When Martha appears at the grove, she introduces herself and the history of the land, which stretches far into the future:

> She said, "I come to pay my respecks. I be's Martha. Martha Mickens."
> . . .
> "Then lemme tell you. Ain't nobody never gone cold-out hungry here. I'se seed the grove freeze to the ground. I'se seed it swivel in a long drought. But Sugar, they was grove here before my folks crossed the big water. They was wild grove here as long back as tongue can tell. Durin' the war for freedom the white ladies used to drive out here in wagons and pick the wild oranges to squeeze out the juice and send it to the sojers. And they'll be grove here right on, after you and me is forgotten. They'll be good land to plow, and mast in the woods for hogs, and ain't no need to go hongry. All the folks here ahead o' you has fit cold and wind and dry weather, but ain't nary one of 'em has goed hongry." (*Cross Creek* 28–29)

Her words serve to comfort Rawlings, but they also introduce several thematic elements that will be important throughout *Cross Creek*. Hunger, racial politics and the history of slavery, and the endurance of nature beyond human life weave throughout the memoir, making Rawlings's rendering of Martha's welcome speech into something like a thesis statement for the book as a whole.

Rawlings's approach to race in *Cross Creek* resists a simple hermeneutics of suspicion. Though she often casts her African American neighbors and grove workers in stereotypical roles—the magical Black woman, the mammy, the dissolute drunk, a gang of convicts who "drove like African emperors" (291)—she also repeatedly aligns herself with the Black women around her. In addition to Martha, who provides continuity to the narrative, Rawlings introduces characters like "Black Kate," who appears on the very first page of the introductory chapter and serves to establish Rawlings as an atypical white woman in an atypical southern setting:

> Black Kate and I between us once misplaced some household object, quite unreasonably.
> I said, "Kate, am I crazy, or are you?"
> She gave me her quick sideways glance that was never entirely impudent.
> "Likely all two of us. Don't you reckon it take somebody a little bit crazy to live out here at the Creek?" (*Cross Creek* 9)

Moments like the above are crucial to the memoir and to understanding the character that Rawlings makes herself into throughout the novel. As Toni Morrison argues in *Playing in the Dark,* it is naïve to assume "that black people signified little or nothing in the imagination of white American writers . . . other than to provide local color" (15). Instead, as Morrison eloquently notes, "the subject of the dream is the dreamer. The fabrication of an Africanist persona is reflexive; an extraordinary meditation on the self; a powerful exploration of the fears and desires that reside in the writerly conscious" (17). When Rawlings centers herself as a character, and aligns herself with these "crazy" and mythic Black women, she forcefully asserts her outsider status: she is outside not only the literary establishment, the urban world of the culture industry, but also outside her own white womanhood. But the Creek is where outsiders belong; it is a haven for the "mad" (*Cross Creek* 10) and the "queer" (*Cross Creek* 9).

Fan mail writers like Alexandra Apostolides and Mary Louise Aguirre responded to Rawlings's depiction of Martha, but she resonated with more than just white readers. Because several of her books were printed in Armed Services Editions, we know that Rawlings was read as well by African American men. Indeed, future Malcolm X biographer Alex Haley responded to Rawlings's depiction of Martha in a letter from 1944:

> It was "Cross Creek" first; naive, ever-interesting, tempestuous Cross Creek where those few never-to-be-forgotten families lived in a world all their own until venerable old Aunt Martha's "Sugar" undertook the must-

have-been-pleasant task of sharing it's [*sic*] joys and heartaches with the world. I read "Cross Creek" a month ago; it was among the first batch of those special servicemen's editions to come out this way. . . .

You see, I am a writer too, but, as yet, definitely amateur. Think as you might, you won't recall my name unless you make a practice of following the pulps or various service magazines. I've ideas, though, and no end of ambition which, coupled with the fact that a few agents and people at large might have been right when they said I "have something," may see me through. Like Aunt Martha, too, I am colored, though that, rather than hindering, spurs me. Do you know, I'd like to meet Aunt Martha—she seems such a sagacious individual. I wonder what she'd think of me.

You'll probably be months getting this because I'll have to mail it to a forwarding address, but I hope you do anyway—that you'll number me among your admirers, proteges or what have you.

Haley identifies himself with Rawlings and with Martha. He uses Rawlings as a model for his own work, while also positioning her as "Martha's 'Sugar,'" creating a complex network of desired associations. Haley writes himself into association with a successful writer, but also a writer approved of and cared for by Martha, and into an association with Martha herself, as container of the 'real' for and in this community. In a 1976 interview published in *The Black Scholar*, Haley confirms that his writing career began in service magazines and the pulps (Allen). But in 1944, he is still, in his words, "an amateur," an admirer or protégé like self-described writers Mary Louise Aguirre, Jack Latham, and Lucille Shearwood, or any of the other servicemen or Book-of-the-Month Club members who wrote to Rawlings.

Haley repeats the expression of pleasure that features in so many of these letters, suggesting that World War II soldiers responded to Rawlings's books in the same ways that teenagers and housewives did. Still, it is worth looking at the particulars of this soldierly pleasure in closer detail, for it has much to tell us about the relationship between regionalism and nationalist propaganda.

In the only published history of the Armed Services Editions, Molly Guptill Manning explains that World War II–era studies demonstrated soldiers' preference for leisure activities that were "relatively independent," such as "writing letters, reading magazines and books, watching a movie, or listening to the radio" (23). Though Manning doesn't elaborate, it is worth noting here that, though these activities were more independent than playing team sports, they also connected the soldiers to a media-saturated world outside their bases and camps. Such activities provided "an escape," improved satisfaction and morale, and helped soldiers adjust to military life, and for these reasons "the War Department concluded that amusements and entertainment were crucial" (Manning 23). Books, Manning notes, provided a "form of recreation that was small, popular, and affordable" (24). When book collection drives and bulk magazine subscriptions proved insufficient (Manning 55–56), a working committee of representatives from several major publishers convened and created the Council on Books in Wartime (Manning 64). The Council, declaring that "books are weapons in the war of ideas" (65), undertook several projects to provide United States soldiers with reading recommendations and material. In the spring of 1943, they hit on the idea of "Armed Services Editions" (ASEs) and set about the project that would "revolutionize" the publishing industry and "reconstruct the book—inside and out" (Manning 74).

The Council designed these books with the war in mind at every step. ASEs were sized to slip into the pockets of standard military uniforms; they were bound on the short side, with two columns of text intended to be easy for the eye to follow despite interruptions, stress, and poor lighting (Manning 76–77). Furthermore, the selection of titles to be printed emphasized variety, and the Council generally "worked to avoid censorship of the soldiers' reading" (Manning 79–80). From September 1943 to June 1947, 1,322 books were printed in Armed Services Editions; print runs began at 50,000 and eventually rose to 155,000 copies per title (Manning 82). The project was "a resounding success," praised by US media outlets, US Army and Navy officials, and the soldiers themselves (Manning 85–87). War correspondents admired the ASEs' widespread popularity and their ability to circulate between units in far-flung locales (Manning 86–91). As Manning notes throughout her book, soldiers stationed across the world took time to write to ASE authors, thanking them for the "pleasure" their books provided.

Marjorie Kinnan Rawlings's inclusion in the Armed Services Editions program made her a touchstone for many soldiers in the United States and overseas during World War II. Like Alex Haley, they read her in "snatches . . . at a time," while at sea, or stationed in New Guinea, or convalescing in hospitals. Eight thousand copies of *Cross Creek,* her first of three books to be printed in an Armed Services Edition, were set aside "specifically for those who would participate in the D-day invasion," alongside an equal number of copies of *The Selected Short Stories of Stephen Vincent Benét*, Betty Smith's *A Tree Grows in Brooklyn*, Willa Cather's *Death Comes for the Archbishop*, Voltaire's *Candide*, Mark Twain's *The Adventures of Tom Sawyer* and *The Adventures of Huckleberry Finn*, and others (Manning 96–97). Like Haley, servicemen from Alaska to Germany to "somewhere in the Caribbean" wrote to Rawlings to praise *Cross Creek* for the "genuine pleasure" it provided. Like Louis Dollarhide, several of them wrote more than once, confirming Rawlings's comment to Ellen Glasgow that she answered all their letters (*Selected Letters* 251). Rawlings kept up this correspondence with US soldiers while her own husband, Norton Baskin, was serving as an ambulance driver in India (Perkins and Rawlings 559). She also saved numerous letters received as part of this correspondence, judging from the many that appear in her archive.

The ASEs were meant to furnish pleasure, to distract soldiers from the hell of war. Books like *Cross Creek*, with its lyrical meditations on an authentic regional, rural locale, also served to remind soldiers of the geography and ecology of the distant homeland for which they were fighting. North central Florida becomes a surrogate for the United States as a whole: region stands in for country, while physical space in the form of land simultaneously stands in for the political and social construct of the nation.

Rawlings would have objected to any characterization of her work as propaganda, for she felt the form was inauthentic. As she writes to Perkins in 1942, over a year before the ASE program would begin, she dislikes anything overtly jingoistic:

> I have suffered over the requests of the Treasury Board and the War Writers' board . . . and tried to write things, but I have decided two things: the forced "Americanism" is both disgusting and unnecessary (the simplest people are aware of the danger and the need for concerted action); and I can do no more than write as I always do. A basic Americanism is implicit in what I write, and the inferred is always more effective than the obvious. An astonishing percentage of my letters about "Cross Creek" is from men in the service. I may have written you what one man in the Army said: "You are writing about the simple things for which we in the Army are fighting." . . . You don't need "propaganda" when people feel that way. (*Selected Letters* 225)

Rawlings did believe her work had something to say about the United States as a global ideal, especially in light of the "danger" of Hitler and National Socialism. Yet to characterize her work, or indeed any of the ASEs, as merely propagandistic is too reductive by far. Nor does it square with the final chapter of *Cross Creek,* which invokes the specter of the atomic bomb and ends by arguing for a compassionate stewardship of the land that contradicts the very idea of war propaganda.

Rawlings uses this final chapter to emphasize the philosophy and ethics for which her book has been reaching. It opens with a humorous story about Albert Einstein mistaking a prune for the gizzards of the cold roast squab he had been served on a fishing yacht, demonstrating her thesis that "our philosophers are usually the most unpractical of men, while very simple folk may have a great deal of wisdom" (*Cross Creek* 371). But the mention of the Nobel Prize winner in physics also reminds us of the threat of atomic warfare that hung over the world. Rawlings wonders if there are "psychic things that are nourished by our annihilation," and then advances a radically pacifistic theory of human life:

> We [at Cross Creek] know only that we are impelled to fight on the side of the creative forces. We know only that a sense of well-being sweeps over us when we have assisted life rather than destroyed it. There is often an evil satisfaction in hate, satisfaction in revenge, and satisfaction in killing. Yet when a wave of love takes over a human being, love of another human being, love of nature, love of all mankind, love of the universe, such an exaltation takes him that he knows he has put his finger on the pulse of the great secret and the great answer. (*Cross Creek* 377)

This mystical worldview suggests why a book like *Cross Creek* encouraged its fans to reach for connection and to express their pleasure. At the same time, it positions US literary fans—Rawlings's fans, fighting "on the side of the creative forces"—against the "evil satisfaction" of fascism and Nazism.

The refrain of the chapter is its title—"Who Owns Cross Creek?"—and possibly a reference to the 1936 book *Who Owns America?,* which "evokes and defends in realist terms an America characterized by small-property ownership, decentralized politics, and responsible stewardship of the nation's natural resources" (Agar and Tate, inside flap). In other words, Rawlings borrows from the New Deal regionalists while also resisting their capitalist ethic. For Rawlings, property ownership is temporary at best, and no human civilization can change that: "The earth will survive bankers and any system of government, capitalistic, fascist or bolshevist. The earth will even survive anarchy" (*Cross Creek* 379). In the final passages of the memoir, Rawlings positions herself alongside the birds and a snake who share her farm, suggesting a retreat from humanism as the only rational response to contemplation of death: "Who owns Cross Creek? The red-birds, I think, more than I. . . . It seems to me that the earth may be borrowed but not bought. It may be used, but not owned. It gives itself in response to love and tending, offers its seasonal flowering and fruiting. But we are tenants and not possessors, lovers and not masters. Cross Creek belongs to the wind and the rain, to the sun and the seasons, to the cosmic secrecy of seed, and beyond all, to time" (*Cross Creek* 380). Moments like this undercut the idea that *Cross Creek* operated as simple US propaganda during World War II. Rather, they build on the space of empathy that Rawlings has constructed in her rendering of Cross Creek, and in doing so, demonstrate what Fetterley and Pryse call the "cultural therapy" that regionalism models. Like the nineteenth-century regionalists they read, Rawlings's memoir "provides an opportunity for the culture as a whole to engage in an act of re-narration, allowing it to tell a different story of itself, one that counters the dominant narrative of individuation and violence with a narrative of empathy, relation, and connection" (359). Nor is this work nonpolitical; as Alison M. Jagger argues, "Critical reflection on emotion . . . is itself a kind of political theory and political practice" (qtd. in Fetterley and Pryse 382). Despite the wish of the Council on Books in Wartime to avoid censoring soldiers' reading, we must note that Rawlings's inclusion in the ASE program appears notable in light of this reading. For what is the point of waging war for "America," Rawlings seems to ask, when the land itself will outlive us and what we try to make of it?

Rawlings's work, especially in *Cross Creek*, follows in the tradition of nineteenth-century regionalism that feminist scholars like Fetterley and Pryse characterize as inherently counter to hierarchical social structures and heteronormativity. Borrowing from queer theorist Michael Warner, Fetterley and Pryse assert that regionalism "participat[es] in the construction of a queer planet" (317); "using the perspective of the so-called queer to suggest the oddity of the so-called normal, and offering empathy as an alternative to terrorism in the approach to difference," regionalism "engages in actively imagining a queer world as both necessary and desirable" (320). For the soldiers, teenagers, retired schoolteachers, and other fans who write to Rawlings, that queer planet is experienced via their pleasure, which is itself decidedly queer.

The pleasure at work in Rawlings's texts enacts Sara Ahmed's assertion that "queer pleasure might challenge the economics that distribute pleasure as a form of property—as a feeling we have" (162). In other words, it challenges a consumer capitalist theory of pleasure, just as Rawlings herself challenges capitalism's notions of property ownership. And, as Ahmed notes, there is "an important spatial relation between pleasure and power. Pleasure involves not only the capacity to enter into, or inhabit with ease, social space, but also functions as a form of entitlement and belonging" (164–65). If, as Ahmed writes, "queer bodies 'gather' in spaces, through the pleasure of opening up to other bodies" (165), we must note that these spaces need not be physical or "real." They can be the imagined spaces of rural Florida known only through a writer's work, or the virtual spaces of letter pages which can only hold those bodies sequentially, as they are written and later read.

The servicemen who write to Rawlings do not explicitly thank her for the book as "cultural therapy" or "queer pleasure," nor do they all plainly acknowledge her work as a model for empathy that has helped them rethink their participation in the war—though Louis Dollarhide's letters come close. In fact, most of them commend Rawlings for one very specific thing: her writing about food. And yet, food in *Cross Creek* (and its companion cookbook, published shortly after the memoir) can help us understand how queer pleasure circulated between Rawlings and her readers.

Cross Creek treats food as a pan-religious experience—as both pagan and Christian ritual that provides spiritual sustenance along with pleasure and emotional engagement. Rawlings titles her chapter on food "Our Daily Bread," in reference to the Lord's Prayer, but this is only the first of many allusions and quotations that make the chapter feel like a recipe scrapbook pasted together from many sources. Rawlings grounds her discussion of food in the books, words, and recipes of others, especially women: she describes how she "wept in nostalgia" upon reading Della Lutes's *A Country Kitchen* and "studied Fanny Farmer as a novitiate the prayer book," hoping to carry on the food traditions of her mother, grandmother, and mother-in-law (*Cross Creek* 216–17).[25] Rawlings characterizes "native and local" Florida foods as "queer" (*Cross Creek* 217) and "exotic" (236)—rattlesnake, cooter, swamp cabbage, squirrel pilau—but they are no less ritualistic. As her neighbor Ed Hopkins demonstrates to her, in Florida one can "gather . . . a dinner directly from the land," trusting that "The Lord will provide" (*Cross Creek* 237). But while her Florida Cracker neighbors speak in biblical rhetoric, Rawlings muses on a lineage of feminine divinity that links her and her Black neighbors to both modern art and myth. The bananas that Martha cooks sprout blossoms "exotic past description, so that only Georgia O'Keeffe could do [them] justice with her brush and palette"; pomegranates hold "a magical connotation" given their link to the myth of Ceres and Proserpine that enchanted Rawlings a child (*Cross Creek* 235).

The extravagant bounty of food both creates and feeds a "nostalgic hunger" (*Cross Creek* 223) that is a theme for Rawlings throughout the memoir. This hunger may be physical, but it is more often spiritual, and Rawlings's descriptions of meals "prepared in the middle of the St. John's River," in cast iron instead of "modern aluminum," and eaten at camp surrounded by "great live oaks . . . and palms tall against the aquamarine evening sky," under a bright full moon (*Cross Creek* 222) confirm Martha's early reassurance that no one at the Creek goes hungry. The food rationing that began in 1942 seems not to threaten Cross Creek at all; Rawlings notes that she keeps Jersey cows that provide almost endless cream and butter (*Cross Creek* 217), and the land around is rich in meat, vegetables, and fruits.

All this food talk struck a chord. Readers such as Robert Soderberg write in pleasurable agony: "I have one complaint to make. You should put some sort of forward [*sic*] in your stories telling patients in army hospitals to avoid certain chapters in your book . . . namely, that one on food. As I read it . . . I began to suffer such ghastly pangs of hunger that I arose from the proverbial bed of pain." For readers, many of whom were facing restricted diets due to rationing or military service, the nourishment of this hunger is only spiritual or aesthetic, but it is powerful. William Loveridge explains that his enjoyment of *Cross Creek* "may have been enhanced by my present fare, which is limited to canned beef and a very small selection of vegetables, also canned." Jerome D. Countess writes of the "woe" he feels as a self-proclaimed "gourmand" that he has read about such exotic meals but cannot eat them. Still, his reading experience was a pleasurable one: "How can I tell you," he asks, "with what delight we sampled the words of those foods?"

Many, like Countess above, characterize the book itself as sustenance. For Zetta Davison, it is the first among "the books I have been hungry for." Helen Bodley writes: "A few weeks ago I read 'Cross Creek.' I saw it dealt with earth +

growing things and I was hungry for them. But I found, as so many other must, food for a deeper hunger." Rawlings's food descriptions help readers navigate their own physical and aesthetic hunger, to find pleasure in it, and to use it, like religious fasting, to better understand their spiritual selves and their relationship to the earth.

In turn, the outpouring of responses about food gave Rawlings her next project, a cookbook based on *Cross Creek,* which she released six months later. Rawlings intersperses among the recipes of *Cross Creek Cookery* vignettes mostly adapted from the memoir, and some descriptions of the letters that prompted its creation. She revels in the hyperbolic pleasure-pain of her fans, describing letters from cadets and corporals who call for her book to be banned from encampments:

> "Lady," [an officer] wrote, "I have never been through such agonies of frustration."
>
> Men in the Service have written me from Hawaii, the Philippines, Australia, Ireland and Egypt. Always there was a wistful comment on my talk of foods; often a mention of a boyhood kitchen memory. Eight out of ten letters about Cross Creek ask for a recipe, or pass on a recipe, or speak of suffering over my chat of Cross Creek dishes.
>
> "Bless us," I thought, "the world must be hungry."
>
> And so it is. Hungry for food and drink—not so much for the mouth as for the mind; not for the stomach, but for the spirit . . . It was not only the squab-sized chickens stuffed with pecans, the crab Newburg and Dora's ice cream for which he longed, but the convivial gathering together of folk of good will. Country foods, such as those of Cross Creek, have in them not only Dora's cream and butter and a dash of cooking sherry, but the peace and plenty for which we are all homesick. (*Cross Creek Cookery* 2)

Rawlings thus positions her cookbook as a response to the hunger she has stimulated in her audience, but also as an extension of her pacifism in the face of the war. She looks to pass on not just her recipes but also "the delight of the surroundings in which they have been eaten" (*Cross Creek Cookery* 3), the leisure and pleasure that accompany them. It is a wish to recirculate the pleasure her fans have expressed to her, to keep those queer good feelings moving among the network created by a writer and her readers.

After *Cross Creek Cookery*, Rawlings found one more use for her large collection of fan correspondence, though one much more bitter than her sumptuous cookbook. The letters became evidence in the "Cross Creek Trial," a libel suit brought against Rawlings by former friend Zelma Cason in January 1943. Rawlings had written about Zelma in a chapter of *Cross Creek*, using her real name and describing her as "an ageless spinster resembling an angry and efficient canary" (*Cross Creek* 56); Zelma's suit charged "that several passages in the book had caused her severe pain and humiliation" (*Selected Letters* 229). In February 1943, Rawlings wrote to her lawyer Philip May about the defense they were mounting:

> I think the bulk of letters I have received show that the imagination in question not only is not gross and depraved, but is humanitarian, kindly and generous. . . .
>
> I shall bring to you several envelopes of letters that you can cull over for items useful to prove both my lack of maliciousness, and the sense in the general reading public, including many men in the service of our country, that they have had a feeling of spiritual uplift in the book—which would not be possible if there were any taint of unkindness in the writing. (*Selected Letters* 235)

The suit dragged on for five and a half years, during which time Rawlings continued to collect those fan letters that she felt best proved the "spiritual uplift" provided by *Cross Creek*. Indeed, it seems likely that the bulk of the letters in Box 39 of the Rawlings archive were assembled to serve as trial evidence. Many passages of praise for *Cross Creek* are indicated with checkmarks made in red pencil; many envelopes are marked "KEEP" and "SUIT" in Rawlings's hand.

The latest letters in the box are dated February 1946; Rawlings and Cason went to trial in May of that year. Rawlings was initially acquitted of the charge, which had been changed from libel to invasion of privacy, but Cason's lawyers appealed (*Selected Letters* 230). The Florida Supreme Court found for Cason in August 1948, ordering Rawlings to pay her one dollar in damages plus court costs (*Selected Letters* 312). All those fan letters mattered little for the suit in the end. Rawlings was worn out after nearly six years of "major distraction and hindrance to her writing," and the suit had ended up costing her more than eighteen thousand dollars in legal fees (*Selected Letters* 230).

Cross Creek was Rawlings's last full-length book set in the Florida that she had become known for depicting. Soured on the area by the lawsuit, she left Cross Creek for good in 1947. Her final two books, *Mountain Prelude* (serialized in the *Saturday Evening Post*) and *The Sojourner*, are set elsewhere; neither matched the critical or public success of her Florida stories. Furthermore, they were published without the editorial guidance of Maxwell Perkins, whose 1947 death was yet another blow to Rawlings's work and life.

Rawlings died of a cerebral hemorrhage on December 14, 1953, in her cottage in Crescent Beach, Florida. She was buried near Island Grove, "only a few miles from the weathered farmhouse in the orange grove at Cross Creek" (*Selected Letters* 404). Her tombstone carries the inscription, "Through her writing she endeared herself to the people of the world," a sentiment that her fan mail absolutely bears out.

Fan History and Contemporary Fan Tourism

Enchantment lies in different things for each of us. For me, it is in this: to step out of the bright sunlight into the shade of orange trees; to walk under the arched canopy of their jadelike leaves; to see the long aisles of lichened trunks stretch ahead in a geometric rhythm; to feel the mystery of seclusion that yet has shafts of light striking through it. This is the essence of an ancient and secret magic. It goes back, perhaps, to the fairy tales of childhood, to Hansel and Gretel, to Babes in the Wood, to Alice in Wonderland, to all half-luminous places that pleased the imagination as a child. . . . And after long years of spiritual homelessness, of nostalgia, here is that mystic loveliness of childhood again. Here is home.

—MARJORIE KINNAN RAWLINGS, *Cross Creek*

These days, it is possible to step off the highway and inside Marjorie Kinnan Rawlings's rusty gate as only the boldest could have done when she was alive. Rawlings willed her Cross Creek farm and house to the State of Florida after her death, and the property is now open to the public as Marjorie Kinnan Rawlings Historic State Park. Tourists and students can tour the homestead, gather oranges in season, and experience firsthand the rural Floridian "enchantment" about which Rawlings wrote.

The park makes Rawlings's literary legacy into an interactive domestic exhibition, adapting her 1930s regionalism to speak to twenty-first-century concerns over sustainable food and "spiritual homelessness." In doing so, it embodies a fascinating brand of literary fan tourism that extends Rawlings's own invitation to join her in the "mysterious heart" of her world. Past the rusty gate, a Florida state park sign in familiar brown and yellow frames every visit: before the hammock breaks to reveal the orange trees, the barn, and the house, Rawlings's words set the scene (see fig. 10). This sign ensures that every visitor who stops to read it will have at least a small taste of Rawlings's mystical literary version of the farm they are about to see.

FIG. 10. A sign bearing a slightly modified passage from *Cross Creek* greets visitors to the Marjorie Kinnan Rawlings Historic State Park. Photograph by the author, 2017.

The grounds are free to wander. The park's rangers have replanted her kitchen garden exactly as she described it, and keep chickens and ducks as she did. During the day, the chickens perch in the orange trees. The ducks clack together around the yard, and just as they did in Rawlings's day (*Cross Creek* 263), they wait to be enclosed in their pen every evening. Visitors familiar with *Cross Creek* can find the infamous outhouse—door-less, located in full view of the dining room—and marvel at the chayote squash plant, whose "luxurious vine" is once again trained "for shade over [the] Mallard duck pen" (*Cross Creek* 227). A stray cat, fiery orange, has taken up residence in the nearby scrub; the rangers and docents call him "Penny," after the red-haired father in *The Yearling*.

For a small fee, park docents guide visitors through Rawlings's house, where her furnishings and books have been meticulously preserved. Tours gather hourly at the barn, where docents in period dress introduce visitors to Rawlings's literary career and the Florida of her era before leading them through the house (fig. 11). Though each docent has his or her own style and favored stories, some elements remain consistent: the "Cracker daybed" on the porch where Rawlings would nap through the heat of summer, the typewriter on a table where she wrote most of her books, the hidden "firewater" cabinet built during Prohibition, the corncob broom used to clean the hard pine floors (visitors are encouraged to take pictures holding it), and the icebox where Racket the racoon once surprised the iceman (*Cross Creek* 171). Docents are volunteers—some are students and administrators from nearby University of Florida in Gainesville, some retired snowbirds who serve as "campground hosts" at state parks across the country, and one is an eighty-five-year-old former Studebaker factory worker from South Bend, Indiana, who lives at the nearby fish camp—and every single one I spoke to had something in common: they love Rawlings's writing so much that they feel compelled to spend time at Cross Creek however they can. More than the visitors, the docents are the "fans" driven to re-create, reinterpret, and reinvigorate the magic of Cross Creek and their beloved "Marjorie."

This magic looks different for each of them. A history student revels in the gossipy details of Rawlings's life, divulging to tour groups the damaging extent of Rawlings's alcoholism and speculating about where the infamously tall Gregory Peck slept when he visited during the filming of MGM's *The Yearling*. Jack, the Studebaker man, is a romantic; he has read the love letters Rawlings wrote to her second husband, Norton Baskin,[1] and provides a running commentary on their marriage throughout his tour. Another volunteer comes once a month to provide tours of the tenant house (fig. 12), where Martha Mickens and her husband, Will, lived until they passed away in the 1960s.[2] He says he fell in love with the farm and with the history of the African American residents of Cross Creek. He honors their memory with his tours, and he tells me he recently tracked down Martha Mickens's poorly marked gravestone and cleaned it up a bit. He loves Marjorie too, but, he says, he isn't interested in presenting her as a saint, the way some volunteers do.

There's room for many versions of Rawlings at the park—saint, drunk, independent woman, devoted wife, literary celebrity, and even Gregory Peck's lover—but it is the Rawlings of *Cross Creek* who most comes alive. She is equal parts mystic and hostess, still feeding the spiritual hunger of her readers and fans. At the penultimate stop on the house tour, visitors are ushered into Rawlings's kitchen to see her original wood-burning stove. Cabinets hang open, displaying period-accurate food packaging. The rangers and volunteers regularly make bread, jams, and preserves in the kitchen (see fig. 13), and the walk-in pantry is stocked with glass jars full of edible creations. Park ranger Carrie Todd

FIG. 12. The tenant house at the Rawlings historic site. Photograph by the author, 2015.

stresses the interpretative work of the kitchen: both the 1930s food artifacts and the cooking demonstrations help visitors to better understand how Rawlings and her contemporaries lived and ate.

Moreover, the park's attention to food proves that what spoke to Rawlings's World War II–era readers still speaks to us today. Though the United States is not currently under rationing, and though we are not fighting in anything called a "world war," concerns about climate change and global hunger have driven a resurging interest in sustainable agriculture, locally grown food, and homesteading. Carrie Todd tells me that she often looks to social media sites like Pinterest and Instagram for "fads" that she can use for program inspiration. She cites both an "old-fashioned ice cream making" event and working with Gainesville's Forage Farm and their Southern Heritage Seed Collective as examples of successful recent programming that married Rawlings's literary legacy with the contemporary "local food movement."

To celebrate the seventy-fifth anniversary of the publication of *Cross Creek* and *Cross Creek Cookery* in 2017, Todd and her park staff organized a full year of food-related events. I visited in late January for a "Campfire Cooking" program inspired by the description of an especially delicious meal prepared in cast iron

FIG. 13. Rawlings's kitchen table is used by volunteers to prepare apple and sweet potato soufflé. The recipe, from Rawlings's own *Cross Creek Cookery*, is propped on a stand for the cooks' reference. Photograph by the author, 2017.

over an open fire (*Cross Creek* 222; see chapter 3). The day was cold and overcast, but more than thirty park visitors huddled around the fire and watched a volunteer campground host cook chicken, greens from the garden, apple and sweet potato soufflé, and "Zelma's Ice Box Rolls" (*Cross Creek Cookery* 33) in cast-iron Dutch ovens (see fig. 14). Before serving us, Todd and her staff read aloud relevant passages from *Cross Creek* and the *Cookery*. Rawlings's words became prayers, gracing us and our meal.

The park is a fiction. The barn has been rebuilt, and the current tenant house was moved from a neighboring property to stand in for the demolished original. A microwave hides behind a curtain in the kitchen's back room, and the house's small park office contains extra docent costumes. But it is a fiction crafted with love: beside those costumes hangs a "library sign-out sheet" where volunteers note which of Rawlings's books they've borrowed to read. There is no gift shop, and other than the small tour fee, no money changes hands on the property—at Rawlings's request. Here, unlike almost anywhere else in the tourist-trap of Florida, the fannish gift economy rules.

FIG. 14. Antique cast-iron pots arranged around hot coals at the campfire-cooking demonstration at the Rawlings historic site. Photograph by the author, 2017.

CONCLUSION

Fandom Is Literary,
Fandom Is Historical

Mimicry is an art in itself. If it is not, then all art must fall by the same blow that strikes it down.

—ZORA NEALE HURSTON, "Characteristics of Negro Expression," 1934

Fan studies scholars have characterized the field as being broken into three distinct, roughly chronological approaches: "fandom is pathological"; "fandom is beautiful"; "fandom is complicated." Jonathan Gray, Cornel Sandvoss, and C. Lee Harrington coined the middle phrase to describe the work of John Fiske and Henry Jenkins—work that followed Michel de Certeau in asserting the value of popular culture, while also pushing back against earlier scholars who saw fandom as unhealthy obsession or psychological mania (Gray, Sandvoss, and Harrington 1). The reaction to this reaction—"fandom is complicated"—has sought to avoid celebrating all fannish activities as inherently good, asserting instead that fandom as a social and cultural practice is value neutral and can be leveraged toward texts, causes, and ends that range from progressive to conservative, even regressive.

As the preceding chapters of this book have demonstrated, I would like to lobby for an additional approach: "Fandom is literary." And perhaps, another: "fandom is historical." By the time the word "fanfiction" came to mark a specific transformative writing practice, American women in both white and African American fan and proto-fan communities had been transforming existing literary texts to speak to their own positionality for at least one hundred years—since well before the coining of the terms "fan" and "fandom." These literary and historical components of fandom and fan cultures are understudied; as I wrote in the introduction, I hope this book intrigues both literary and fan studies scholars to turn their attention in this direction.

What does attention to the historical, and more specifically the literary historical, aspect of fandom make possible? To illustrate one possibility, let me return to something I wrote in the introduction to this book. In outlining the myriad ways that I saw fannish practices in use throughout the history of women's writing, I suggested that I read Nella Larsen's 1930 story "Sanctuary" as a proto-example of "racebending," a practice in which a fanfiction author or artist reimagines the white characters of a text as people of color.[1] As a means of concluding this book, I'd like to spend a little time with this interpretation.

The stakes of this rereading are high. When *Forum* published "Sanctuary" in 1930, several readers wrote the magazine to point out that it appeared to be plagiarized from Sheila Kaye-Smith's 1922 *Century Magazine* short story "Mrs. Adis." *Forum* defended Larsen and published an author's note in which Larsen defended herself, but the damage was done. Though she received a Guggenheim fellowship and continued to write, Nella Larsen never published again.

Critics and scholars have struggled for decades to explain "Sanctuary" and the narrative of plagiarism that surrounds it. In the 1990s, those who approached the story found it "embarrassing" (Larson 98), a "failed experiment" (Wall 133), an adaptation or theft undertaken "unconsciously" (Wall 133–34; Douglas 86), and even an "act of literary suicide" (Haviland 302). That Larsen plagiarized is affirmed and emphasized repeatedly in these explications. But more recent scholarship has sought to place the act of so-called "plagiarism" within nonwhite cultural contexts—that is, to understand how the story's Blackness might forestall accusations of plagiarism. For Hildegard Hoeller, "Sanctuary" is an intervention into the "racial hypocrisy of modernism's appropriation of 'other' texts, voices, and traditions" (421). But Hoeller sees this intervention as a "partial" failure, due to the fact that "literature, like the hospital [that appears in Nella Larsen's author's note] is run by white superintendents who punish black workers for 'infractions of rules' and 'neglect of duty'—both defined by whites and rooted in white print culture and a white-defined sense of authorship, originality, and authenticity" (431). In other words, "Sanctuary" fails because it cannot overturn centuries of white literary culture.

Other recent scholarship has left aside the question of whether or not "Sanctuary" failed, preferring instead to read the story in the context of Black artistic practices. For Kelli A. Larson, the story is an example of "recasting" that was common to African American theater of the time (83). Barbara Hochman reads it as "an act of bitter defiance and declaration of defeat," a version of "minstrelsy" in which Larsen "imitates, parodies, puns, and distortedly mirrors her sources" (510–11). Finally, Mollie Godfrey returns to Hoeller's argument that "Sanctuary" is meant as an intervention, though she contextualizes this reading by emphasizing the story's participation in the black artistic form of "repetition and revision" that Henry Louis Gates Jr. calls signifyin' (126). Signifyin' works, like "Sanctuary" but also the mocking "cakewalk" dance, are meant to "challenge white aesthetic forms and structures of power" (Godfrey 126–27).

I pause here to ask: why perform yet another rereading of "Sanctuary"? It may be that connecting the story to the tradition of signifyin' is enough. Certainly, Larsen deserves to be read in the context of African American artistic traditions, not as a failure or "literary suicide" but as a sophisticated Black writer in full control of her choices and literary tools. But I resist readings that liken "Sanctuary" to minstrelsy and the cakewalk, for little in the story suggests that it is meant to be seen as parody or mockery. Rather, it is an earnest exploration of how a narrative changes when its characters are Black Americans instead of poor white British. Nor do the scholarly readings above attempt to connect Larsen's work in "Sanctuary" to other literary texts; they rely on reference to dance, theater, and visual arts. But this is an opportunity to say yes: yes, her story is signifyin', and yes, it is also modeling a practice that will come to be known in the twenty-first century as "racebending," and yes, both of these readings make the story part of the long history of transformative textual practices with which this book has been concerned.

The term "racebending" originated during a protest against the whitewashed casting of the film *The Last Airbender,* a live-action adaptation of Nickelodeon's animated series *Avatar: The Last Airbender.* The animated fantasy series, set in a world in which certain people can "bend" (i.e., control) the elements of earth, air, fire, and water, incorporated East Asian and Inuit cultural practices, clothing, and architecture, and featured no white characters. But when the film adaptation's cast was first announced in 2010, it contained no people of color. Fans created Racebending.com as a hub to coordinate their protests and discuss the long history of white-washed casting in Hollywood. As scholar Lori Kido Lopez notes, "By referencing 'bending' the activists mark their fandom and attachment to the world of the franchise, even as they use the same term to articulate their frustration with an industry where roles are systematically taken from Asian Americans and given to white actors" (433). But the term soon outgrew its origins: Elizabeth Gilliland explains, "'racebending' has become the code word for fan casting characters of color into traditionally white franchises" (3). Gilliland notes that though the terminology may be new, the practice itself is not; she links it specifically to Afrofuturism. The Afrofuturist movement, in turn, may also be relatively newly named ("Afrofuturism" was coined in 1991 by Mark Dery), but as Paul Youngquist's "The Afro Futurism of DJ Vassa" demonstrates through its rereading of *The Interesting Narrative of Olaudah Equiano* (1789), the term did not invent the practice. Rather, both terms—racebending and Afrofuturism—belatedly give name to traditions that have been practiced for centuries. Youngquist reads the *Interesting Narrative* as an Afrofuturist text in response to challenges to the "authenticity" of Equiano's work. Here I suggest that we can apply racebending to Larsen's "Sanctuary" to similar ends.

Sheila Kaye-Smith's "Mrs. Adis," published in *Century Magazine* in 1922, is a brief tragedy about class solidarity set in the woods surrounding Scotney Castle in Sussex. In the story, Mrs. Adis hides a neighbor, Peter Crouch, who is on the run from the castle's gamekeepers. While poaching, Crouch shot a man he presumes to be a keeper; hidden in her home, Crouch overhears the keepers inform Mrs. Adis that the man he shot was her son. Though she could give him up to the keepers, Mrs. Adis lies that she hasn't seen Crouch, providing him, as the story ends, with the possibility of escape. The story is itself a transformative text; as Mollie Godfrey points out, it is based on a sixteenth-century Christian parable by St. Francis de Sales (130). Kaye-Smith has recast the parable to speak to the conditions of life for poor white British people living in the shadow of the landed gentry. Kaye-Smith's version comments repeatedly on the hardscrabble appearance of her main characters: Crouch is "evidently of the laboring class, but not successful, judging by the vague grime and poverty of his appearance," while Mrs. Adis has "a brown, hard face" and looks older than her forty-two years, because "life treats some women hard in the agricultural districts of Sussex, and Mrs. Adis's life had been harder than most" (Kaye-Smith). Their misfortunes are tied as tightly to their class positions as to the district where they live—the two combining to determine the quality of life and labor available to them.

Nella Larsen's further transformation of this text stems from a simple question: how would the story change if these characters were African American? Thus Peter Crouch becomes Jim Hammer, "a big, black man with pale brown eyes in which there was an odd mixture of fear and amazement," who has "streaks of grey soil on his heavy, sweating face and great hands, and on his torn clothes," and "wooly hair" full of "bits of dried leaves and dead grass" (Larsen 22). Mrs. Adis becomes Annie Poole, "a tiny, withered woman—fifty perhaps—with a wrinkled face the color of copper, framed by a crinkly mass of white hair" (Larsen 23). While drawing on Kaye-Smith's story, these descriptions emphasize each character's Blackness and poverty as inherently linked—with no need to narrate the relative hardness of their lives. Furthermore, Larsen transposes the setting to the American South in a manner that purposefully draws attention to her source material—not de Sales's parable but Kaye-Smith's magazine story. "Mrs. Adis" begins: "In northeast Sussex a great tongue of land runs into Kent by Scotney Castle" (Kaye-Smith); "Sanctuary" opens: "On the Southern coast, between Merton and Shawboro, there is a strip of desolation some half mile wide and nearly ten miles long between the sea and old fields of ruined plantations" (Larsen 21). Nothing is "unconscious," as earlier Larsen scholars have tried to claim, about this mirroring. Rather, it is the purposeful transformation of a text, meant to draw out both the similarities and the differences between the lives of the British laboring class and African Americans in the Jim Crow South. What difference is there, Larsen's opening line asks, between Scotney Castle and the ruined plantations?

Yet her story does not maintain the close mirroring of its source material, and in these gaps between source and transformation we can see her working out answers to the question she posed to herself. There are two major changes I want to focus on here. First, "Sanctuary" is more clearly fixed in a specific time. "Mrs. Adis" lacks reference to any markers of modernity, beyond the passenger train that lets us know the story is set sometime after 1832. But "Sanctuary" is more specifically modern: the road walked by Jim Hammer "is little used, now that the state has built its new highway to the west and wagons are less numerous than automobiles" (Larsen 21). Instead of poaching—there is nothing to poach from a ruined plantation, nor anyone to poach from—Hammer has been caught trying to steal tires from the garage behind the local factory (Larsen 26). This factory is in fact the American stand-in for Scotney Castle, policed not by keepers but by the white local sheriff. This engagement with capitalist modernity is one of the ways Larsen's story answers its own question. America may not have an aristocracy, but it has a power structure all the same.

Larsen's second major change to the story is its ending. Mrs. Adis hides Crouch in a "lean-to" off the kitchen of her cottage. When the keepers bring in the body of her dead son, she asks them to put him in the bedroom. As the story ends, she unlocks the door to the lean-to and then closes herself in the bedroom. Crouch is left to guess at her intentions, and the final lines of the story are ambiguous and open-ended: "Peter Crouch knew what he must do—the only thing she wanted him to do, the only thing he possibly could do. He opened the door and silently went out" (Kaye-Smith). Though Mrs. Adis lied to protect Crouch, her grief has made her unable to communicate with her son's accidental killer. She is silent, and as the story's third-person narration is limited to Crouch's perspective, we as readers can only guess with him as to Mrs. Adis's thoughts and feelings. But Larsen's Annie Poole is not so silent, giving "Sanctuary" a final beat that emphasizes again her choice to recast these characters as Black Americans living in the South around 1930. Annie Poole hides Jim Hammer in her featherbed (Larsen 23), so that her son's body cannot be brought into the privacy of her bedroom. Instead she must confront Hammer, after lying to the sheriff that she hasn't seen him (26). Annie Poole's grief is not expressed through silence but in "a raging fury in her voice," and the final lines of the story are her words directly to Hammer: "Get outer mah feather baid, Jim Hammer, an' outen mah house, an' don' nevah stop thankin' yo' Jesus he done gib you dat black face" (27). Larsen's ending heightens the classical strain of tragedy in the tale, for it is ironic that the one thing that saved Jim Hammer—his Blackness—can also be seen as the thing that doomed him to his seemingly inescapable poverty and desperation in the first place. Larsen replaces the unspoken grief of Kaye-Smith's story, instead giving voice to the rageful helplessness felt by her characters.

These changes demonstrate Larsen's purposeful transformation of "Mrs. Adis" into what we could today call a racebent version of the original story. But without a fan-culture framework in which to understand "Sanctuary," Larsen's transformative work has been misunderstood, even vilified. The plagiarism accusations seem to have prevented her from ever publishing again. Though she continued to write, she was no longer a "professional" writer, and this change in status can make it feel as though Larsen's story, her experiment, indeed her entire career, "failed" (to echo the word used by Hoeller). Thus, scholars of the past thirty years have been driven to explain this failure, without being able to speak to the transformative literary context of Larsen's work. In this case, I am not suggesting that a different reading could restore a text in our esteem; I am suggesting, rather, how a historical reading could have prevented the loss in the first place. By understanding the literary and historical elements of fandom, we might never have lost Larsen as a publishing writer in the first place, let alone have seen her work alienated from its legacy.

After "Sanctuary" came Gwendolyn Brooks's *Annie Allen,* the anti-Helenic epic that transformed and critiqued white modernism (see chapter 1), for which Brooks won the 1950 Pulitzer Prize for Poetry. After this came novels like Jean Rhys's *Wide Sargasso Sea* (1966) and Alice Randall's *The Wind Done Gone* (2001), which retell famous stories from the perspectives of formerly marginal or invisible characters of color. And after all of these came Racebending.com and the pre-production protests against *The Last Airbender,* which convinced the studio to add an actor of color to the cast. And since then, corporate media giants have begun to see some value in breaking up the hegemonic whiteness of their franchises. Thus, more recently, the stage play *Harry Potter and the Cursed Child* (2016) reimagined Hermione as a Black woman; the continuation of the *Star Wars* saga (2015–19) added multiple actors of color to each successive film; and Marvel Studios' *Black Panther* (2018) stacked both cast and crew with Black creatives and won Academy Awards for its Afrofuturist production design and costuming—with both awards going to African American women for the first time in the Academy's history.

It's a long and winding road from the ruined plantations between Merton and Shawboro to Wakanda, and Nella Larsen certainly didn't make the journey alone. "Sanctuary" is just one entry in a body of archontic literature still pushing against the white authority of the culture industry. Moreover, I don't deny that, as contemporary fan studies scholars assert, "fandom is complicated." Though I have grouped the above examples together to suggest the shifting ways that corporate media responds to fan practices like racebending, neither racebent fanworks nor "inclusive" casting are inherently antiracist practices. Samira Nadkarni and Deepa Sivarajan have explored the "limits of racebending," a practice that they argue "exists parallel to the practice of deraced casting in theater, television, and film" (122). Both practices, they find, can "inadvertently create or further systems of violence within racial and cultural hierarchies" (124). Furthermore, as Rukmini Pande points out in the context of the new *Star Wars* films, even fan communities that see themselves as "progressive" can react to diversified media properties in ways that are implicitly or explicitly racist (9–14).

We do well always to keep in mind that the transformative project that connects Nella Larsen to award-winning Black superhero stories is the same transformative project that made the letter columns of *Amazing Stories* a gathering place for anti-Semites and white supremacists. As I have argued here, both are worth studying further, to deepen our understanding of Western media fandom's origins and, simultaneously, our understanding of American literature and culture since at least the 1880s—that watershed decade when loving baseball was so exciting that it demanded new language.

So much has changed in the intervening 140 years, but that language—the language of fans and fandom—is still with us. It still marks specific cultures, with specific practices. And there are still stories to tell: about fans, and what they do with texts, and why it is important. I've told a few here, but this book barely begins to describe all the ways that fans, fan culture, and literature overlap and interact.

What other stories can we say yes to?

NOTES

Introduction: Fanaticism, Yes!

1. "Western media fandom" is an umbrella term used to describe a collection of various individual fandoms dedicated to Western media products like television series and film franchises. It is distinct from fan cultures such as anime fandom, sports fandom, and Korean pop music (K-pop) fandom, though it may share certain practices with each.

2. The Bronze message boards were named after the location where characters in *BtVS* hung out, a local all-ages club with live music. Posters to the boards maintained this interactive transmedia fiction by textually performing as though the Bronze (forum) were the Bronze (club). They described the outfits they were (fictionally) wearing for a night out and wrote about threads (messages and their responses) as if they were real locations, using spatial metaphors to describe their virtual participation. For example, if an interesting conversation were going on in another thread lower down the list, a poster might write that they were "running downstairs to join the party." For more about the Bronze, see Tuszynski.

3. See Sawyer; Coppa; and Hellekson and Busse.

4. The history of the term "fanfiction" (or "fan fiction") can be difficult to trace, but most sources agree that it came into regular use in the 1940s. Its meaning has shifted over the decades: early usage often marked fictional stories written *about* fans. By the 1970s, the now-common meaning—of fictional stories written within the fictional worlds of existing media properties—was in use (see "Fan fiction, N."). However, it is worth noting here that, again, this etymology originates in science fiction fandom and may reflect that fan culture's biases.

5. The *Oxford English Dictionary* gives the following definition for the word "fan": "in modern English (orig. U.S.): a keen and regular spectator of a (professional) sport, orig. of baseball," with examples dating back to 1889.

6. As Janice Radway points out, the early twentieth century's "explosion of print" caused a backlash in which arbiters of taste sought to reinforce the cultural hierarchy "through the rhetoric of brow levels. Popular literary taste was branded as the 'low' to literature's 'high,' demonstrating with the allusion to phrenology that a social cartography was being overlaid upon an aesthetic one. This racist biological innuendo defamed the literary tastes of many, including women, working people, immigrants, and African Americans" ("Learned and Literary Print Cultures" 199). For this reason, I use the words "highbrow," "middlebrow," and "lowbrow" sparingly and designate them with quotation marks.

7. See Wanzo; and Pande.

8. Archives and sites hosting fanfiction have changed over the years; currently, fic is likely posted to the noncommercial Archive of Our Own (for more on this archive, see Edwards, "*Orlando*: A Fan Fiction").

9. As Lewis Hyde argues, "Any exchange, be it of ideas or of goats, will tend toward gift if it is intended to recognize, establish, and maintain community" (101). Taking the concept of the "gift" even further, some fans participate in formalized fanfic gift exchanges, either one-to-one or Secret Santa–style, where every writer is also the recipient of a fic. And the Archive of Our Own has a system by which fic writers can designate their stories as "gifts" for other Archive members.

10. These unspoken rules even apply to fanfiction based on literature in the public domain—that is, even when media texts are not protected by current copyright laws. I once witnessed an extensive argument between fans who were offended that a fanfic writer had accepted paid commissions for her *Les Misérables*–inspired stories. Despite the fact that Victor Hugo's 1862 novel is out of copyright, and therefore the writer was not breaking any laws, these fans were angered by the exchange of money for a product (fanfic) that they felt should have been a gift.

11. There is a link between fandom's gift economy and its nonhierarchical structure. As Hyde writes, "Gifts are best described, I think, as anarchist property" (110).

12. See Campbell v. Acuff-Rose Music, Inc. 510 U.S. 569 (1994).

13. This identificatory practice has been encouraged most heavily by the Organization for Transformative Works (OTW), a nonprofit dedicated to protecting and preserving fanworks. The OTW's flagship project is the Archive of Our Own, mentioned above; other projects include a legal team helping to defend fans whose work has been challenged for copyright infringement, and a partnership with the University of Iowa to preserve physical and digital fanwork archives.

14. "Any text is a mosaic of quotations; any text is the absorption and transformation of another" (Kristeva 66).

15. See Lothian, Busse, and Reid.

16. "Slash" refers to the slash mark used to denote which pairing a fanfiction story features. Kirk/Spock or K/S is the first recognized slash pairing.

17. Kink memes are dedicated online communities where fans can post story prompts for other fans to fill by writing fanfiction. They are usually anonymous, which allows "both prompters and fillers to have fewer inhibitions in making and filling requests, and may be a way for new fans to feel more comfortable about participating" ("Kink Meme"). Prompts and fills can be but are not always sexually explicit. ("Kink" here has two definitions: it can be mean either non-normative sexual acts, or simply story tropes and concepts that a fan especially enjoys.) "A/B/O" fic is the abbreviation for "Alpha/Beta/Omega" fanfiction, a trope wherein some or all characters are part of an animalistic sexual mating hierarchy. Instead of Western society's sex/gender/sexual orientation matrix, a character's identity as "alpha," "beta," or "omega" dictates their biology and sexual preferences ("Alpha/Beta/Omega").

18. For a powerful cultural history of such eradications, see Vito Russo, *The Celluloid Closet: Homosexuality in the Movies* (HarperCollins, 1987).

19. Or, as in the saying my fandom friend Renne taught me, "Queer as in fuck you."

20. Like Tom Stoppard's *Rosencratz and Guildenstern Are Dead* and Jean Rhys's *Wide Sargasso Sea,* both of which have been compared to fanfiction (see Grossman, as well as chapter 2 of this work).

21. See Huyssen's *After the Great Divide,* especially the chapter "Mass Culture as Woman," which examines why cultural products made for and by women have been schematically undermined since the nineteenth century, and why this "feminization of culture" has been crucial to the definition of modernism.

22. See Rubin's *The Making of Middlebrow Culture,* which argues that the "middlebrow" presented a middle road between the "highbrow" avant-garde of the post–World War I era and the mass media sensibility of Hollywood and the pulps.

1. Intimacy and Transformation in Literary Fan Communities

1. Worldcon still happens every year, in much the same format, as do hundreds of other fan conventions, gathering not just science fiction fans but also fans of television shows, video games, comics, horror films, and My Little Pony.

2. The *Oxford English Dictionary* gives the following examples of "assemblies of historic note, as the Convention of Congregational Ministers of Massachusetts organized early in the 18th c.; the Albany Convention of 1754, the first movement of the colonies towards concerted action; the American Convention of Abolitionists, founded in 1793; the Hartford Convention of 1814, with a view to the possible division of the Union, etc." ("Convention, N.").

3. See, for example, the public outcry that female *Twilight* fans were "ruining San Diego Comic-Con," which dominated pop culture news in the summer of 2009 (Buchanan; O'Brien; Ohanesian; Sciretta)—as though women had not always been present at Comic-Con.

4. As a substitute for higher education, clubs were also able to adapt their reading material to better speak to the concerns of their members' social positions. In addition to reading canonical European and American texts, clubwomen from stigmatized groups worked to broaden the category of literature by including texts that spoke to their needs—including those written by living women writers, African American activists, and working-class exposé writers (see Gere 219–28).

5. See Jenkins 27, 32; Certeau 175; and Kaplan 150.

6. Stowe also went to great lengths to conceal her authorship, doctoring one of her essays so that the paper looked old and yellowed (Tonkovich 147). The Semi-Colon Club members played with anonymity and pseudonymity; members often asked friends to copy out their papers so that the handwriting could not be identified (Tonkovich 147). In this we can see a parallel to contemporary online fan communities, like Tumblr and the Archive of Our Own, where pseudonymity is maintained.

7. We can compare these private physical spaces to contemporary internet fandom communities, which have a complicated relationship to open access and privacy. In 2015, for example, fanfiction writers were outraged when news broke online that their publicly available stories were being assigned as part of a college seminar. The class required students, many of whom were not members of fandom, to leave feedback on the stories; fans saw this outsider feed-

back as an unwelcome incursion into their private space. In the words of one fan whose work appeared on the syllabus:

> As is often the case in this kind of conflict, the basic problem was a misunderstanding of the difference—and overlap—between private and public Internet spheres. While most fanfic is published on easily accessible platforms, it's often posted with the tacit understanding that it will only be read by its target audience—and for the most part, it is. Fanfic authors are *definitely* not expecting their writing to be scrutinized by people who aren't familiar with the source material or with fandom in general. (Baker-Whitelaw, original emphasis)

8. For more on club privacy, see Gere 44–45.

9. Despite these utopian descriptions, clubs could also be sites of restriction and exclusion. Most clubs I have read about were segregated (though some clubs organized "reciprocity days" so that white and African American clubwomen could meet jointly [Knupfer 115]). African American women's clubs were not allowed to join state and national federations, and thus had to form their own federating body (E. Long 486).

10. See Campbell v. Acuff-Rose Music, Inc. 510 U.S. 569 (1994).

11. "A New Experience in Millinery," published in *Recreation* in February 1900, protested the killing of birds to make hat trim and decorations (J. R. Long 148).

12. For more on literary contests, see chapter 2.

13. The story centers on a set of mistreated farm animals, who stage "the strike at Shane's" to protest their abuse at the hands of an ill-tempered farmer. The book, as described by Judith Reick Long, reads like a fable about the US labor movement that had gained force in the mid-1880s (127–28).

14. That house, known as the Limberlost Cabin, is now a state historic site. Visitors can tour the cabin and the surrounding wetlands. For more on literary tourism and fandom, see the postlude.

15. Take, for example, this passage:

> Of Nature in her varying moods he feasted and feasted, and was never filled. Hear him saying:

> "I think I could turn and live with animals,
> They are so placid and self-contained.
> I stand and look at them, and long and long,
> They do not sweat and whine about their condition;
> They do not lie awake in the dark and weep for their sins;
> They do not make me sick discussing their duty to God;
> Not one is dissatisfied, not one is demented with the mania of owning things;
> Not one kneels to another, nor to his kind that lived a thousand years ago;
> Not one is respectable or unhappy over the whole earth."

> It has been truly said that his book, *Leaves of Grass,* and the Declaration of Independence were the only strictly Democratic things in America. Look to his life; see

him boarding round, meeting all sorts; see him travel America from shore to shore, consorting with whoever came in his way. Look at the equanimity of mind with which he goes through great cities, accepting the want, squalor, hunger, prostitution, equally with the wealth, beauty, and refinement. See him during the war absolutely refusing to have party or politics, giving as his reason for nursing that he was the wellest man alive, therefore fittest to nurse the ill, absolutely refusing to be of North or South, going where he listed, caring for whoever needed him, walking nearer in the footsteps of Jesus on earth than any other man has ever trod. (Stratton-Porter, qtd. in Meehan 91)

16. See Hogue; Goldstein; Phillips; and Ryan, "The 'Girl Business.'"

17. Stratton-Porter does not appear in Fetterley and Pryse's book-length study of women regionalists or their companion anthology, but several writers studied by Stratton-Porter's club do appear: Harriet Beecher Stowe, Sarah Orne Jewett, and Grace King, about whom Stratton-Porter wrote and presented a paper to the club in 1894.

18. Were Stratton-Porter writing today, I would comfortably classify *The Harvester* as a published example of Real Person Fiction (RPF), a fanfiction genre that treats celebrities as "texts" that can be appropriated and transformed like other media texts. RPF stories often explore the sexuality of their celebrity characters.

19. In fictionalizing herself, Stratton-Porter prefigures fans' textual performances of themselves in virtual spaces (see Kristina Busse, "My Life Is a WIP on My LJ: Slashing the Slasher and the Reality of Celebrity and Internet Performances," *Fan Fiction and Fan Communities in the Age of the Internet: New Essays,* ed. Karen Hellekson and Busse [McFarland, 2006]: 297–24).

20. Stratton-Porter did not initially plan to have the lovers marry. In the original ending, Freckles was crushed to death by a falling tree limb. But Stratton-Porter's publishers would only release the book if she would "add the conventional happy ending" ("My Life" 13).

21. This narrative technique, representing emotion through its intense bodily affects, can also be found in Jane Austen and contemporary fanfiction (see Edwards, "In the Regency Alternate Universe," 15).

22. For more on the relationship between whiteness and nature in Stratton-Porter's novels, see Edwards, "Hollywood Regionalism: What the Studio System Did with Gene Stratton-Porter's Nature Novels," *Feminist Media Histories* 6.2 (March 2020).

23. There is no scholarly convention for how to refer to Inez Travers Cunningham Stark Boulton. She appears in different accounts by various last names, and many scholars seem unaware that all of these Inezes are in fact the same woman. I've chosen to refer to her by her first name to prevent confusion.

24. For more on creative writing workshops and participatory culture, see Chasar, chap. 5.

25. For more on the Benéts, see chap. 2.

26. Examples of this work in television fandom include the fanfiction tradition of "slash," romantic stories about same-sex character couples, which rewrites television shows in the image of the queer women who enjoy them, and "racebending," the practice of imaginatively recasting an existing media property with actors of color, which serves to both reimagine the property and point out the overwhelming prevalence of white characters in popular media. For more on racebending, see the conclusion of this work.

27. I use "pseudo-fan community" here to distinguish the Chicago Poet's Class from the earlier women's club movement, which predated the invention of the term "fan," and from contemporaneous communities that self-consciously used the term "fan club" to describe themselves.

2. Fandom in the Magazines

1. These scrapbooks include details of their successful petition to have Sidney Lanier enshrined in the Hall of Fame for Great Americans at the former University Heights campus of New York University (now Bronx Community College).

2. See, for example, *Spectator*, no. 406, June 16, 1712.

3. I use "spread" here purposefully to echo the language of Henry Jenkins, Sam Ford, and Joshua Green in their book *Spreadable Media: Creating Value and Meaning in a Networked Culture*, and, in doing so, also follow Margaret Beetham's argument that periodicals and the internet operate in similar ways.

4. The Sherlock Holmes stories have been a subject of particular fannish devotion since at least 1893, when Arthur Conan Doyle tried to kill off his famous detective character (in "The Final Problem"), only to have readers demand his return to the pages of the *Strand Magazine* so fervently that Doyle finally had to comply.

5. For more on advertisements in "middlebrow" periodicals, see Ellen Gruber Garvey, *The Adman in the Parlor: Magazines and the Gendering of Consumer Culture, 1880s to 1910s* (Oxford University Press, 1996).

6. In this case, the story was a novelization of *The Virginian* (dir. Cecile B. DeMille, 1914), a silent Western produced by Jesse Lasky, adapted from a stage play by Kirk La Shelle that was based on a novel by Owen Wister. The "novelette" is credited to Harold S. Hammond and illustrated with pictures from the film, making it an early example of what we might now think of as adaptive transmedia (*Photoplay* November 1914: 3).

7. Perhaps the most enduring example of Grantland Rice's mock-heroic sportswriting is "The Four Horsemen," published in the *New York Herald Tribune*, October 18, 1924. In it, Rice recasts the four horsemen of the biblical apocalypse as University of Notre Dame football players, creating what we might now call a mythology AU RPF story—that is, a piece of Real Person Fiction set in an Alternate Universe where mythology is real and defines the rules of the world.

8. It is worth noting that Edna Ferber's prize-winning career as a novelist depended in large part on the multiple successful film adaptations of her stories. See J. E. Smyth, *Edna Ferber's Hollywood: American Fictions of Gender, Race, and History* (University of Texas Press, 2010).

9. Lee Server explains the unsavory implications of these story contests. Contest entries often became the sole property of the magazines, meaning that even nonwinning entries "could be published without remuneration" (18). We might see significant similarities with contemporary fandom issues of affective fan labor being exploited by corporations for profit, like the ones Sara K. Howe examines in her article on *Twilight* fandom.

10. The friending meme is "an activity to encourage fans with similar interests to find each other and 'friend' or 'follow' one another's social media accounts. . . . The original poster often

provides a set of questions such as name, age, country of origin, favourite fandoms/pairings/characters, hated fandoms/pairings/characters, etc." ("Friending Meme"). Examples can be found at http://fandomfriendingmeme.tumblr.com.

11. It is also worth noting, as Chasar does, that established literary-intellectual figures like *Poetry* editor Harriet Monroe were often critical of radio poetry programs and their fans (89). But, following Radway, I would argue that the need to assert cultural hierarchy shows just how intertwined various forms of media were in the early twentieth century.

12. See Lynch.

13. A hierarchy that, in light of the history above, begins to look less like a pyramid and more like a sprawling web.

14. It would be anachronistic to call this story fanfiction—the term did not exist in 1924—and yet it performs the same kind of playful literary appropriation of Wells's work and life as contemporary Real Person Fiction (RPF).

15. Like the "convention," it seems that the science fiction fan clubs of the mid-twentieth century shared the "federation" organizing structure with women's clubs.

16. An Alternate Reality Game is "an interactive fusion of creative writing, puzzle-solving, and team-building, with a dose of role playing thrown in. It utilizes several forms of media in order to pass clues to the players, who solve puzzles in order to win pieces of the story being played out" ("Unfiction.com History"). The term and the earliest-known examples of such games date from the mid-1990s.

17. Edith Wharton's praise is printed on the back cover of the Penguin edition of *Gentlemen Prefer Blondes*. James Joyce, *Letters of James Joyce*, vol. 1, ed. Stuart Gilbert (Faber and Faber, 1957); William Faulkner, *Selected Letters of William Faulkner*, ed. Joseph Blotner (Random House, 1977), 32.

18. Despite having the same title, Loos and Emerson's 1920 *How to Write Photoplays* does not appear to be the same text as Elbert Moore's 1915 book. But, as editors Cari Beauchamp and Mary Anita Loos note in *Anita Loos Rediscovered*, Loos and Emerson's how-to book is presumably the work of a ghostwriter (43).

19. That the ad uses images from the 1923 silent film *Isle of Lost Ships*, based on a novel by Crittenden Marriott, further demonstrates the interconnectedness of multiple media in this era—and magazine advertising's casual relationship to truthful representation.

20. A scholar of comparative literature at the University of Georgia told me in conversation that the Russian translation of *Blondes* completely abandons any attempt to render Lorelei's writing style, which is the source of so much of its "fun."

21. For more on the connections between Harlow and Monroe, see Karina Longworth, "Marilyn Monroe: The Beginning," audio blog post, *You Must Remember This* (podcast), Panoply, March 2, 2017.

22. Sayers may or may not have considered herself a "fan" of Anita Loos, but, as a member of the Sherlock Holmes Society of London, she was no stranger to fan communities and their playful approach to literary texts. According to Michael Dirda, Sayers not only played "The Game"—a social and scholarly exercise in pretending that Holmes and Dr. Watson were real—she also mischievously insisted that it be played "without cracking a smile" (The Browser).

3. Fan Mail as Communal Literary Practice

1. I borrow the concept of the "workshop" created via textual interpretation and appropriation from Mike Chasar's writing on poetry scrapbooks (Chasar 61–62).

2. And unlike the correspondence schools for writing advertised in the back pages of magazines, the fan mail workshop remained within the gift economy. Elizabeth Bishop wrote about her 1930s work for a correspondence school in her 1968 story "The U.S.A. School of Writing," *Prose* (Farrar, Straus and Giroux, 2011) 100–109. Bergen Evans lent his name to one in the 1960s and 1970s, until it was exposed as fraudulent by muckraking journalist Jessica Mitford ("Let Us Now Appraise Famous Writers," *Atlantic Monthly* July 1970).

3. One notable exception is Jennifer Parchesky's "'You Make Us Articulate': Reading, Education, and Community in Dorothy Canfield's Middlebrow America." Parchesky notes that "the frequency with which the term *fan letter* is placed in quotation marks suggests that this was a well-known genre" (252–53n12, original emphasis).

4. As Gaul and Harris point out, "early newspaper editors filled their columns with the contributions of 'correspondents'—letter writers, not formal journalists" (10).

5. The parenthetical citations for Bates's article refer to the section and paragraph number.

6. Unfortunately, none of the essays quoted here reprint a complete fan letter, so I have had to rely on quoted fragments.

7. It is interesting to note that, in these early days of the film industry (Bow's career peaked in the 1920s), very few fans quoted by Orgeron mention having *seen* Bow's films, despite statistics that suggest fifty million Americans went to the movies every week (Kyvig 79). Multiple letters refer to having *read* about the films in fan magazines—suggesting that issues of uneven access necessitated a textual engagement with the cinema, at least in its infancy, and/or that those fans who wrote were also those who read.

8. Cather did choose to write back to some of these letters, but I want to suggest that the actual response is less important than its possibility, in terms of motivating fans to write. In this we can see the fannish gift economy at work: the gift of the letter is offered, motivated by the possibility, but not the certainty, that it will be returned. Again, this element of the gift delineates how fan letters differed from correspondence schools. It also suggests what fan mail might have in common with contemporary fan practices like tweeting at singer Harry Styles, hoping against the odds that he will reply.

9. "Cracker" generally denotes poor white residents of the US South and has been in use since the mid-eighteenth century. In Florida, the word has come to describe white residents whose families have lived in the region for generations. As such, the term is used with pride and tends not to carry pejorative connotations. For more on the complicated history of the word, see Dana Ste. Claire's *Cracker: The Cracker Culture in Florida History* (University Press of Florida, 2006). I retain the term here as the most accurate description of the poor, white, long-term resident population of Rawlings's Florida.

10. Other potential fan letters are filed with her general correspondence, chronologically, in thirty boxes, suggesting that this range of letters was kept separate, for a specific purpose. For more on the trial, see the end of this chapter.

11. The story of Fatty Blake's "doin'" appears again in Rawlings's 1942 memoir *Cross Creek* (discussed below), with minor edits that somewhat smooth out these issues of narrative voice. Rawlings chose the middle path in her changes: "can't to can't" with its double explanation just becomes "can't-see to can't-see" (*Cross Creek* 251), while the vernacular spelling of "pilau" is dropped entirely.

12. Christopher Rieger describes this juxtaposition as distinctly pastoral and argues that southern writers like Rawlings, alongside Erskine Caldwell, Zora Neale Hurston, and William Faulkner, use the pastoral as a device to reinterpret the relationship between southerners and the natural world (*Clear-Cutting Eden* 2).

13. The schottische, a slow polka, appeared in several regionalist novels, including Willa Cather's *My Ántonia* (1918) and William Faulkner's *Absalom, Absalom!* (1936).

14. For John Duvall, this kind of encounter between the regional and the modern offers a way of thinking about regionalism as a segment of a broader body of "modernist" literature (242–43).

15. Rawlings would have been horrified to learn that her friend Margaret Mitchell tried to answer every piece of fan mail she received after the publication and film adaptation of *Gone with the Wind* (1936, 1939)—a time-consuming practice that may help explain why she never published another book.

16. This letter and all subsequent fan letters to Rawlings quoted in this chapter are held in the Marjorie Kinnan Rawlings Papers at the University of Florida.

17. Rawlings had editorial trouble with this alligator, which she described as being thirty feet long in drafts of the novel. A librarian from Florida who read the manuscript questioned the credibility of this claim, and the second printing of *South Moon Under* reduced his size to twenty feet ("First Novels"). But Shields's letter suggests Rawlings may have been correct after all.

18. Rawlings wrote to Perkins that she was "interested in seeing which reviewers notice that the period [of *The Yearling*] is actually one year, almost to the day" (Perkins and Rawlings 339)—suggesting that the time frame was definitive but presented only in context clues throughout the novel.

19. Much like Mark Twain before her—think Huck Finn in drag.

20. I have identified nine fan letters sent around the time of the publication of *The Yearling* and referring to that novel.

21. The textual reinterpretation and representation of character is typical of fan texts; as Deborah Kaplan has noted, fan writers often use narrative to develop individualized interpretations of a source text's characters, combining the given facts of a text with the fan's own particular "interpretative play" (150). The fans quoted here "play" with Rawlings's characters by imagining them outside the bounds of the text, by making friends with them and treating them like members of their own communities, as Ronald Zboray wrote of antebellum literary characters and their readers.

22. These expressions prefigure how contemporary media fandom conveys emotions. Fans in internet communities have developed a complex set of tools for expressing their feelings about media properties, including posting pictures of their facial expressions, using premade

"reaction gifs" (animated images that play like digital flipbooks), emojis and emoticons, and rendering emotional actions via textual commands like "/sobbing," where the slash mark indicates how to read the text that precedes it.

23. Christopher Rieger argues that Florida in this era tended to be depicted as "a lost garden of plenty," in tones ranging from "lament[ing]" to "elegiac and mournful," largely due to the state's population boom and the ensuing damage to the environment (55).

24. Fetterley and Pryse maintain that the nineteenth-century tradition of regionalism has a definitive end point (9), citing 1910 and 1920 as potential dates (15). Again, my intention here is to demonstrate that Rawlings continued this tradition of regionalism, even into the 1940s.

25. The Rawlings archive at the University of Florida holds the copy of Fannie Farmer's *Boston Cook Book* to which Rawlings here refers.

Postlude: Fan History and Contemporary Fan Tourism

1. Published in *The Private Marjorie: The Love Letters of Marjorie Kinnan Rawlings to Norton S. Baskin*, ed. Roger L. Tarr (University Press of Florida, 2004).

2. And where Zora Neale Hurston once slept—though Rawlings was later ashamed that she hadn't had Hurston sleep in the main house, as befit a friend.

Conclusion: Fandom Is Literary, Fandom Is Historical

1. Somewhat confusingly, the term "racebending" originated to critique the whitewashing of East Asian and Inuit characters in the film *The Last Airbender*. Its meaning has since expanded to include the definition above, that is, both the corporate problematic and the crowd-sourced solution (see Gilliland, 2–3, and the remainder of this conclusion).

WORKS CITED

Adorno, Theodor W., and Max Horkheimer. "The Culture Industry: Enlightenment as Mass Deception (1944)." *Dialectic of Enlightenment*. Ed. Gunzelin Schmid Noerr. Trans. Edmund Jephcott. Stanford University Press, 2007. 94–136.

Agar, Herbert, and Allen Tate. *Who Owns America? A New Declaration of Independence.* Houghton Mifflin, 1936.

Ahmed, Sara. *Queer Phenomenology: Orientations, Objects, Others.* Duke University Press, 2006.

"Alpha/Beta/Omega." Fanlore.org. fanlore.org/wiki/Alpha/Beta/Omega. March 15, 2017.

Altman, Janet Gurkin. *Epistolarity: Approaches to a Form.* Ohio State University Press, 1982.

Anderson, Benedict. *Imagined Communities: Reflections on the Origin and Spread of Nationalism.* Rev. and extended ed. Verso, 1991.

Armitage, Kevin. "On Gene Stratton Porter's Conservation Aesthetic." *Environmental History* 14.1 (2009): 138–45.

Bacon-Smith, Camille. *Enterprising Women: Television Fandom and the Creation of Popular Myth.* University of Pennsylvania Press, 1992.

Badia, Janet. *Sylvia Plath and the Mythology of Women Readers.* University of Massachusetts Press, 2011.

Baker-Whitelaw, Gavia. "What Not to Do When Teaching a Class about Fanfiction." *Daily Dot,* February 23, 2015, sec. IRL. www.dailydot.com/irl/berkeley-fanfiction-class-backlash/.

Baring-Gould, William Stuart. "Little Superman, What Now?" *Harper's Magazine,* September 1946: 283–88.

Bates, Courtney A. "The Fan Letter Correspondence of Willa Cather: Challenging the Divide between Professional and Common Reader." *Transformative Works & Cultures* 6 (March 2011).

Beetham, Margaret. "Periodicals and the New Media: Women and Imagined Communities." *Women's Studies International Forum* 29 (January 1, 2006): 231–40. doi: 10.1016/j.wsif.2006.04.002.

"Belding's Page." *Journal of Education* 111.3 (January 20, 1930): 62.

Benét, William Rose. "The Phoenix Nest." *Saturday Review of Literature* 1.1 (August 2, 1924): 22.

———. "The Phoenix Nest." *Saturday Review of Literature* 10.20 (December 2, 1933): 309.

———. "The Phoenix Nest." *Saturday Review of Literature* 27.44 (October 28, 1944): 32.

———. "The Phoenix Nest." *Saturday Review of Literature* 28.5 (February 3, 1945): 28.

———. "The Phoenix Nest." *Saturday Review of Literature* 30.1 (January 4, 1947): 32.

Benjamin, Walter. "The Work of Art in the Age of Mechanical Reproduction." 1936. *Illuminations.* Ed. Hannah Arendt. Trans. Harry Zohn. Schocken, 1985. 217–52.

Bigelow, Gordon E. *Frontier Eden: The Literary Career of Marjorie Kinnan Rawlings.* University of Florida Press, 1966.

Bloch, Julia. "'Shut Your Rhetorics in a Box': Gwendolyn Brooks and Lyric Dilemma." *Tulsa Studies in Women's Literature* 35.2 (December 9, 2016): 439–62. doi:10.1353/ tsw.2016.0033.

Bone, Robert, and Richard A. Courage. *The Muse in Bronzeville: African American Creative Expression in Chicago, 1932–1950.* Rutgers University Press, 2011.

Boone, Joseph A., and Nancy J. Vickers. "Introduction—Celebrity Rites." *PMLA* 126.4 (October 1, 2011): 900–911. doi:10.1632/pmla.2011.126.4.900.

Bourdieu, Pierre. *Distinction: A Social Critique of the Judgement of Taste.* Trans. Richard Nice. 1984. Routledge, 2013.

Brodhead, Richard H. *Cultures of Letters: Scenes of Reading and Writing in Nineteenth-Century America.* University of Chicago Press, 1993.

Brooks, Gwendolyn. *Annie Allen.* 1949. *Selected Poems.* Harper Perennial, 2006.

———. *Report from Part One.* Broadside, 1972.

The Browser. "The Essential Sherlock Holmes: Michael Dirda's Recommendations." *Daily Beast,* December 2011. www.thedailybeast.com/articles/2011/12/09/the-essential-sherlock-holmes-michael-dirda-s-recommendations.

Buchanan, Kyle. "Why Must Twilight-Obsessed Women Ruin Comic-Con for Avatar-Obsessed Men?" *Movieline,* July 10, 2009. movieline.com/2009/07/10/why-must -twilight-obsessed-women-ruin-comic-con-for-avatar-obsessed-men/.

Busse, Kristina. "Geek Hierarchies, Boundary Policing, and the Gendering of the Good Fan." *Participations* 10.1 (2013): 73–91.

Canby, Henry Seidel. "Timely and Timeless." *Saturday Review of Literature* 1.1 (August 2, 1924): 1.

cereiscrown. "One of My Favorite Things." *Tumblr,* 2014. cerseiscrown.tumblr.com /post/47472366665/one-of-my-favorite-things-about-fandom-is-that-the.

Certeau, Michel de. *The Practice of Everyday Life.* Trans. Steven F. Rendall. 3rd ed. University of California Press, 2011.

Chasar, Mike. *Everyday Reading: Poetry and Popular Culture in Modern America*. Columbia University Press, 2012.

"Convention, N." *OED Online*. Oxford University Press. www.oed.com.proxy-remote. galib.uga.edu/view/Entry/40714. February 3, 2017.

Coppa, Francesca. "A Brief History of Media Fandom." *Fan Fiction and Fan Communities in the Age of the Internet: New Essays*. Ed. Karen Hellekson and Kristina Busse. McFarland, 2006. 41–60.

De Kosnik, Abigail [Derecho]. "Archontic Literature: A Definition, a History, and Several Theories of Fan Fiction." *Fan Fiction and Fan Communities in the Age of the Internet: New Essays*. Ed. Karen Hellekson and Kristina Busse. McFarland, 2006. 61–78.

Dinan, John. *Sports in the Pulp Magazines*. McFarland, 1998.

Douglas, Ann. *Terrible Honesty: Mongrel Manhattan in the 1920s*. Farrar, Straus and Giroux, 1995.

Duvall, John. "Regionalism in American Modernism." *The Cambridge Companion to American Modernism*. Ed. Walter Kalaidjian. Cambridge University Press, 2005.

Edwards, Alexandra. "In the Regency Alternate Universe: Jane Austen and Fan Fiction Culture." *Jane Austen*. Ed. Gabrielle Malcolm. Intellect, 2015. 10–18.

———. "Literature Fandom and Literary Fans." *A Companion to Media Fandom and Fan Studies*. Ed. Paul Booth. Wiley-Blackwell, 2018.

———. "*Orlando*: A Fan Fiction; or, Virginia Woolf in the Archive of Our Own." *Journal of Modern Literature* 44.3 (Spring 2021): 49–62.

Eisner, Eric. *Nineteenth-Century Poetry and Literary Celebrity*. Palgrave Macmillan, 2009.

English, Elizabeth. *Lesbian Modernism: Censorship, Sexuality and Genre Fiction*. Edinburgh University Press, 2015.

Evans, Bergen. "Fantasia." *Scribner's Magazine* 101.4 (April 1937): 55–57.

"Fan, N." *OED Online*. Oxford University Press. February 3, 2017.

"Fan fiction, N." *The Oxford Dictionary of Science Fiction*. Ed. Jeff Prucher. Oxford University Press, 2006.

Ferber, Edna. "The Eldest." *McClure's Magazine*, June 1916: 14–17.

Fetterley, Judith, and Marjorie Pryse. *Writing out of Place: Regionalism, Women, and American Literary Culture*. University of Illinois Press, 2003.

"First Novels: Marjorie Kinnan Rawlings." University of South Carolina Libraries—Rarebooks and Special Collections. library.sc.edu/spcoll/rawlings/novels.html. February 24, 2017.

Fiske, John. *Understanding Popular Culture*. 2nd ed. Routledge, 2010.

Foote, Stephanie. *Regional Fictions: Culture and Identity in Nineteenth-Century American Literature*. University of Wisconsin Press, 2001.

Franklin, Benjamin. *The Autobiography and Other Writings*. 1771. Bantam, 1982.

"The Friend in Need." *Love Story Magazine* 64.1 (May 25, 1929): 148.

"Friending Meme." fanlore.org/wiki/Friending_Meme. March 3, 2017.

Frost, Laura. "Blondes Have More Fun: Anita Loos and the Language of Silent Cinema." *Modernism/modernity* 17.2 (2010): 291–311.

Fuller, Kathryn H. *At the Picture Show: Small-Town Audiences and the Creation of Movie Fan Culture*. 1996. New ed. University of Virginia Press, 2001.

Garvey, Ellen Gruber. "Scissorizing and Scrapbooks: Nineteenth-Century Reading, Remaking, and Recirculating." *New Media, 1740–1915*. Ed. Lisa Gitelman and Geoffrey B. Pingree. MIT Press, 2003. 207–28.

Gaul, Theresa Strouth, and Sharon M. Harris. Introduction. *Letters and Cultural Transformations in the United States, 1760–1860*. Ed. Strouth and Harris. Ashgate, 2009. 1–14.

Gere, Anne Ruggles. *Intimate Practices: Literacy and Cultural Work in U.S. Women's Clubs, 1880–1920*. University of Illinois Press, 1997.

Gere, Anne Ruggles, and Laura Jane Roop. "For Profit and Pleasure: Collaboration in Nineteenth Century Women's Literary Clubs." *New Visions of Collaborative Writing*. Ed. Janis Forman. Boynton/Cook, 1992. 1–18.

Gernsback, Hugo, ed. "Correspondence." *Amazing Stories* 1.10 (January 1927).

———. "Correspondence." *Amazing Stories* 2.5 (August 1927).

———. "Correspondence." *Amazing Stories* 2.7 (October 1927).

Gilliland, Elizabeth. "Racebending Fandoms and Digital Futurism." *Transformative Works and Cultures* 22 (2016).

The Girl from Missouri. Dir. Jack Conway. Perf. Jean Harlow, Franchot Tone, and Lionel Barrymore. Metro-Goldwyn-Mayer, 1934.

Godfrey, Mollie. "Rewriting White, Rewriting Black: Authentic Humanity and Authentic Blackness in Nella Larsen's 'Sanctuary.'" *MELUS* 38.4 (2013): 122–45.

Goldman, Jonathan. *Modernism Is the Literature of Celebrity*. University of Texas Press, 2011.

Goldstein, J. "A Daughter's Place: The Intertextuality of Gene Stratton-Porter's *Laddie* and Louisa May Alcott's *Little Women*." *Remembrances of Childhood*. Spec. issue of *Canadian Children's Literature*. Ed. C. H. Carpenter. 111/112 (2003): 50–59.

Grasso, Linda. "'You Are No Stranger to Me': Georgia O'Keeffe's Fan Mail." *Reception: Texts, Readers, Audiences, History*, no. 1 (2013): 24–39.

Gray, Jonathan, Cornel Sandvoss, and C. Lee Harrington. "Introduction: Why Study Fans?" *Fandom: Identities and Communities in a Mediated World*. Ed. Gray, Sandvoss, and Harrington. New York University Press, 2007. 1–16.

Grossman, Lev. Foreword. *Fic: Why Fanfiction Is Taking Over the World*. Ed. Anne Jamison. Smart Pop, an imprint of BenBella Books, 2013. xi–xiv.

Haley, Alex. "Alex Haley Interviewed by Robert L. Allen." *Black Scholar*, 1976. www
.alex-haley.com/alex_haley_robert_allen_interview.htm.

Hammill, Faye. *Women, Celebrity, and Literary Culture between the Wars*. University
of Texas Press, 2007.

Hancock, La Touche. "The Motion Picture Fan." *Motion Picture Story Magazine*, June
1911: 93.

Haviland, Beverly. "Passing from Paranoia to Plagiarism: The Abject Authorship of
Nella Larsen." *Modern Fiction Studies* 43.2 (1997): 295–318.

Hellekson, Karen, and Kristina Busse. "Introduction: Why a Fan Fiction Studies
Reader Now?" *The Fan Fiction Studies Reader*. Ed. Hellekson and Busse. University of Iowa Press, 2014. 1–18.

Hillyer, Robert. *First Principles of Verse*. Rev. ed. The Writer, Inc., 1950.

Hochman, Barbara. "Love and Theft: Plagiarism, Blackface, and Nella Larsen's 'Sanctuary.'" *American Literature* 88.3 (September 2016): 509–40.

Hodge, Lamont Foster, and Arthur Lee. *A Manual in Elementary English, to Accompany
Elementary English*. C. E. Merrill, 1922.

Hoeller, Hildegard. "Race, Modernism, and Plagiarism: The Case of Nella Larsen's
'Sanctuary.'" *African American Review* 40.3 (2006): 421–37.

Hogue, Beverly J. "From Mulberries to Machines: Planting the Simulated Garden." *Isle:
Interdisciplinary Studies in Literature and Environment* 15.1 (Winter 2008): 101–10.

Horton, D., and R. Wohl. "Mass Communication and Para-Social Interaction: Observation on Intimacy at a Distance." *Psychiatry* 19 (1956): 215–29.

Howe, Julia Ward. "How Can Women Best Associate?" *Papers Read at the ... Congress
of Women*. Vol. 1. Mrs. William Ballard, Book and Job Printer, 1874. 5–10.

Howe, Sara K. "Teams, Tears, and Testimonials: A Rhetorical Reading of the Twilight
Time Capsule." *Reception: Texts, Readers, Audiences, History* 5.1 (July 18, 2013):
61–75.

Hurston, Zora Neale. "Characteristics of Negro Expression (1934)." *Within the Circle*.
Ed. Angelyn Mitchell. Duke University Press, 1994. 79–94.

Huyssen, Andreas. *After the Great Divide: Modernism, Mass Culture, Postmodernism*.
Indiana University Press, 1986.

Hyde, Lewis. *The Gift: Creativity and the Artist in the Modern World*. 25th anniversary
ed. Vintage, 2007.

Jaffe, Aaron. *Modernism and the Culture of Celebrity*. Cambridge University Press, 2005.

Jaffe, Aaron, and Jonathan E. Goldman, eds. *Modernist Star Maps: Celebrity, Modernity,
Culture*. Ashgate, 2010.

Jagose, Annamarie. *Queer Theory: An Introduction*. New York University Press, 2010.

Jamison, Anne. *Fic: Why Fanfiction Is Taking Over the World*. Smart Pop, an imprint
of BenBella Books, 2013.

Jeewells, H. [Christopher Ward]. "The Nightmare." *Saturday Review of Literature* 1.1 (August 2, 1924): 6–7.

Jenkins, Henry. *Textual Poachers: Television Fans & Participatory Culture.* Routledge, 1992.

Jenkins, Henry, Sam Ford, and Joshua Green. *Spreadable Media: Creating Value and Meaning in a Networked Culture.* New York University Press, 2013.

Jones, Carolyn M. "Race and the Rural in Marjorie Kinnan Rawlings's Cross Creek." *Mississippi Quarterly* 57.2 (Spring 2004): 215–30.

Kaestle, Carl F., and Janice A. Radway. "A Framework for the History of Publishing and Reading in the United States, 1880–1940." *Print in Motion: The Expansion of Publishing and Reading in the United States, 1880–1940.* Vol. 4 of *A History of the Book in America.* Published in association with the American Antiquarian Society by the University of North Carolina Press, 2009. 7–21.

Kahan, Benjamin. "Queer Modernism." *A Handbook of Modernism Studies.* Ed. Jean-Michel Rabaté. John Wiley, 2013. 347–61.

Kaplan, Deborah. "Construction of Fan Fiction Character through Narrative." *Fan Fiction and Fan Communities in the Age of the Internet: New Essays.* Ed. Karen Hellekson and Kristina Busse. McFarland, 2006. 134–52.

Kaye-Smith, Sheila. "Mrs. Adis." *Joanna Godden Married and Other Stories.* Project Gutenberg Canada.

"Kink Meme." fanlore.org/wiki/Kink_Meme. March 15, 2017.

Knupfer, Anne Meis. *Toward a Tenderer Humanity and a Nobler Womanhood: African American Women's Clubs in Turn-of-the-Century Chicago.* New York University Press, 1996.

Kristeva, Julia. *Desire in Language: A Semiotic Approach to Literature and Art.* Columbia University Press, 1980.

Kyvig, David E. *Daily Life in the United States, 1920–1940: How Americans Lived through the "Roaring Twenties" and the Great Depression.* Ivan R. Dee, 2004.

Lanier Literary Club Scrapbooks, 1937–1993. MS158 NC Collection. Special Collections at Pack Memorial Library, Asheville, NC.

Larkin, Mark. "What Happens to Fan Mail." *Photoplay,* August 1928.

Larsen, Nella. "Sanctuary." 1930. *The Complete Fiction of Nella Larsen.* Anchor, 2001.

Larson, Kelli A. "Surviving the Taint of Plagiarism: Nella Larsen's 'Sanctuary' and Sheila Kaye-Smith's 'Mrs. Adis.'" *Journal of Modern Literature* 30.4 (2007): 82–104.

Latham, Sean, and Robert Scholes. "The Rise of Periodical Studies." *PMLA* 121.2 (2006): 517–31.

Lichtenberg, Jacqueline. "Alien Romances: Star Trek, WorldCon, & Alien Romance." *Alien Romances,* August 15, 2006. aliendjinnromances.blogspot.com/2006/08/star-trek-worldcon-alien-romance.html.

"The Log-Book." *Argosy,* October 27, 1917: 765–70.

Long, Elizabeth. "Aflame with Culture: Reading and Social Mission in the Nineteenth-Century White Women's Literary Club Movement." *Print in Motion: The Expansion of Publishing and Reading in the United States, 1880–1940.* Ed. Janice A. Radway and Carl F. Kaestle. Vol 4. of *A History of the Book in America.* Published in association with the American Antiquarian Society by the University of North Carolina Press, 2009. 476–90.

Long, Judith Reick. *Gene Stratton-Porter: Novelist and Naturalist.* Indiana Historical Society, 1990.

Loos, Anita. *"Gentlemen Prefer Blondes: The Illuminating Diary of a Professional Lady"; And, "But Gentlemen Marry Brunettes."* Penguin, 1998.

———. *Kiss Hollywood Good-By.* Ballantine, 1974.

Loos, Anita. *Anita Loos Rediscovered: Film Treatments and Fiction.* Ed. Cari Beauchamp and Mary Anita Loos. University of California Press, 2003.

Loos, Anita, and Ray Pierre Corsini. *Fate Keeps on Happening: Adventures of Lorelei Lee and Other Writings.* Dodd, Mead, 1984.

Lopez, Lori Kido. "Fan Activists and the Politics of Race in *The Last Airbender.*" *International Journal of Cultural Studies* 15.5 (September 2012): 431–45.

Lothian, Alexis, Kristina Busse, and Robin Anne Reid. "'Yearning Void and Infinite Potential': Online Slash Fandom as Queer Female Space." *English Language Notes* 45.2 (Fall/Winter 2007): 103–11.

Lynch, Deidre Shauna. *Loving Literature: A Cultural History.* University of Chicago Press, 2015.

Manning, Molly Guptill. *When Books Went to War: The Stories That Helped Us Win World War II.* Houghton Mifflin Harcourt, 2014.

Marson, Una. "Kinky Hair Blues." *The Moth and the Star.* Self-published, 1937. http://ufdc.ufl.edu/UF00077395/00001. March 1, 2017.

McCullough, Kate. *Regions of Identity: The Construction of America in Women's Fiction, 1885–1914.* Stanford University Press, 1999.

McHenry, Elizabeth. "Reading and Race Pride: The Literary Activism of Black Clubwomen." *Print in Motion: The Expansion of Publishing and Reading in the United States, 1880–1940.* Ed. Janice A. Radway and Carl F. Kaestle. Vol. 4 of *A History of the Book in America.* Published in association with the American Antiquarian Society by the University of North Carolina Press, 2009. 491–510.

"Media Fandom." fanlore.org/wiki/Media_Fandom. March 13, 2017.

Meehan, Jeannette Porter. *Life and Letters of Gene Stratton-Porter.* Hutchinson, 1928.

Melhem, D. H. *Gwendolyn Brooks: Poetry and the Heroic Voice.* University Press of Kentucky, 1987.

"MLA Convention Statistics." www.mla.org/Convention/Convention-History/MLA
-Convention-Statistics. February 1, 2017.

Moore, Marianne. "Baseball and Writing." *Complete Poems.* Penguin, 1994.

Morris, Mary. "The Friendliest Corner." *Love Story Magazine* 64.1 (May 2, 1929):
143–47.

———. "The Friendliest Corner." *Love Story Magazine* 64.4 (August 24, 1929): 142–47.

Morrison, Toni. *Playing in the Dark: Whiteness and the Literary Imagination.* Harvard
University Press, 1992.

Motion Picture Magazine, February 1924.

Motion Picture Story Magazine, April 1911 and November 1911.

Nadkarni, Samira, and Deepa Sivarajan. "Waiting in the Wings: Inclusivity and the
Limits of Racebending." *Fandom, Now in Color.* Ed. Rukmini Pande. University
of Iowa Press, 2020. 122–35.

Najar, Lubna. "The Chicago Poetry Group: African American Art and High Modernism at Midcentury." *Women's Studies Quarterly,* no. 3/4 (2005): 314–23.

National Women's History Museum. "Rights for Women: The Suffrage Movement
and Its Leaders." www.nwhm.org/online-exhibits/rightsforwomen/SenecaFalls
.html. February 1, 2017.

Nolan, Michelle. *Ball Tales: A Study of Baseball, Basketball, and Football Fiction of the
1930s through 1960s.* McFarland, 2010.

O'Brien, Daniel. "4 Reasons to Hate Comic-Con." July 31, 2009. www.cracked.com
/blog/4-reasons-to-hat-this-comic-con/.

Ohanesian, Liz. "Comic-Con's Twilight Protests: Is There a Gender War Brewing?"
L.A. Weekly, July 28, 2009. www.laweekly.com/arts/comic-cons-twilight-protests
-is-there-a-gender-war-brewing-2373110.

Olson, Liesl. "Across Stark Lines." *Centennial: A History of the Renaissance Society,
1915–2015.* Ed. Karen Reimer. Renaissance Society, 2015. 50–59.

O'Neill, Bonnie Carr. "'Does Such a Being Exist?': *Olive Branch* Readers Respond to
Fanny Fern." *Letters and Cultural Transformations in the United States, 1760–1860.*
Ed. Theresa Strouth Gaul and Sharon M. Harris. Ashgate, 2009. 161–77.

Orgeron, Marsha. "'You Are Invited to Participate': Interactive Fandom in the Age of
the Movie Magazine." *Journal of Film and Video* 61.3 (Fall 2009): 3–23.

Page, Yolanda Williams. "May Miller." *Encyclopedia of African American Women Writers.*
Greenwood, 2007.

Pande, Rukmini. *Squee from the Margins: Fandom and Race.* University of Iowa Press,
2018.

Parchesky, Jennifer. "'You Make Us Articulate': Reading, Education, and Community
in Dorothy Canfield's Middlebrow America." *Reading Acts: U.S. Readers' Interac-*

tions with Literature, 1800–1950. Ed. Barbara Ryan and Amy M. Thomas. University of Tennessee Press, 2002.

Penley, Constance. *NASA/Trek: Popular Science and Sex in America.* Verso, 1997.

Perkins, Maxwell, and Marjorie Kinnan Rawlings. *Max and Marjorie: The Correspondence between Maxwell E. Perkins and Marjorie Kinnan Rawlings.* Ed. Rodger L. Tarr. University Press of Florida, 1999.

Phillips, Anne K. "Of Epiphanies and Poets: Gene Stratton-Porter's Domestic Transcendentalism." *Children's Literature Association Quarterly,* no. 4 (1994): 153.

Photoplay, November 1914.

"The Press: Amazing! Astounding!" *Time,* July 10, 1939: 34. content.time.com/time /magazine/article/0,9171,761661,00.html.

Publishers' Weekly 99.26 (June 25, 1921): 1882.

Radway, Janice A. *A Feeling for Books: The Book-of-the-Month Club, Literary Taste, and Middle-Class Desire.* University of North Carolina Press, 1997.

———. "Learned and Literary Print Cultures in an Age of Professionalization and Diversification." *Print in Motion: The Expansion of Publishing and Reading in the United States, 1880–1940.* Vol. 4 of *A History of the Book in America.* Published in association with the American Antiquarian Society by the University of North Carolina Press, 2009. 197–233.

Rawlings, Marjorie Kinnan. "Cracker Chidlings." *Scribner's Magazine* 89.2 (February 1931): 127–34.

———. *Cross Creek.* 1942. Simon and Schuster, 1996.

———. *Cross Creek Cookery.* 1942. Simon and Schuster, 1996.

———. Marjorie Kinnan Rawlings Papers. Special and Area Studies Collections, George A. Smathers Libraries, University of Florida, Gainesville.

———. *Poems by Marjorie Kinnan Rawlings: Songs of a Housewife.* University Press of Florida, 1997.

———. *Selected Letters of Marjorie Kinnan Rawlings.* University Presses of Florida, 1983.

———. *South Moon Under.* 1933. Armed Services Edition. Council for Books in Wartime, 1943.

———. *The Uncollected Writings of Marjorie Kinnan Rawlings.* Ed. Rodger L. Tarr and Brent Kinser. University Press of Florida, 2007.

———. *The Yearling.* 1938. Aladdin, 2001.

Rice, Grantland. "At Random in Fandom." *McClure's Magazine,* June 1916: 13.

Richards, Bertrand F. *Gene Stratton Porter.* Twayne, 1980.

Rieger, Christopher. *Clear-Cutting Eden: Ecology and the Pastoral in Southern Literature.* University of Alabama Press, 2009.

Roosevelt, Mrs. Franklin D. "Proceedings of the Twenty-Fifth Annual Convention of the American Federation of Arts: Washington, D.C., May 14, 15, 16, 1934." *American Magazine of Art* 27.12 (December 1, 1934): 1–47.

rossetti. "time is an ocean." *Dreamwidth*. rossetti.dreamwidth.org. March 4, 2017.

Rubin, Joan Shelley. *The Making of Middlebrow Culture*. University of North Carolina Press, 1992.

Ryan, Barbara. "The 'Girl Business' + the Bachelor of Nature: Romancing Thoreau." *Journal of American & Comparative Cultures* 25.1/2 (Spring 2002): 185–98.

———. "A Real Basis from Which to Judge: Fan Mail to Gene Stratton-Porter." *Reading Acts: U.S. Readers' Interactions with Literature, 1800–1950*. Ed. Ryan and Amy M. Thomas. University of Tennessee Press, 2002.

———. "Teasing Out Clues, Not Kooks: The Man Nobody Knows and Ben-Hur." *Reception: Texts, Readers, Audiences, History* 5.1 (July 18, 2013): 9–23.

Ryan, Barbara, and Charles Johanningsmeier. "Guest Editors' Introduction: Fans and the Objects of Their Devotion." *Reception: Texts, Readers, Audiences, History* 5.1 (July 18, 2013): 3–8.

Sales Management 28 (1931): 396.

Sawyer, Andy. "Fables of Irish Fandom: Fan Fiction in the 1950s and '60s." *Fic: Why Fanfiction Is Taking Over the World*. Ed. Anne Jamison. Smart Pop, an imprint of BenBella Books, 2013. 77–83.

Sayers, Dorothy Leigh. *Have His Carcase*. HarperPaperbacks, 1995.

Scheiner, Georganne. "The Deanna Durbin Devotees: Fan Clubs and Spectatorship." *Generations of Youth: Youth Cultures and History in Twentieth-Century America*. Ed. Joe Austin and Michael Willard. NYU Press, 1998. 81–94.

Sciretta, Peter. "Will Twilight Ruin This Year's Comic-Con?" *Slashfilm* July 10, 2009. www.slashfilm.com/will-twilight-ruin-this-years-comic-con/.

Sedgwick, Eve Kosofsky. *Tendencies*. Routledge, 1994.

Server, Lee. *Danger Is My Business: An Illustrated History of the Fabulous Pulp Magazines*. Chronicle, 1993.

Silverman, Al. "The Fragile Pleasure." *Reading: Old and New*. Spec. issue of *Daedalus* 112.1 (Winter 1983): 35–49.

Smith, Dora V. "Composition, Public Speaking, Vocabulary, Grammar, Spelling, and Handwriting." *Review of Educational Research* 13.2 (April 1, 1943): 162–89. doi:10.2307/1168513.

Sorensen, Leif. "A Weird Modernist Archive: Pulp Fiction, Pseudobiblia, H. P. Lovecraft." *Modernism/Modernity*, no. 3 (2010): 501–22.

Spencer, Amy. *DIY: The Rise of Lo-Fi Culture*. New York: Marion Boyars, 2005.

Spencer, Richard V. "Thumbnail Biography." *Photoplay*, November 1914: 168.

Stratton-Porter, Gene. *Freckles*. 1904. Indiana University Press, 1986.

———. *A Girl of the Limberlost.* 1909. Indiana University Press, 1984.

———. *The Harvester.* 1911. Grosset and Dunlap, 1916.

———. *Homing with the Birds: The History of a Lifetime of Personal Experience with the Birds.* John Murray, 1919.

———. "My Life and My Books." *Ladies' Home Journal,* September 1916: 13, 80–81.

Todd, Carrie. Personal interview by the author. January 27, 2017.

Tonkovich, Nicole. "Writing in Circles: Harriet Beecher Stowe, the Semi-Colon Club, and the Construction of Women's Authorship." *Nineteenth-Century Women Learn to Write.* Ed. Catherine Hobbs. University Press of Virginia, 1995. 147–75.

Travers, Inez. "News of the Chicago Women's Clubs." *Chicago Tribune* November 7, 1915. archives.chicagotribune.com/1915/11/07/page/D3/article/news-of-the -chicago-womens-clubs.

Tuszynski, Stephanie. "Excerpt from 'IRL (In Real Life): The Bronze Documentary Project.'" *Transformative Works and Cultures* 6 (September 7, 2010). journal.trans-formativeworks.org/index.php/twc/article/view/238.

"Unfiction.com History." www.unfiction.com/history/. March 6, 2017.

Wall, Cheryl A. *Women of the Harlem Renaissance.* Indiana University Press, 1995.

Wanzo, Rebecca. "African American Acafandom and Other Strangers: New Genealogies of Fan Studies." *Transformative Works and Cultures* 20 (July 22, 2015). journal. transformativeworks.org/index.php/twc/article/view/699.

"The Wednesday Club." *Geneva Herald,* May 18, 1894. cdm16066.contentdm.oclc.org /cdm/ref/collection/p15078coll6/id/17.

———. *Geneva Herald,* June 15, 1894. cdm16066.contentdm.oclc.org/cdm/ref/collection /p15078coll6/id/18.

———. *Geneva Herald,* July 6, 1894. cdm16066.contentdm.oclc.org/cdm/ref/collection /p15078coll6/id/19.

———. *Geneva Herald,* October 19, 1894. cdm16066.contentdm.oclc.org/cdm/ref /collection/p15078coll6/id/20.

The Wednesday Club. "Programme." cdm16066.contentdm.oclc.org/cdm/ref/collection /p15078coll6/id/22. Accessed January 9, 2017.

Wertenbaker, G. Peyton. "On Parody." *Saturday Review of Literature* 1.3 (August 16, 1924): 54.

"What Is a Fanzine?" fanlore.org/wiki/File:Whatisafanzine.jpg. March 3, 2017.

Whitehead, Jessica Leonora. "Local Newspaper Movie Contests and the Creation of the First Movie Fans." *Transformative Works and Cultures* 22 (September 15, 2016). journal.transformativeworks.org/index.php/twc/article/view/723.

Whitman, Walt. *Leaves of Grass.* New American Library, 2000.

Willey, Malcolm M. "'Identification' and the Inculcation of Social Values." *Annals of the American Academy of Political and Social Science* 160 (March 1, 1932): 103–9.

Willis, Ika. "Keeping Promises to Queer Children: Making Space (for Mary Sue) at Hogwarts." *Fan Fiction and Fan Communities in the Age of the Internet: New Essays.* Ed. Karen Hellekson and Kristina Busse. McFarland, 2006. 153–70.

Youngquist, Paul. "The Afro Futurism of DJ Vassa." *European Romantic Review* 16.2 (April 2005): 181–92.

Zboray, Ronald J. "The Letter and the Fiction Reading Public in Antebellum America." *Journal of American Culture* 10.1 (Spring 1987): 27–34.

INDEX

Note: Page numbers in *italics* refer to illustrations; those followed by "n" indicate endnotes.

Emerson, John, 76
Emerson, Ralph Waldo, 23, 25–26, 32, 33, 35, 37
Emerson, Zelie, 26, 34
emojis and emoticons, 154n22
emotional and affective responses in letters, 87–88, 106, 108
empathy, 114–15, 124
Empson, William, 75
emulation trope in letters, 88–89, 106
English, Elizabeth, 13
epistolary studies, 81–83. *See also* fan mail
Equiano, Olaudah, 140
Evans, Bergen, 79–83, 89, 116, 152n2

Fair Use, 10, 28–29
fandom (media fandom): fan cultures, 5, 6; fan identity, 4, 51, 54, 58, 67; gift economy theory, 9–10; as pathological, beautiful, complicated, literary, historical, 137; "poaching" model and gleaning metaphor, 8–9; science fiction creation myth, 2, 3, 50–51; stereotypes of, 8; transformative works theory, 10–11; Western media fandom as term, 145n1. *See also* fan mail; film fandom; magazine fandom; women's clubs
fandom history, alternate: baseball, 56–58; cross-media tie-ins, 61–62; film magazines, 53–56; letter columns, 51; male-dominated, sci-fi myth, 50–51; networked interactive print culture, 52–53; pulp magazines, 58–61; technology changes and, 52
fanfiction: fan cultures vs., 5; gift economy and, 9–10, 146n9; internet treatment of, 9; Real Person Fiction (RPF), 149n18; slash, 11, 13, 149n21, 149n26; term, history of, 145n4; unspoken rules, 146n10
fan mail: *Amazing Stories* letter column, 51, 144; *Amazing Stories'* "The Shaver Mystery" and, 69–71; archival practices,

86; epistolary studies, 81–83; Evans's "Fantasia" essay on, 79–81, *80;* film fan magazines, 83–84; film stars, 79–81; gift economy and, 152n2; private and public realms and, 84; radio and, 61–62; Rawlings and, 92–96, 99–102, 105–12, 115–22, 126–28; regional literature and, 89–92; from students, 84–85; tropes of, 85–89, 106; virtual communities and, 83; as workshop space, 81, 88, 93
Fantasy Commentator, 70
Far, Sui Sin, 17
Far and Near, 24
Faulkner, William, 72, 75, 153n12
Ferber, Edna, 58, 150n8
Fern, Fanny, 85, 89
Fetterley, Judith, 12, 17, 36, 114–15, 124, 149n17, 154n24
Fic (Jamison), 50
fiction factories, 61
film fandom, 53–56, 79–81, 83–84, 86–88, 152n7
Fiske, John, 7–8, 137
Fitzgerald, F. Scott, 74, 90, 95
Foote, Stephanie, 17, 89, 92, 114
Franklin, Benjamin, 21, 23
Freckles (Stratton-Porter), 36, 37–40
Friday Club, 25–26, 44
friending memes, 59, 150n10
"Friendliest Corner, The" (*Love Story Magazine*), 59, *60,* 71
Frost, Laura, 74
Frost, Robert, 42, 63, 67
Fuller, Kathryn, 54, 56
Fuller, Margaret, 32
Fuller, Mary, 55

"Garnishing the Aviary" (Cunningham), 43
Garvey, Ellen Gruber, 8–9
Gates, Henry Louis, Jr., 139
Gaul, Theresa Strouth, 81–82, 108, 152n4
General Federation of Women's Clubs, 23

O'Keeffe, Georgia, 86–88, 108, 109, 126
Olive Branch column (Fern), 89
O'Neill, Bonnie Carr, 85, 89
Organization for Transformative Works (OTW), 28, 146n13
Orgeron, Marsha, 84–88, 152n7

Pande, Rukmini, 6, 143
Parchesky, Jennifer, 86, 152n3
participatory cultures, theory of, 7–9
pastoral, the 153n12
Paterson (Williams), 43
Peck, Gregory, 133
periodicals. See magazines
Perkins, Maxwell, 95–103, 105, 110, 122, 129
Peterkin, Julia, 92
Phillips, Anne K., 37
"Phoenix Nest" (Benét), 65–68
Photoplay, 54–56, 55
plagiarism narrative, 138–44
Playing in the Dark (Morrison), 119
pleasure, 108–11
"poaching" model, 8–9, 29
popular culture, 2, 7–8, 52, 137
Pound, Ezra, 44
private space: internet fan communities as, 147n7; Love Story Magazine and, 59; women's clubs and, 26–27
Pryse, Marjorie, 12, 17, 36, 114–15, 124, 149n17, 154n24
pseudonymity, 147n6
Publishers' Weekly, 58
pulp fiction: Benét's "Phoenix Nest" and, 67–68; Haley and, 120; magazines, 58–61, 71; modernist poetry and, 44; science-fiction, 49–51, 68–71. See also Amazing Stories; "lowbrow"; magazines

queerness: defined, 12; internet fan communities as queer female space, 27, 35; media fandom and, 11–13; queer female spaced prefigured in women's clubs, 35; in

Rawlings, 104–5, 110–11; regionalism and, 12, 92, 124–25

race: Afrofuturism, 140, 143; cultural "brow" levels and, 145n6; plagiarism narrative and, 138–39; in Rawlings's Cross Creek, 118–19; white beauty norms, challenges to, 45; white supremacy and anti-Semitism in Amazing Stories letters, 144; whitewashing, 139; women's clubs and segregation, 148n9
racebending, 138–44, 149n21, 154n1
radio programs, 61–62, 84, 151n11
Radway, Janice, 52, 109–10, 145n6, 151n11
Randall, Alice, 143
Rawlings, Charles, 102
Rawlings, Marjorie Kinnan: about, 81, 89–90; Armed Services Editions and, 119–24; Blood of My Blood, 90; "Cracker Chidlings," 93–95, 96; Cross Creek Cookery, 127–28, 134–35; death of, 129; fan mail to, 92–96, 99–102, 105–22, 126–28; homestead of, 91; lawsuit against, 93, 100, 128–29; literary canon, exclusion from, 90–91; Marjorie Kinnan Rawlings Historic State Park, 130–35, 131, 132, 134–136; Mountain Prelude, 129; narrative voice and, 96–98, 104, 113; Perkins, relationship and correspondence with, 95–103, 105, 110, 122, 129; regionalism and, 89–92, 99, 105, 114–15, 124–25; "Regional Literature of the South" lecture, 91–92; "Songs of the Housewife" column, 90; The Soujourner, 129; South Moon Under, 93, 96–103, 110, 114; The Yearling, 90, 92–93, 102–9, 110, 132–33, 153n18. See also Cross Creek
reaction gifs, 154n22
Real Person Fiction (RPF), 149n18, 151n14
Red-Headed Woman (Brush), 74, 76
Red-Headed Woman (film), 74, 77
regionalism: as cultural therapy, 124; as emotional tutorial, 114–16; end point,

purported, 154n24; marginalization and, 105; modernism and, 17–18, 99, 153n14; queer, 12, 92, 124–25; Rawlings and, 89–92, 99, 105, 114–15, 124–25; World War II and, 89

"Regional Literature of the South" (Rawlings), 91–92

Renaissance Society, University of Chicago, 41

Report from Part One (Brooks), 41–42

Rhys, Jean, 50, 143

Rice, Grantland, 48, 57, 58, 150n7

Richards, Bertrand F., 31

Rieger, Christopher, 153n12, 154n23

Rittenhouse, Paul, 107

Roberts, Elizabeth Madox, 92

Robinson, Edwin Arlington, 63

Rogers, Howard Emmett, 76

Roop, Laura Jane, 26–27, 29

Rosencrantz and Guildenstern Are Dead (Stoppard), 50

rossetti, 1, 12

Ryan, Barbara, 36

"Sanctuary" (Larsen), 138–44

Sandvoss, Cornel, 137

Santayana, George, 63

Sappho, 3

Saturday Morning Club, 23–24, 27

Saturday Review of Literature, 50, 63–64, 73

Sawyer, Andy, 50

Sayers, Dorothy L., 72, 77–78, 151n22

Scholes, Robert, 62

science fiction fandom, 2, 3, 20, 50–51. See also *Amazing Stories*

scrapbooking, 8, 48

Sebree, Charles, 41

Sedgwick, Eve Kosofsky, 11–12

Semi-Colon Club, 25–26, 147n6

Server, Lee, 61, 150n9

sexuality: kink memes and A/B/O fic, 11, 146n17; Loos's Lorelei Lee and, 74, 149n21; Real Person Fiction (RPF) and,

149n18; slash fanfiction, 11, 13, 149n21, 149n26; Stratton-Porter and, 34–40. *See also* queerness

Shakespeare, William, 65

"Shaver Mystery, The" (*Amazing Stories*), 68–71

Shearwood, Lucille, 93, 106, 108, 120

Sherlock Holmes Society of London, 151n22

Sherlock Holmes stories (Doyle), 54, 150n4

Shields, John Franklin, 93, 101–2

Sidney, Philip, 10

signifyin,' 139

Silverman, Al, 109

Sitwell, Edith, 63

Sivarajan, Deepa, 143

slash fanfiction, 11, 13, 149n21, 149n26

Smith, Betty, 122

Soderberg, Robert, 126

"Songs of the Housewife" column (Rawlings), 90

Sorensen, Leif, 44

Soujourner, The (Rawlings), 129

South Moon Under (Rawlings), 93, 96–103, 110, 114

Spencer, Richard V., 54

Stanton, Elizabeth Cady, 21

Stark, Inez Cunningham, 40–42

Starrett, Vincent, 63

Star Trek, 1, 11, 22, 49, 50

Star Wars films, 143

Stein, Gertrude, 13, 72

Stewart, Mary, 27

Stoppard, Tom, 50

Stowe, Harriet Beecher, 17, 23, 25, 29, 32, 34, 112, 147n6, 149n17

Strachey, Lytton, 63

Stratton-Porter, Gene: about, 14, 23, 30; emotional responses from readers, 87–88; *Freckles*, 36, 37–40; *A Girl of the Limberlost*, 36, 37; *The Harvester*, 36–37, 40, 149n18; "The Strike at Shane's," 30–31; the Wednesday Club and, 31–32, 36–37; Whitman essay, 32–35, 148n15

Printed in the USA
CPSIA information can be obtained
at www.ICGtesting.com
BVHW031049030923
669018BV00002B/116